COVENTRY LIBRARIES

Please return this book on or before
the last date stamped below.

EAR

AGE CONCERN (7X)
2/08

TILE HILL
Age Concern (15) E/G

FINHAM

TRANS FROM EAR
DTIL 1/09

8 MAY 2015
KN 9/16

07 JAN 2010

11 FEB 2010

1 AUG 2010

TANYARD 9/2

AGE CONCERN 1

17 DEC 2013

Age Concern
(12) E/G

Tile Hill
2 3 DEC 2021

5 Oct

KU-411-054

To renew this book take it to any of
the City Libraries before
the date due for return

Coventry City Council

CHAMPAGNE AND
POLAR BEARS

CHAMPAGNE AND POLAR BEARS

Marie Tièche

WINDSOR
PARAGON

First published in Great Britain 2007
by Summersdale Publishers
This Large Print edition published 2009
by BBC Audiobooks Ltd
by arrangement with
Summersdale Publishers Ltd

Hardcover ISBN: 978 1 408 42793 4
Softcover   ISBN: 978 1 408 42794 1

British Library Cataloguing in Publication Data available

Printed and bound in Great Britain by
CPI Antony Rowe, Chippenham, Wiltshire

CONTENTS

PROLOGUE

Those eyes. They were the faded blue of a clear winter sky, a luminous, translucent, glacier blue. They had spoken to me, invited me into a strange new world of isolation and loneliness, treacherous weather, icebergs and danger. And I had accepted. What had I done? I'd only met him in the pub an hour ago and I'd just agreed to go with him on his scientific expedition to a deserted, glaciated island 600 miles (1,000 kilometres) from the North Pole. Just the two of us. Me and him. No one else. We'd live alone in a little wooden hut with just two huskies for company and to protect us from polar bears; you know, those huge, white, ferocious, man-eating creatures. They would be our neighbours for a year. A whole year. No going home halfway through if the going got tough. Twelve months or not at all. Giving up was not an option. I must be completely mad. Round the bend. Out of my tiny mind.

But that's how it all began.

CHAPTER ONE

BAITING THE HOOK

Snow-devils waltzed and tangoed down the road, scouring the glossy ice-bound surface and turning it to frosted glass. Under the clear skies it looked a bitter, raw night, cold wind blowing off the glacier. Going to bed with a good book was an attractive proposition, but I was getting fed up with my own company of an evening and it was, after all, Friday night. Come on. Make an effort. I drew the curtains together with a vigour I wasn't really feeling.

Shrugging myself into my warm brown jacket, I locked the door to the bedsit and trotted silently down the stairs in my thick wool socks. In the entrance hall I could hear, coming from the room off to one side, the hum of the huge communal freezer shared by all 12 residents of the building. Running a freezer in these arctic temperatures was a bit strange, but leaving frozen food outside would only encourage foxes, mice and thieves. Three pairs of cross-country skis stood in one corner, poles leaning drunkenly across each other in mutual support, and a rainbow of thick jackets and scooter dresses (a bit like romper suits for adults) hung on the coat racks above the twenty or so pairs of assorted boots, shoes and slippers left haphazardly on the floor. Some were old and dusty, their owners having long since departed their bedsit, and probably Longyearbyen too. I assumed most of the people came up here to work in an exotic surrounding and to save money for the future, for instance to get married or buy a house. I wondered how many of the people were English like me. (My name makes me sound a foreigner to almost everyone, whatever their nationality, but I was named after my Aunty Jean's French pen-friend and ended up with a Swiss father-in-law when I got married.)

I had come to Spitsbergen because that was where my old flame and good friend Edwin just happened to be living. He threw me Spitsbergen as a lifeline, a place to regroup and recover from the stress of my failed marriage. It could just as easily have been Borneo. I'd stayed with him for six months on arriving in Longyearbyen, hoping that we could finally mesh together in a successful partnership, but it didn't work, and I moved out into my own place here. We were a bit estranged at the moment, but time would get us back onto a steady footing once more. We would always be special to each other.

Dodging the melt puddles I shoved my feet into my sensible, brown leather shoes, pulling on my snug hat and windproof gloves as I pushed open the heavy, glass-panelled door and braced myself for −20°C. The snow was hard and rutted with scooter and ski tracks criss-crossing through those of boots and the occasional dog. In between, the thin layer of hard-compressed, slippery-smooth snow awaited the unwary and unlucky.

Cautiously, I walked around to the end of the long, wooden building and crept past the metal rubbish skips and down the slope to the path, the snow a dull amber under the street lamps, and breathed in the clean, cold air of a Spitsbergen night. On the left, sandwiched between more rows of timber flats and bungalows and the now frozen,

2

snow-hidden river beyond, the main road headed up the hill behind me, passed the school and sports centre before petering out at Nybyen, an outlying hamlet near the upper end of the valley where most of the handful of students attending the tiny university lived. Theirs was a journey of unequal halves, whizzing downhill on their bicycles all the way from the top end of town to the lower in the morning and toiling back up the steady incline at the end of the day, a distance of some two kilometres each way.

The wooden church with its steeply pitched roof, standing on the slopes on the opposite side of the river, was illuminated from outside in creamy light and looked welcoming as ever as honey-coloured rays of the interior lighting percolated through the square windows along its length. Above, stars struggled vainly to be noticed in the debilitating glow of the street lighting, and on the far side of the frozen, snow-dusted fjord, a three-quarters moon shone high over the silhouette of Hiorthfjell mountain ahead of me, silvering the snow on its solid flanks and snow- and frost-glued scree slopes, its broad ridge a hard line against the cloudless blue-black sky beyond. At the foot of the mountain, the dim, yellow glow of an oil lamp shone from a single hut, a smudge of smoke, barely visible, hanging in the air above its roof.

I scrunched my way downhill in the cut-glass air, watching the wind play with the snow. Wave upon wave of snow-sand skittered and snaked on the frozen land, hissing and eddying in the sharp, cold wind blowing off the glacier. It drifted low and hard, fanning out in fine, white-edged waves before gathering into mini tornadoes that exploded into nothingness moments later. It blew towards the little town, most of which lay before me in the tadpole-shaped Longyear valley between me and the fjord. Its tail reaches to the blunt face of the Longyear Glacier just above Nybyen, and its nose pushes out into Adventfjord, a seven-kilometre arm of the huge Isfjord, or Ice Sound as it used to be called. The industrial and administrative centre lies to the left of the frozen river of its backbone, the residential and shopping area to its right.

Communal wood-clad blocks of bedsits, built and extended from Portakabins (just like mine), gave way farther down the hill to strings of wooden houses with sharply pointed roofs, their bright colours of chocolate or coffee, pink or green, yellow or orange, beige or turquoise subdued in the night. The residential area spread up the valley sides, making way for the town centre. It was quiet at this late hour of the evening—the few shops having long since closed—but there were some people about, picking up a pizza, popping into the post office foyer to check their mail boxes, or like me, off to one of the numerous hostelries in town to enjoy the start of the weekend.

I had been bored and fidgety at home and thought I would go out earlier than usual. Despite it being 10.30 p.m., I knew it was too early for Longyearbyen, at least another half-hour before it would start to liven up. I thought I'd buy a beer in one of the hotels and maybe read a bit more of a book I'd found in its small library. The Radisson SAS Polar Hotel lay just past the shopping centre and the hospital, and was a popular watering hole for the 1,500 residents of Longyearbyen, not only for morning coffee, but for high-class evening meals in

4

its panoramic restaurant. Tucked unobtrusively into a corner of the hotel was Barents Pub, or 'PubEN' as it was known—my destination for the evening.

The brisk walk down from the bedsit had kept me from feeling the sub-zero temperatures, and after scraping the snow from the soles of my shoes, I heaved open the weighty door to the hotel foyer to be assailed by a wall of warm air from within. Stuffing my hat and gloves back into my pockets, I hung up my jacket on my usual peg in the corner of the cloakroom, recrossed the foyer and into the gloom of PubEN. It must be one of the darkest pubs I have ever been in, and it took me a few moments for my eyes to adjust after the glare of the entrance hall. The dark, sea-blue walls seemed to absorb the light from the enormous, grand chandelier hanging through an orange sail stretched across the ceiling, the bare pine floorboards the only bright spot in the décor. It was a cosy pub, had a lovely, somehow old-fashioned atmosphere, and was generally packed out at weekends, with everyone talking loudly over the foot-tapping, distracting blues and rock music in the background or dancing to the excellent live bands.

At first glance the place was almost deserted, unusual even for this time of night. I couldn't see who was sitting in the dark rear of the pub as I wasn't wearing my glasses, but three or four young people were sitting on the bench seats under the old etchings of whales, and a short, older guy in a woolly jumper was leaning back on the bar, standing beneath a huge poster advertising Otard cognac. I hadn't seen him before and took him for a tourist. We made eye contact as I walked past and ordered myself a half-litre (just doesn't sound as good as a pint) from Johan behind the bar and had a mooch round to see if I could find anyone I knew in the murky depths at the back of the pub. It was quite usual for friends to get together at home in the evening for a 'Vorspiel'—a German word adopted by the Norwegians which means prelude, a curtain raiser, and also foreplay—either eating, drinking, chatting or watching television together, before venturing out on the town later; so, it being a bit early, I wasn't surprised that I knew no one there. They were probably all tourists. I wandered back out of the pub with my 'pint' and over to the tiny hotel shop, thinking I would browse the shelves for a few minutes before settling into one of the comfy armchairs opposite to continue reading my book about a sailing trip to Greenland in the tracks of Leif Eiriksson.

The shop was very small. It was the usual stuff for the tourists, fluffy bears for children, T-shirts, hats, chocolate, biros, books and post cards, jewellery and small stone sculptures, dinner plates printed with a map of Svalbard (as the Norwegians call Spitsbergen)—a surprisingly large amount in such a small space. I was looking at some sew-on patches, wondering about sending a couple back to England for my niece and nephew, when I heard someone behind me speaking Norwegian, though I didn't catch what he was saying. Being a bit nosy, I turned to see the man who had been at the bar standing just outside the door, clutching his pint and obviously talking to me. I apologised in Norwegian as best I could and explained that I hadn't understood as I was English. He gave me a friendly smile and said, 'No problem.' He was not much taller than me (so not very tall at all), with blond-grey hair, an attractive smile and crinkly-twinkly blue eyes—not something I normally notice. His jumper had seen better days but looked well loved, just like most of mine. The yoke was off-white with a black motif, two-tone grey below, with a green trim. He wore boots and some old, dark brown leather trousers, all in all giving the impression of a likeable person, and I warmed to him immediately.

We introduced ourselves, and I discovered he was a German called Hauke and that he was a scientist on one of his numerous visits to Spitsbergen. He asked what an Englishwoman was doing in Longyearbyen and I explained I had been living and working there for the last couple of years. He was exceedingly attentive and I got the full charm offensive. He asked all sorts of questions: was I married; where was I working; did I like the cold; did I like living in the Arctic; had I seen any polar bears? (No, not yet. Spotting them in the area around Longyearbyen was even more unlikely than me winning on the lottery or the Faeroes winning an international football match. In recent memory only one has wandered right through the centre of town in the middle of the night. No one saw him, and his footprints, found in the snow next morning, were the only sign he'd been there.) Then Hauke moved up a gear and started telling me all about his research project, searching for the origin of life in sea ice. I said I'd never heard of that, but if bacteria could live in the vicinity of 'black smokers', superheated hydrothermal vents on the ocean floor, why not at the opposite end of the scale and live in extremely cold conditions? I was fascinated by his ideas, which he explained very clearly and simply in layman's terms, leaving out the scientific terminology so that I would understand. He told me about his last expedition to a place called Mushamna, where he purposely got his yacht frozen

7

into the ice and lived there completely alone with his two dogs, Bjosse and Svarten, studying the ice. He's mad, I thought. He looks really nice, but he's a bit mad. He was a Doctor of Physics too, so I wouldn't have been surprised if there was an old, dark blue London police box somewhere outside and a hidden Dalek or two. I'd always liked K9.

Then he went into overdrive and told me about a planned trip to a place called Kinnvika, which was many kilometres further north on an island called Nordaustlandet (I had never heard of it), and how he was looking for someone to go with him. (The Doctor's new assistant?) Well, not just anyone—a female, actually. It would be for a year and he and this other person would be entirely alone for the whole time, with maybe a couple of huskies, and it would be such a fantastic adventure, never to be repeated—and how would *I* like to go with him? Whew! What? Had I heard correctly? I thought so. He drove home the point by saying we would be living in a little wooden hut and it would be part of the deal that I wasn't allowed to go home halfway through the experiment if I didn't like it any more. It would be an amazing experience, and I didn't have to do the science stuff, and no one else in the last 40 years had had permission to stay in Kinnvika for a whole year, but he had as he was a scientist and so was very privileged; and was I interested? Silly question! I stood there flabbergasted. What could I say? My mind couldn't seem to marshal any sensible thoughts. My tongue was stuck in neutral whilst my brain was racing away trying to get to grips with his extraordinary proposal. Off the top of my head I couldn't think of a single, serious reason for saying no. Too right I was interested.

8

We agreed to talk more about it at a future date, and, with that, he said, 'Well, I'll let you go and find your friends now,' and disappeared back into the pub leaving me standing there with an empty glass in my hand. Didn't even offer to buy me a refill! I didn't know what to think, what to do. I was in a daze. I just stood there for a moment, perplexed. The last hour had flown by. I mentally shook myself awake, realising that I was still standing in the doorway of the little shop. I couldn't stand here all night with a bemused look on my face, and my throat was dry from all the talking, so I got myself another beer from Johan. I still couldn't find any of my friends there, that's the way it goes sometimes, but being Longyearbyen, at that hour, there was always someone to talk to. One of the real plus points of going to the pubs in town was that you could talk to almost anyone without feeling you were being chatted up or propositioned; the friendly ambiance made for relaxed and convivial evenings. My encounter with Hauke had been unusual in more ways than one.

The rest of the evening passed in a blur. I suppose I must have enjoyed myself as I don't remember going home particularly early, probably at closing time at 2 a.m. I kept the whole thing to myself, not mentioning it to anyone. I don't think I could believe the turn of events.

I made my way back up the hill to the bedsit, smiling to myself and going over the evening in my mind. I made a quick note in my diary:

'Met Hauke Trinks in Barents PubEN. Talked about Nordaustlandet. Go??? Professor of physics/physicist, Hamburg. He's German.'

9

As usual at weekends I had already converted the sofa to a bed before I went out, so I gratefully flopped straight into it and fell fast asleep whilst thinking of Hauke and his unconventional offer.

It was the first good night's sleep I'd had in an awfully long time. I appreciated it, waking up refreshed and happy for once, even though Daleks disguised as polar bears croaking 'Exterminate! Exterminate!' drifted in and out of my dreams. I pulled the quilt tighter around my shoulders to keep in the warm fug and thoughts of the previous evening. I felt flattered that he'd asked me. I didn't have a university background but at school I had always done well in biology classes without expending too much effort. I was never very squeamish—quite happy to cut up formaldehyde-yellow rats or a cow's eye from the ready supply from the slaughter house on the far side of the sports field. I enjoyed building worm houses and having races with different coloured maggots. I enjoyed physics too, though I don't recall excelling at it. I liked drawing all the diagrams and colouring them in or fiddling with electrical circuits, batteries and light bulbs, Bunsen burners and wave machines. Great fun! I was, however, a bit envious of those less academic pupils who got to work on the school farm. Looking after the animals seemed a great skive; much better than going to real lessons.

I thought how snug and warm I was here in my little bedsit and what it might be like to live in a wooden hut with no central heating, shower or decent cooking facilities. And yet I closed my eyes and felt the glow of anticipation spread throughout my body. 'I could do this,' I thought. Everything seemed to say 'yes'. I couldn't analyse why I wanted

10

to go, it didn't matter, it just felt right. I had the feeling—I knew—I would be capable of undertaking the expedition. I rolled over onto my side and pulled my knees up to my chest. How could I possibly know it would be all right? I knew nothing about surviving out in the extreme cold and bad weather. I liked to think I wouldn't be entirely stupid if I was caught out in the open in a storm, but it only took one silly mistake or a bad gamble and that would be the end of your life. There were no second chances, only the right decision, or perhaps just lots of luck. And luck didn't seem to be my strong suit. Or was it? If winning on the lottery was luck, then mine was non-existent, but if luck was meeting interesting people, then maybe I had it in spades. Perhaps, more importantly, I had the luck to be optimistic; my glass was always half full, not half empty, nothing was ever as bad as it seemed, things would always get better and a disappointment couldn't make me feel sad forever. Just like the Monty Python song, I tried to always look on the bright side of life.

Real life, of course, isn't quite as simplistic as that, not always so upbeat and wonderful, but generally the down times were maybe not so bad for me as they were for others, with the odd exception here and there, of course. I always seemed to find that small spark ready to fight for life in the dying embers of a difficult time, something wouldn't let me give up on myself, I always sprang back again. I wiggled my toes and smiled. This was one big, fat spark. I would need to think about it in more detail before I gave Hauke my final answer; after all, it was a serious undertaking and deserved, for once in my life, serious consideration. I owed it to myself and to Hauke.

11

'What do you think, Moose?' I asked my cuddly moose who was sharing my bed. He wobbled his antlers and gave me a blank look. No help there. Time for a cup of tea and a bit of breakfast, then. I had a final, luxuriant, back-bending stretch under the quilt and rolled out of the bed and into the kitchen to put the kettle on.

*　　*　　*

After getting up so late, I tidied up the bedsit a bit in what was left of the morning, which didn't take too long. It was one Portakabin in length and one and a half wide, so roughly six metres by three. The main room had full-width windows looking out across the valley which allowed sunlight to flood through even at midnight in full summer, tanning the one long, pine-panelled wall. The others were painted white. The furniture came with the room; a tall book case and a low TV unit, and a large, round coffee table with a red-upholstered chair matching the bed-settee. A miniscule kitchen was equipped with a two-ring electric burner, fridge under, and a storage cupboard with shelves above. Across the narrow passageway from the kitchen was the equally tiny bathroom with a loo, sink and shower unit. You didn't need more. For decoration I had a couple of iceberg posters decorating the walls, a small collection of differently shaded rock core samples and some fossil leaves, both found in summer on my wanderings near the base of the Longyear Glacier.

I went for a walk in the afternoon to get some fresh air and exercise. I decided to do a circular tour and started by heading up the hill, away from town, towards Nybyen. Several snow scooters passed by me, trailing blue smoke from their ear-jarring exhausts, a couple towing trailers full of equipment towards the Longyear Glacier from where they might head out to a weekend hut or perhaps go further afield to Barentsburg, the Russian town on Spitsbergen. The occasional cross-country skier came coasting down the hill in the opposite direction taking a well-earned breather after a long tour, a shoosh of skin-tight, pastel lycra sashed with a rifle. The sky was overcast and a soft, dull grey, leaving the light flat and with little contrast—the scooter drivers would have a hard time picking out the ridges and dips in the ice, making their journey a little bit more exciting, a fraction more dangerous. Just before reaching Nybyen, I took the road going off to the right which cuts across the narrowed valley and makes a dog-leg turn at a big, solid looking building called Huset, the town's multi-functional entertainment centre, to run back parallel on the other side of the valley. Huset looked a little sad painted in dingy pink and grey, broad vertical stripes; the whole place cried out for some money being spent on it to smarten it up a bit, but then maybe it wouldn't be Huset any more. Apart from the everyday café serving burgers and steaks and a daily special, it doubled as a nightclub on Friday and Saturday nights, and had another, fine restaurant with a superb, renowned wine cellar. On Sunday evenings its theatre also became a cinema. Despite its distance from the centre of the town, it could be considered its social heart. It was originally constructed between the homes of the miners and their white-collar bosses in a no-man's-land between the two, so encouraging social contact between the two communities. I decided not to call in today for a coffee (black regulation Norwegian) and slip-walked by on the hard snow to continue back down the far side of the valley.

I stopped and gazed up towards the top of the high cliffs on the left-hand side of the road and listened to the distant cries of the kittiwakes which had started returning from summer latitudes to their nesting sites on the inaccessible ragged-topped rocks. The first ones could usually be heard in early March if weather conditions were favourable, and I looked forward to the early summer and seeing great clouds of them wheeling about above me, twisting and twirling in unison, now silver, now invisible against the intense, heavenly blue of the sky. The snow-white birds are about the size of wood pigeons, a pale, pearly grey across their backs and wings which end in black tips. The feet are black and webbed and the beak, which seemed to me to vary in size and shape, just like human noses, is yellow but, surprisingly, bright red inside. Last summer I had been able to hand-feed one or two of them as they perched on my window ledge. In thanks they spat clear, fishy-stinking liquid over my just-cleaned windows.

Tucked under the snow-decked scree slopes at the base of the high cliffs that form the sides of the valley was a lonely little graveyard, the last resting place of several unlucky coalminers, their lonely crosses in the bleak landscape a reminder of the dangerous nature of their profession even here in the Arctic. The young men lay in the cold, hard ground out of sight of the modern, rust-red wooden Svalbard Church a kilometre further on. The church's big glass windows made it look like a greenhouse with a tangled jungle of plants behind them, luxuriating in

14

the interior warmth. Its sharply angled grey roof, mirroring those of the houses opposite, was surmounted by a short bell tower with a conical roof and weathervane. I smiled to myself as I remembered my first visit there and seeing the stuffed polar bear standing amongst the deep-buttoned armchairs of the comfortable social room alongside the church, his black, untwitching nose pointing towards the kitchen and the scent of coffee and waffles.

I cut down and right on Melkeveien, the middle of three roads crossing the valley, passing behind the remains of the wooden carousel-like structure which in the old days would have directed coal buckets, descending on aerial ropeways from the coalmines that were driven high and deep into the mountainside above, down to the quay below and waiting ships. It was built of massive timbers and still had the rusted turntables and a mass of thick, auburn cables and fittings. All around town there were reminders of the coal industry, past and present; several huge coal buckets were stranded, suspended on a last stretch of overhead ropeway connected to the Taubanensentrum, literally the aerial ropeway centre, the Clapham Junction of the whole system, and standing like a great grey menacing stick insect on long iron legs; tall wooden pyramids that supported the old cables still march up the mountains; lorries rumbling back and forth along the main road between the town and the new mine stain the snow with a light coating of coal dust.

At the point where the road crossed the frozen river, a couple of snow scooters buzzed under the girders of the bridge, drivers muffled up and well insulated against the cold, heads ducking, just in

15

case . . . From there it was just a short walk to the end of the road and into the middle of town. It was Saturday, and most shops had closed at 2 p.m., but the food department of Svalbardbutikken was still open and there was a steady stream of cars pulling in and out of the car park. My little fridge already being full, I popped into the post office foyer to check my mail box. Arranged around the wall were about 500 blue metal boxes of assorted sizes, the smallest above and the larger ones below. I didn't quite need the kick-step to reach the lock, but I couldn't see inside so had to stretch up to feel the interior of the box. Inside I found a grey, fuzzy-papered little envelope waiting for me. I ripped it open. Talk about quick work: it was a letter from Hauke inviting me out to a pizza at Kroa, a bar and restaurant in town, to talk over the expedition. He must have posted it early that morning. He left his phone number and asked me to get in touch soon as he was going back to Germany in a few days' time. In the cold, sober light of day, I became a bit nervous. I now had to make the approach to him. I would have to do some concentrated thinking before I phoned him. Did I actually want to take part in this expedition, or had I said yes last night just because I was flattered by his advances and persuasive talk? It was no longer a bit of fun in the pub. It struck me properly for the first time that this was a serious proposal and not to be fooled around with. I couldn't treat it flippantly like an invitation to a party thrown by someone I didn't know too well. Was I really going to do this thing? Had he actually asked me? Had I actually said yes? I must be as mad as him. And yet, although it might well be a completely crazy thing to do, right here, right now, it didn't

16

seem a bad idea at all. Well, there's being asked out and being asked out. But this was Spitsbergen, and nothing here was quite normal. This was for real and no backing out of it once committed. All or nothing. Shit. I stood quietly in front of the open box, gently nodding my head, numbed. Shit, I thought, again. Bloody hell. I folded up Hauke's note, slipped it back into its envelope and tucked it into my jacket pocket. I relocked the door of the shallow blue box and went home. More tea, I think.

*   *   *

All through the next day I tried to analyse my thoughts about the expedition. There was no denying that I was interested. I drew up on a piece of paper 'for' and 'against' columns. The biggest and obvious drawback would mean giving up my three part-time jobs and my sunny bedsit as I couldn't afford to keep it while I was away for the year. On my return to Longyearbyen after the expedition I would have nowhere to live and no money coming in. I could hope to sleep on a friend's sofa for a while or rent a spare room, but unless I got a job very quickly I couldn't afford even that for long. I had a little bit of money saved up in the bank, not too much, and if I decided I wanted to return to England I would need to ensure I had enough to get home. I also had to have funds for paying solicitors' fees for my upcoming divorce. I'd no idea how I would possibly pay them if I was away for a year, but I supposed as long as I explained how inaccessible I was going to be, they would be OK about the late payment of bills. And if it took a bit longer to sort everything out . . . Well, after 14 years of being together, a few

17

months' delay would hardly make a lot of difference. I wouldn't be paid for participating on the expedition—that had been made very clear at our initial meeting in PubEN—but all my food and equipment would be provided, so it would cost me nothing financially to go. My monthly income barely exceeded my outgoings, despite three jobs and being thrifty, so going on the expedition would hardly affect my bank balance. But could I live with a man I had only just encountered and knew nothing about for a whole year, in a hut hundreds of miles from anywhere, with no one else to speak to? How would I cope if it all went sour and we hated each other? What if he turned out to be a secret axe murderer? I might be chopped up into little pieces and fed to the dogs; no one would know what had really happened, no witnesses to the crime . . . Be serious! Would I be bored out of my mind? What about the bears? A whole year could seem an awfully long time. More boring than an FA Cup Final.

And yet these seemingly important factors to me were almost insignificant. (I was trying not to think about the bears.) Maybe there were lots of things I should have been adding to my list, but for now the 'against' list seemed very short.

The arguments for going were much easier to come up with.

It would be the experience of a lifetime, good or bad, and I would never forget it. I liked Hauke so far. Should first impressions be trusted? No idea. I've met a few people I thought I liked and they had turned out to be right horrid pieces of work. Nevertheless, Hauke stayed in the 'for' column. Being out in the middle of nowhere and living with

18

nature and the elements was a wonderful challenge. Even if I was scared at the thought, seeing polar bears would be amazing, observing them in their natural habitat, learning about their behaviour. Getting close to other creatures would be possible too, like seals and walrus. Being just two people looking after each other and trying to survive the conditions didn't seem to me a major drawback. I tried not to think of problems where none were likely to arise, to be objective. Things like cooking and washing would be no different from how it's been done for hundreds of years, it was just a case of getting used to not having a washing machine again and an electric stove. And to live amongst the icebergs, experience the isolation, experience a completely dark polar night and watch the Northern Lights and the stars. There's no sodium lighting in Kinnvika to pollute the night sky as in Longyearbyen and most other places—in fact no lighting at all. And to have dogs at home (I missed having a dog) and explore the terrain with them would be a real plus. Hopefully, I would enjoy Hauke's company and be able to assist him with his research. A whole year could seem an awfully short time.

Oh, I was sure I wanted to go to Kinnvika. Something inside me said I would enjoy it immensely; I just wished I could stop saying 'Why not?' all the time and be more objective. Oh, so what! The 'fors' were winning by a country mile.

What I should have been doing if I seriously wanted to go was to give Hauke a ring and discuss it further to see if there was anything I had neglected to consider, but I was scared to phone him, and the longer I left it the harder it became. I put it off. As usual.

*   *   *

Monday was a busy day for me as I had to be up early for work at Isbjørnbutikken, a sort of corner shop located beside the car park, selling newspapers, sweets and souvenirs, and renting out videos. On Mondays and Wednesdays I worked there in the mornings, using the company van to drive to various warehouses to fetch all the goods needed to restock the shelves. Usually it was cans and bottles of soft drinks, part-baked bread, ice cream and sausages from the warehouse near the harbour, T-shirts, cigarettes and cuddly toys from the store near the coal-fired power station, then all the way on up to Nybyen to the bakery to fetch the bread rolls for the hot dogs. After that I went to the post office to pick up the newspapers, magazines, post and parcels and delivered them back to Isbjørnbutikken or to Motekroken, the ladies' and gents' clothing shop where I also worked part time, or to Sport1, the outdoor sport and casual clothing shop, both located in the Lompensenter. This particular Monday morning there was a mountain of boxes at the post office, full of new clothing for both the clothes shops. I was already running late and now had no chance to catch up. It would be a late start at Randi's sewing room where I worked weekday afternoons, but I could work later into the afternoon to make up for it.

There were so many packages that I had to make two trips to get them delivered, and I was sweating profusely by the time I'd dropped off the first batch, despite the cold weather. They weren't particularly heavy, just bulky, and a fraction too big for me to get my fingers comfortably around the far corners. I was getting a bit agitated about being so behind, and feeling a bit short-tempered as a result when, in the middle of dropping off the last parcel, unable to see for the huge box in my arms, I literally bumped into Hauke. His face lit up into a huge grin as we said hello, and straight away he asked about the pizza date. I apologised rapidly about not really having the time to talk now; pushed past him into the shop, dumped the box on the floor, said 'I'll call you later' as I whisked past him and shot out of the shopping centre and back out to the van, driving the short distance across the car park back to Isbjørnbutikken far too fast. Was this a subconscious sign that I didn't want to see Hauke again, that I didn't want to go on the expedition with him, or just that I hadn't had enough time to come to a concrete decision? Or just bad timing? I wasn't sure. I just knew I was hot and bothered and late for my next job and I'd been exceedingly rude to him. After all, if you're already half an hour late, another couple of minutes doesn't make much difference. If I worked 1–5 p.m. instead of 12–4 p.m., Randi didn't mind as long as I got the work done. So why the panic?

And yet I still didn't phone Hauke.

*　　*　　*

Towards the end of the afternoon a couple of days later I was queuing up at the checkout after doing some food shopping in Svalbardbutikken, looked to see who was waiting next in line, and looked straight into Hauke's face. We were both surprised as he hadn't realised I was in front of him either. Being caught at the till, I had no chance to escape. It was crunch time. Like a schoolboy asking his first girl out on a date, Hauke's face flushed as red as a robin as he pestered me for a day to meet him. We agreed on the following Monday. It was with some trepidation that I awaited the coming rendezvous, knowing that the outcome of the meeting could decide my immediate future. Was my next job to be as expedition assistant? I was feeling very nervous. Then, to make matters worse, Hauke phoned me at Randi's to cancel the date as emergency repairs had to be made to the water pipes in the middle of town, so the restaurant would be closed, but if it was OK by me, he had rearranged it for the following evening. My calendar wasn't exactly full, so yes, it was OK. Another 24 hours to wait. Blaaaaaah!

*　　　*　　　*

'Kroa' means 'The Pub' in Norwegian, and not 'The Crow' as I first thought when I came to Spitsbergen, though its wooden cladding painted blue-black didn't help to dispel that idea. Inside, the toffee-coloured wood panelling was covered in black and white photos of characters from Spitsbergen's mining and hunting heritage, provision lists, animal skins, maps and a huge, gory painting of a bloody polar bear lying dead in the snow. A bust of Stalin (or was it Lenin?) adorned one end of the bar. The heavy tables were long, thick slices of varnished pine, the seats chunky logs, their tops covered in sealskin. At the bar, the stools were made from iron pit props.

Hauke was sitting at a table by one of the picture windows at the side, wearing the same boots, jumper and leather trousers I'd seen before, nursing a half-litre of beer. Was he more nervous than me? He couldn't be. As I approached the table, he stood up and we shook hands and exchanged broad grins and warm greetings before I made myself comfortable on the bench opposite. Any tension we were feeling disappeared as fast as an Arctic tern and we relaxed into the evening, talking animatedly over a beer and our pizzas like old friends.

Conversation was friendly and we learnt much about each other. It wasn't until later that I realised just how loaded Hauke's seemingly innocuous questions were. He was determined to get a thorough knowledge of the capabilities of his prospective expedition assistant. It was the funniest interview I'd ever had. In fact it didn't seem like one at all. We laughed and joked the whole time.

We talked about our families, discovering we were both separated, but whereas I had no children, he had three, and seven grandchildren of whom he was obviously very proud. He was 15 years older me, but that didn't bother me as I've never been an ageist person. You either like someone or you don't. I've often got on better with people older than me. It was curious to find that I was 43 and he was born in '43, he was 58 and I was born in '58, this year the only year when these reverses could possibly occur. Spooky.

What was my profession? Well, I didn't really have one. I was always interested in so many things that I could never decide what I should do for a living when I got older, and as a result—and with no regrets—had ended up without a 'career' as such. I had trained as a dispenser, a pharmacy assistant making up prescriptions; worked as a postlady delivering letters and later as a counter clerk; could sew proficiently and make upholstery and hoods for old cars; and lately worked as librarian at the National Motor Museum at Beaulieu in Hampshire. I was very practical, and could often fix and service my own cars, motorbikes and sewing machines.

Hauke raised important questions concerning my health, as being in such a remote location meant that medical assistance could be several hours or days away if the weather was bad when an emergency arose. Did I require regular medication? No. Did I get depressed after the winter when the sun returned? No, I didn't. This was a common ailment in the Arctic, often leading to the confiscation of weapons by the police until the owner recovered. How fit was I? I was quite fit and sporty. In England I had been an enthusiastic member of the Lymington rowing club, rowing on the sea out in the Solent, and here I kayaked on the fjord in summer and did circuit training in the sports hall in winter. Could I ski? I could fall over a lot! How about secretarial skills? Well, I could find my way round a keyboard and produce tolerably good documents as long as one wasn't in a hurry, but I was no typist and had had no training. What about a rifle? Did I own one here for protection against polar bears? Yes, I had a Ruger. Ah, but can you use it, he asked. This'll show him, I thought. I'd been .22 rifle shooting since I was 16, had been clay pigeon shooting in the New Forest after I'd got married, and here in Longyearbyen went to shooting practice nearly every week. Yes, I could shoot.

Hauke was mentally ticking off his list of questions, and only he knew if I'd come up with the right answers, but I thought I probably had as he wouldn't have continued otherwise.

Over a bottle of red wine Hauke persisted in his surreptitious interrogation. He probed my attitudes to life and difficult situations, my optimism and experience. I told him about going off walking and camping on my own, he told me about his sailing trips across the Atlantic single-handed and more about his first expedition to Mushamna. We found we were both practical (a bit unusual, I thought, for a scientist, but what did I know) and had a similar view of life, preferring to get on with it rather than whinge and ask for help or handouts. I found myself frequently agreeing with many things he commented on: 'I feel the same way' or 'That's just what I would do' sprang out of my mouth so often it was uncanny.

It was fun to giggle and tease each other, great to find another grown-up who liked to be silly sometimes. On the other hand, have I ever really been grown up?

The hands of the clocks seemed to race around the dial, and a change of venue was declared. Let's go to PubEN. Hauke, like the gentleman I thought him, generously paid for dinner and we wriggled into our elusive-sleeved jackets and set off down the hill.

I refused to drink any more alcohol—I'd had enough—and ordered a coffee, but by the time it had arrived it looked more like a large brandy to me. A young man that Hauke knew joined us. I wondered how come I'd never met him before because he was a chef in the restaurant there and was English to boot! Anthony and I introduced ourselves and we too hit it off straight away.

All three of us decanted, somewhat unsteady on our feet, to Karlsberger pub back in the middle of town for a last drink before going home. I'd had a

25

great evening and reckoned I'd made two good friends in Hauke and Anthony.

During the evening the wind had increased and fine, hard snow like white sand was slashing down, stinging exposed skin, scratching at the eyes like a cat's claws. As we left the pub, Anthony asked if I was going home, in which case he'd walk with me as he lived close by, or was I going with Hauke. 'Going with Hauke' was the instant reply, so we all said our goodnights and left Anthony to walk home alone. Hauke and I pulled up our hoods, linked arms, and with hunched shoulders and heads down against the lazy wind, set off downhill towards Hauke's place. Wherever that was.

By the university, we took the road towards the airport, meeting the full blast of the rising wind. I tightened the hood of my jacket so I could hardly see out and hung on to Hauke so I didn't lose him. We crossed the bridge, where in summer the river roars and roils and tumbles over rocks out into the fjord, and turned right down a lumpy track that led to the sailing club where the kayaks were stored. It was difficult to see where I was going as my eyes were screwed up tight to protect them from the micro-daggers of snow, so I hoped no bear was lurking about, though it was highly unlikely. No one bothered toting a rifle in town. We cut left through the odd assortment of sailboats and motorboats looming out of the dark, sitting on their cradles, stranded, most awaiting the brief freedom of ice-free summer; one, I knew, was lived in; others appeared forgotten or abandoned. Battling the gusty wind and razor-sharp snow, we approached an old, tarpaulin-covered, wooden boat, the *Silje Marie* (or the *Silly Marie* as I called it), parked adjacent to a two-storey

26

wooden naust, or boathouse, opposite the Sailing Club. Hauke pulled a key from his pocket and ducked under the boat's fat red bottom, and opened a door in the naust. We slammed the door on the foul weather and pulled off our hoods, revealing faces glowing rosy warm. Bare wooden steps like a loft ladder led steeply to the yellow glow of light spilling from the upper floor living space.

'Tea?' enquired Hauke, reaching for a flask on the kitchen unit—identical to mine in the bedsit. I was soon to learn that Hauke's tea was made with one teabag in a flask of hot water and drunk black without milk or sugar, but, more importantly, he always had a flask ready for when he came out of the cold to help thaw himself out. In an emergency you could even warm up frozen fingers in the tea, provided it was only lukewarm.

The ceiling was high on one side, dropping almost to the floor on the other side where an array of rucksacks, books and clothing were stored in the semi-darkness. One small window in the triangular wall let out the light. To enhance the atmosphere, Hauke lit some candles stuck into the hollow centres of reindeer backbones which looked like little simplistically carved folk art animals. Either side of a long, low coffee table were two old sofas, and we sat close together, talking, laughing and drinking our tea. Snuggling up closer made us even more friendly, and it was obvious I wasn't going back to my place once my mug was empty. No sign of a bedroom, though. But, Hauke, being a practical man, hauled away the coffee table and shoved the two sofas together. He produced a sheet, pillows and two quilts from behind a third sofa in the darkest, lowest corner of the room and we made ourselves a cosy

27

nest and concluded the job interview.

The morning, far from bringing the morning-after-the-night-before embarrassment, brought more good humour and lots more tea. After descending the steps backwards, the safest way to negotiate them, Hauke escorted me as far as the car park in town as I was due in at Isbjørnbutikken again. He said he had to return to Germany in the early hours the day after tomorrow, but still to take a little time to think about Kinnvika before letting him know in a week or two, because if I declined, he would need to have time to try to find someone else. We gave each other a big hug and I went skipping off to work smiling.

Mulling over the events of the previous evening, I realised that our meeting had quickly progressed from seeing if we could work and live together through the year-long expedition to something on a more personal level. Hauke was in a hurry to find an expedition partner so I comprehended his directness and intensity. The formalities of employer assessing a prospective employee had been completed, the salient points had been addressed, but in such a way that the evening had eventually felt more like a date than an interview. If I'd met Hauke in other circumstances, I wondered, would the outcome have been any different? We'd both enjoyed our brief time together, but I was unsure how this would translate into a whole year. 'Marry in haste, repent at leisure' crossed my mind, though in not such a literal way. I still thought of myself as a prospective expedition assistant, but the border lines between that of employer/employee seemed to have been distorted like the snowdrifts in last night's strong winds. An ill-defined line existed between us and I

28

wasn't at all sure how far across it I was prepared to step. I wasn't unhappy. It was nice being hugged by someone my size.

I picked up my post on Friday. There was an envelope with a picture of a polar bear and a map of Spitsbergen on it, Kinnvika marked and labelled in red by Hauke in case I wondered exactly where it was. The note inside read:

With thanks for a wonderful evening, night, morning!

Enclosed with the note, hanging from a silver chain, was a little polar bear. Hauke was being very persuasive. I wanted to thank him personally, but he was already gone, up in the air somewhere between Oslo and Hamburg on the last leg of his journey home that had started at 2 a.m. that morning. I smiled to myself, tears pricking my eyes. I felt happy, sad, lonely.

See you soon.

CHAPTER TWO

TESTING TIMES

Hauke Trinks. What did I know about him? He was a scientist, a professor and Doctor of Physics, so obviously an intelligent man. An outdoors, adventurous man, practical too, who had overwintered before in his own yacht. He had also sailed single-handed in that yacht across the Atlantic Ocean a couple of times by the cold northern route, so didn't mind his own company and had the determination and perseverance to see a tough project through to the end. He was direct, decisive and a fast mover, talked a lot and could be rather sneaky (in a nice sort of way). He was a family man, very personable, a gentleman, sexy, fun to be with and liked a beer or two. And he liked me. Quite a lot to learn about someone in just one evening. What else could I find out about him?

The library upstairs at the Lompensenter kept back-copies of the local weekly newspaper, *Svalbardposten*, and I felt sure there would be reports of Hauke's expedition to Mushamna within their pages. I could also try the web, and so booked myself a half-hour session on the library's computer.

There were thousands of hits, though all seemed to be in German, not unnaturally, many in connection to his overwintering in Mushamna in 1999–2000. (Overwintering, for me, meant surviving from when the sun disappeared below the horizon for the last time in late October until it reappeared again in the middle of February the following year. On Spitsbergen, it meant much more than just 'spending the winter'.) I had no idea where to start. I was completely overwhelmed by the sheer volume of stuff to look at. I scanned the first couple of pages, trying to find a likely one to try, but I was lost in all the German. I picked one at random that had an automatic translator flagged at the end of the reference, turning the article into passable, but occasionally very strange, English. I learned that Hauke had been the president of the Technical University at Hamburg-Harburg (TUHH) just prior to embarking on his expedition to look for the origin of life in luggage ice. In what? Was I being a bit dim? I stared at the phrase. I couldn't work out for the life of me what they were trying to say. I was having as much trouble as some of my Norwegian friends had when I tried to talk their language. Then the penny dropped. Pack ice. It was going to take forever if I carried on like this. Perhaps this wasn't such a good idea after all. I logged off the computer. Maybe I would be safer with the newspapers.

I pulled out the volumes for 1999 and 2000, the years covering his first overwintering in his yacht. I worked my way through each issue page by page and eventually found three references in total, five full pages in all. My understanding of Norwegian wasn't perfect, so I photocopied the pages and took them home to read at leisure with the aid of my Norwegian–English dictionary and a cup of tea.

The first article from July 1999 was entitled 'To Life's Extreme Limits to Find Life's Beginning', which I guess summed up the aim of his adventure. Perhaps in a few years' time, I mused, the title would apply to me. A new beginning for me, anyway.

It recorded that Hauke was a very sporty character and had not only completed the 40-kilometre ski marathon on Spitsbergen, where, for him, 'the first twenty kilometres were training and the rest was the race', but he also kayaked and walked all the way to Austfjordneset (at the southern end of Wijdefjord and lying at a little over 79 degrees north, roughly due north of Longyearbyen), to visit one of his ex-students, who was himself overwintering there as a hunter. Even with my limited knowledge of the terrain up here I knew it must have been a very difficult journey to make alone, even for an experienced adventurer. The article also said that he was looking forward to his forthcoming overwintering, his scientific work and to becoming attuned to the slow rhythms of nature. I thought about how strange it must have felt to sail away alone and not expect to see anyone for a year. How do you prepare for that? I supposed his time spent sailing would help, but a few weeks at sea are not the same as a year. Was he worried about his yacht being crushed by the ice? How concerned was he about not coming back? No one seemed to have asked him the question. Perhaps they didn't like to worry him.

In May the following year, the editor of the newspaper, Arne Holm, and a couple of his friends made a scooter tour to visit him. They were impressed by his enthusiasm for his subject—at one point he got so carried away that he scattered coffee cups and test tubes all over the table. Hauke was convinced, Arne wrote, that life started in sea ice and that there was an 'incredibly huge amount of life in [and on] the ice, everything from molecules to polar bears'. He'd seen 51 of those. (That's a lot, I thought, more than one a week since he'd set sail on 20 July 1999.) He'd had time to write a book contrasting his life in Mushamna with that of an old lady in his home village, Helga Maruska. He said he remembered her story about how to slaughter a pig, which was very useful as he did the same to the first seal he shot. (So he wasn't squeamish, then).

I turned to the third article about his return to Longyearbyen in late July 2000. The journalist asked how he would sum up his experience. Apart from 70 bear visits (so many!) he said he had had 'experiences in the solitude that were difficult to describe, but had found an inner peace'. (Would that be how I felt after a year in Kinnvika? I had no idea, but I could do with some of that.) He was glad that he had done it and that it was now all over, and he'd not likely be doing it again. (Got news for you, sunshine!) That sent an interesting message to me. I couldn't imagine how hard it must have been for him to cope with being alone for so long with almost no visitors. The stress must have been enormous at times; surely he had problems with the yacht in the ice, and the bears, and having no one to talk to about it all would make it harder. Perhaps that was why he was looking to take a companion with him. Would I, at the end of the year, feel that enough was enough, never again? Would being in Kinnvika be so stressful? There was no way to tell, but I had the feeling I would be in good, experienced hands.

I poured myself another mug of tea and thought a bit more about what I had read. It hadn't crossed my mind before; but knowing *Svalbardposten* there must be something in it about his plans for this latest expedition to Kinnvika.

I went back next day to check. Sure enough, in

June 2001, an article talked about his latest adventure, and how much the Governor's office 'liked researchers like him, demanding little in the way of resources and leaving no trace of his stay'. This time they 'preferred he had a companion'. Hauke commented that he had 'done it alone and now it was time to share the experience with someone, and he'd rather prefer it was a woman— that would be his new challenge'. (So I was a challenge, eh? I reckoned that was true, but he didn't know that yet. Or did he?)

The article also gave me my first real information about Kinnvika. It was a group of huts built by the Swedes for the International Geophysical Year of 1957/58 (so constructed the same year as me). I asked the librarian if she had more information on Kinnvika. There wasn't much, but it was comprehensive. In a book called *High Latitudes*, fortuitously in English, by a Swede called Gösta H. Liljequist, it described in detail, and with several photographs, the setting up of the buildings, the life of the scientists (all seeming to sport trendy, straggly beards and de rigueur Norwegian jumpers) and the results they obtained on the Kinnvika station. Importantly, for me, they didn't see many polar bears, a big plus. It made fascinating reading, doing nothing to dissuade me from confirming my acceptance of Hauke's invitation.

Not long afterwards I went to a film show at the university (given by Jason Roberts, Longyearbyen's well-known Australian film-maker) about polar bears, which was to be one programme in a series called *The Blue Planet* for the BBC. It was hot from the cutting room, so perhaps we got the world premiere. It gave an insight into the harsh life cycle

34

of the polar bear and was set against the glorious backdrop of the Arctic. As luck would have it, when I went to the Polar Hotel for a late-night coffee before going home, Jason was there talking to some friends. I felt a bit rude interrupting them, but I had a few questions I wanted to ask about polar bears on Spitsbergen. Fortunately he was very polite and said he didn't mind. Take a seat and fire away.

'Were there many on Nordaustlandet?' I queried.

'Quite a few,' he replied.

'How about in the Kinnvika area?' His brow furrowed as he seemed to put two and two together. 'No, not many at all. It's not on their migration route.'

I didn't know it at the time, but Jason knew Hauke and of his planned overwintering, and had no doubt read about his search for a companion. No one else was likely to be asking such specific questions about Kinnvika unless they were thinking of going there. Jason's not daft. He was the first to know of my intentions.

I wanted to ask other people about what it was like to overwinter, but I knew no one that had. I tried asking my friends in a roundabout, nonchalant way who had overwintered before, trying to keep my enquiries discreet and private. No chance. Soon the rumour that I was thinking of going with Hauke was widespread in Longyearbyen; hardly surprising in such a small, close-knit community. John W. (pronounced Yon Dobbelt-vay; never known as anything else to his friends) who ran the gallery and the adjoining Kunstnersenter (or artists' centre, where Randi's sewing room was located), suggested I talk to Karin Stensson, one of the other girls who rented a workshop there. She had overwintered with her

35

husband Anders, living as hunters, for two years at Austfjordneset, something I hadn't known about before, but which now explained the white fox furs and seal claws in her atelier. (We were both a bit embarrassed when I asked what the other little bones were. Only male seals have them and they make good cocktail stirrers.) Once the subject was broached, I found her full of useful information. She had made a study of women in Arctic Spitsbergen, and to the best of her knowledge, none had overwintered at over 80 degrees north, so if I stayed at Kinnvika I would be the first woman as far as we knew to do so. (Wow! Really?) She gave me an excellent tip for scaring away polar bears too: walk towards the bear banging two saucepans together. It worked every time, apparently. But the most important thing she told me was that the years spent in Austfjordneset were the best two years of her life, and given the chance, she would love to do it again. That was really encouraging, and another tick in Hauke's favour.

In the sewing room one day, Randi and I were chatting away as we worked. She steered the conversation around to Hauke and the topic of Kinnvika.

'Are you thinking of going?' she enquired of me at last.

'Errrr. Yes.'

'No!' she cried, throwing down her work and banging her hands on the table. 'No!'

In all honesty I don't think she was at all surprised that I was going to go, but she was just about to lose her very capable assistant. Where (and I'm trying to be modest here) would she find another as good as me? I did feel a bit guilty, but sometimes a gal's got to do what a gal's got to do.

My worst worry (I was still trying not to think about the bears) was about seeing the same person day in, day out, for a whole year. I knew of instances in the past where it had all gone horribly wrong between couples, married or otherwise, but for others it had been a success. Karin had done it with her husband for two years and loved it, but I was going with a complete stranger. On the other hand, if we got on as well as we had so far, there was no reason why I shouldn't enjoy it as much as she had. I would just have to trust to luck.

If nothing else, I was in the fortunate position of being able to say yes if I wanted to. I lived alone and had no immediate family of my own to consider, no bank loan or mortgage to repay, no career to take a setback—after all, I was little more than an underdog working in Longyearbyen, a very minor cog in the great scheme of things. I could please myself. The last few months had not been all that easy for me and I'd been trying to decide what direction my life ought to take. The answers to my problems had seemed shrouded in dense mist, then suddenly the bright and breezy Hauke had punched a hole through the clouds and shone a bright light down the road ahead. He'd pulled me up short in my aimless wanderings and had just handed me a map of my future with the way ahead clearly marked out for me. Life had suddenly been given direction and purpose. A lift. What the heck. Just do it!

*   *   *

Hauke phoned me one day.
'I'm coming to Kinnvika with you,' I declared.
'Really? You're sure? Absolutely sure?'

37

'Yes.'

'Really, really sure?'

'Yes! Yes! Yes!'

I could feel the electricity flickering back and forth across the wires, sense the broad grin, the twinkling blue eyes lighting up; I could picture him jumping around his office—though surely very sensible professors don't do that.

'Yes. Really coming with you. Absolutely certain. Is that OK?'

'Of course it's OK. I'll see you soon—I'm coming up to Spitsbergen shortly to take a few more measurements and to start preparing equipment for the expedition. I'm really pleased you're coming. We'll have fun. See you in a couple of weeks. Bye.'

So it was done, confirmed. My face flushed with pleasure and embarrassment at his enthusiasm. My heart thumped double-time and I wiggled my fingers and grinned too. In about four months I'd be off to a tiny corner of the world, with a man I hardly knew, and I was looking forward to it immensely. It felt good. I had just one more task to do. To tell my old friend Edwin before he heard it from someone else. If it hadn't been for him, I would never have ended up on Spitsbergen and be faced with the adventure of a lifetime.

I saw him in PubEN late one night, and we stood chatting over a coffee under the chandelier. We'd first met over thirty years ago in connection with the Rangers—for those girls over 16 in the Guide movement—when he was in the army working with youth groups, and we'd had an on–off relationship (mostly off) over the intervening years, but always remaining close. I'd already thought about how I would tell him.

38

'I don't think I'm going to be in Longyearbyen much longer,' I opened. Edwin rocked back on his heels in shock, almost spilling his coffee down his front. (It was the first time I'd actually seen anyone rock back on their heels—I'd previously only read about it in novels.)

'Oh!' he said.

'I'm going to be in Kinnvika!'

'Oh!' he replied, relieved that I wasn't leaving Spitsbergen. 'I know you. You'll love it,' he said. 'You'll love it.'

And that was good enough for me.

*   *   *

Hauke was back in town and rang me at the sewing room.

'Have you got your snow scooter with you?'

'Yes.'

'OK. See you there at four o'clock when you finish work. We're going out.'

Where we were going he didn't tell me, but I soon learned. Punctually (very German), at four, he turned up. We were going down inside the Longyear Glacier. Oh my goodness! I pulled on my scooter dress, hat and thick gloves, yanked the scooter into life and followed Hauke as we wormed our way up towards the glacier at the head of the valley, crossed the foot of it, then climbed the narrow, steep, snow-packed defile on the right-hand side, standing up slightly, leaning forward and twisting the accelerator hard to get up the last, sharply inclined section before racing over the broad, flat expanse of snow-covered ice. We headed across to a small, roped-off area marking the entrance to the tunnel in the glacier. Hauke was well equipped, producing ropes, lamps and ice axes as well as a couple of spotlights and a medium-sized digital video camera. We attached the camera to its tripod and set it up to film us at the entrance. Hauke pulled back the old door covering the entrance and we roped ourselves together.

I slid about three metres below the surface to a large, semi-circular platform cut into the ice. Hauke slid the rucksack containing all the other equipment down to me, and I grabbed it to make sure it didn't drop straight down the dark, vertical shaft to the side.

After a few seconds Hauke slid down after it with a dramatic little squeal. The sequence captured on film, Hauke climbed back up to the surface and retrieved the camera, returning it to the rucksack after we'd made some space in it by strapping lamps to our heads. We checked that they were working correctly, then edged across to the gaping hole where, I saw for the first time, a narrow rope ladder was firmly fixed to the ice wall with thick metal spikes. Hauke shouldered the rucksack, reached across to the ladder and swiftly clambered down with me following, at a more sedate pace, until we reached the bottom, about fifteen metres below.

A long, gently sloping tunnel ran off close by, its water-worn concave walls glinting in the pale lamplight. By turns filming and collecting ice samples for Hauke's research, we bent knees and heads and set off into the unknown depths of the tunnel. I felt as if I was Jonah in the belly of the whale as we emerged into a bigger section of the tunnel. Its walls, slate grey and deeply ribbed, were encrusted with thick frost, glinting under our lights as we gazed in amazement at the sculpted forms. The scooped walls of the tunnel were spirally grooved like rifling in a gun barrel in places, formed in summer by the immense excavating force of the glacier's melt-water powering its way through the ice to the moraine at the foot of the glacier, where a multitude of frothing streams would join together to form the wide, shallow river than ran through town. We slipped and slithered, crawled and crept along the sometimes narrow, sometimes vaulted corridors in the bowels of the glacier, marvelling at the frost flowers growing thickly on the walls or the fronds of short icicles fanning out almost horizontally like many-fingered hands, formed where the cold breeze had blown the dripping water and it had frozen stiff. Other icicles, some over a metre long, hung vertically from the ceiling like glass stalactites while still more were hidden away in deep water-scoured alcoves in the tunnel walls. The floor was strewn with rocks that were temporarily glued in place until the thaw. Other sloping stretches were worn smooth, so we slid down on our bums like children on a playground slide.

We sat on the cold floor and turned off our lamps, and in the perfect dark, listened to the unadulterated silence, scary and thrilling in its purity. I waved my hand an inch in front of my nose. Nothing. The dark was absolute, almost solid, impenetrable as a black fog.

Breaking the spell after five very long minutes, we turned on our feeble lights and grinned at each other. We had been using a couple of big lamps to illuminate the tunnels while we were filming, and they were now starting to fade with use and the cold, so before our headlamps gave out too, we retraced

41

our steps in the slippery darkness back to the foot of the rope ladder. With all the equipment restowed in the rucksack, Hauke climbed up the ladder like a monkey, disappearing from view as he reached the ice platform. I followed slowly, the ladder jerking and twisting suddenly from side to side as I climbed. I couldn't believe how incredibly tired I was; every rung I gained took a lot of effort and I felt totally exhausted. Hauke was shouting at me after a few minutes:

'Where are you?'

'Only halfway!' I shouted back.

It took an eternity to get to the top, unbelievable hard work: was I so unfit? I flopped down gratefully onto the platform, chest heaving, calf muscles protesting, and took a well-earned rest. Hauke looked a bit concerned at my hard breathing and pale face, but I soon recuperated and we scrabbled up the last few metres into the fading daylight and dropped the door back over the opening. We checked watches. No wonder I was tired. We had been down over three hours. So long? As Hauke stowed everything safely on the back of his scooter, I switched on the ignition on mine and yanked on the starting cable, the engine roaring to life at the third pull. Hauke flicked his into life with the electric starter and we whizzed back across the glacier, swooped down the declivity and switch-backed our way into town, stopping off at the Funken Hotel. As if exploring tunnels in the glacier wasn't enough, Hauke took me to the 'ice bar', which is carved into the huge wind-blown bank of snow alongside the hotel. Inside, candles and night lights glowed from niches cut into the walls, and tables and benches were hacked from the solid ice and snow. It was beautiful, magical; the soft lighting suffusing the walls in shades of golden yellow and palest blue. We drank Jaegermeisters, naturally chilled, and toasted each other as we relived our adventure. Hauke seemed to be impressed with my game spirit, so I had the feeling I had just passed one of his tests. What would be next, I wondered.

It was to be a walk.

* * *

After packing spare clothes and warm slippers into my rucksack and shouldering my rifle, I left the bedsit and met Hauke at the naust. We redistributed the food and other goods between his rucksack and mine, though Hauke's remained inordinately heavy. It was late in the day when we set out as I had been working until 4 p.m. in the sewing room, and the soft light under the thin, patchy white cloud was already fading and turning everything to a muted blue-grey.

We were going for the weekend to Hauke's little hut on the far side of Adventfjord, to a place called Revneset—the fox's nose. It was effectively to be a trial run to see how well we got on living together within the confines of four small, wooden walls. As a precursory expedition, it was likely to be a bit unrealistic, for surely we'd both be on our best behaviour, and only a prolonged time cooped up together would reveal our worst habits, but there was little chance to test ourselves in any other way. I was a bit concerned that we'd suddenly find nothing to say to each other and Hauke would expect better things of my cooking, but I was feeling optimistic and looking forward to learning more about him. I wondered what Hauke had up his sleeve this time?

We couldn't walk directly across the fjord to the hut as the ice was weak and unsafe, so we made our way a little further up Advent Valley and crossed where the ice was thick and solid. Even here, the ice was cracked under the pressure of the tides ebbing and flowing unseen beneath our feet. Snow encrusted the surface like wave-formed sand, hard-packed by the wind, crimped by the cloven hooves of meandering reindeer. The going was easy here, the delta naturally flat, but it was over an hour's brisk walk to the distant opposite bank where we scrambled over the tidal ridges and furrows of ice and onto firm land. At Hiorthhamn, the scant covering of snow barely concealed the odd lengths of twisted railway line, gnarled timber sleepers and rusted cables lying around, remnants from the coalmining activities high up in the mountainside above our heads. An enormous rusting engine with cylinders the size of soup plates, shrouded in a snow-sheet, lay near a large, old wooden building perched high upon stilts made of steel girders. This too was a leftover from the old mining days, when the large coal buckets came down the mountainside by the aerial ropeway, just like the one in town, and ended their journey here.

It was very cold, perhaps −15°C; but no wind stirred the air, and it was warm work walking energetically with our heavy packs on the hard-frozen, rutted ground. We had no need of our thick jackets if we kept moving, just chunky jumpers, gloves and hats and the obligatory long, blue wool underwear underneath it all. The sky turned a darker, harder shade of blue and a near-full moon rose, pouring mercury across the crisp snow and casting our shadows long and grey as we walked. We had 12–15 kilometres to cover, and at a little over halfway, a long-abandoned wooden boat signalled our resting place. It was a relief to set down the heavy rucksack and my thigh muscles felt light being released from their burden. We pulled on our jackets to keep in the warmth and Hauke produced a thermos of coffee, some cognac and two bars of chocolate to keep us going. It was too cold to sit long on the canted hull of the ash-grey boat, and the coffee cooled as fast as us, so, shouldering our gear once more, we continued, following the coastline for a few more kilometres before turning uphill and inland as the night closed in around us. We kept a sharp lookout for polar bears as we walked, making 360-degree sweeps of the landscape every few minutes. Each reindeer we spied in the dark was a potential bear in disguise, and we took no chances, standing and observing very pale ones until we were certain they were just that and nothing more.

We talked as we walked, matching our conversation to the rhythm of our stride, helping us to forget the tiredness in our legs. Hauke told me the story of Nils Holgersson, who flew the length of Sweden on the back of a goose, describing the landscape as he went, so giving Swedish children a geography lesson in the telling of the tale. Eventually a break in the wall of mountains to our right indicated the river valley we had to cross, which, much to my relief, meant we were getting near to our destination. The land shelved gently down towards the gully where it dropped away more steeply to the striated, solid river bed. Whilst struggling to keep our feet going down the bank, we saw that in the middle, a smoothly polished dome of

45

blue ice about one metre high and two metres across, like some stupendous opal set in white gold, had forced itself up through the surface like a monstrous blister on the cold finger of the river.

We heaved ourselves up a narrow gully in the far river bank, turned right up the last, steep slope and directed our feet the short distance towards Hauke's hut, dark against the darker background, the moonlight reflecting in the unshuttered windows.

I waited outside, panting, desperate to shed my backpack, while Hauke unlocked the door and lit some candles to give off a soft, welcoming glow throughout the little hut, as cold in as it was out. We dumped our rucksacks indoors, hanging our rifles on stout nails high in the wall by the door, then set about warming up the hut. The fire was ready laid in the woodburning stove in the corner of the main room, and just a match was needed to bring it to life. It had taken us four hours to get here and we were tired and hungry. An hour later the hut was just warm enough to take our jackets off, but by then we had fried up some *'pitt i panne'*—a mixture of potatoes, onions, root vegetables and bacon, all finely diced—had another coffee-cognac and put away everything we'd brought with us. I couldn't believe the amount of stuff in Hauke's rucksack. Food, wine, camera, spare clothing, a book to read and a thick, down quilt for the bed which was in the tiniest of bedrooms (more like a large cupboard) to conserve heat.

It was a simple rectangular hut, simply furnished with old sofas, a coffee table and a bureau. There was an open-plan kitchen with a bottled-gas stove and a small area for hanging coats and parking boots and saws, and the floor was covered in woven cotton rag rugs and reindeer skins. On the pine-panelled walls in the seating area dozens of brightly coloured pictures, painted by young schoolchildren in Germany, showed Hauke's yacht frozen into the ice in Mushamna. Some were excellent, well detailed and technically quite accurate; a couple were so similar that the two children must have been sitting next to each other in class, copying each other; and others had the strangest creatures I'd ever seen outside of old sailing maps. 'Here be Monsters', indeed! It was hard to tell if they were bear, fox, reindeer, dog or seal. The drawings were fascinating, and I spotted more and more details in them as the weekend progressed and marvelled at the children's imagination.

Through the big square windows, unprotected by shutters even in winter, we could see across the mouth of Adventfjord. Light from the gold-ringed moon caressed the icy surface and scattered stars nestled in the soft black velvet of the Arctic sky.

We stoked up the woodburner with logs, shut it down for the night and climbed into the cold, cold bed, shutting the door on ourselves and drawing the thin curtains. We snuggled up close for warmth in the dark shoebox of a bedroom, pulling the quilt tight around our shoulders, and were soon curled up together like a couple of hibernating mice, fast asleep.

Come the morning, Hauke coaxed the fire to life and he let it heat up the hut while he dived back under the quilt to check out how well his new assistant had recovered from yesterday's exertions. After yesterday's filming, cynical thoughts of casting couches flashed through my mind. Silly really. I'd already got the job. I was in bed with

47

Hauke, trying to keep active, alluring and warm with a quilt around my shoulders, because here was where I wanted to be. We knew instinctively that we had clicked together though we avoided talking about what might develop in the future. It was still a 'business' relationship, after all. Yesterday afternoon we had discussed the experiences of other overwintering couples such as Karin and Anders, and decided that, however we felt now, the expedition was time restricted, and at the end of the year we could do as we pleased with no pressure to stay together or keep in touch. We told ourselves, by inference, that our growing relationship was also time restricted, which left me feeling a bit confused.

Eventually, Hauke hopped out of bed and made some tea, which I drank still snug under the quilt, while he dressed and checked over the hut, inside and out. At last even I emerged from my pit, rapidly pulling on my woolly undies, thick socks and felt slippers before I had a chance to get cold again. Over a long, leisurely breakfast of cereals, bread and cheese, boiled eggs (just one had got cracked in the well-stuffed rucksack) and lots and lots of tea, we decided what to do during the day. The weather seemed set fair, the sun was smiling on us, so it was a good day to practise using the video camera.

The ice around Revneset had the appearance of being quite solid farther out into the mouth of the fjord, but it was much cracked around the coastline, at least six inches (15 centimetres) thick and moving under the influence of the sub-ice seawater. It was tinged a pale turquoise and groaned and creaked like old door hinges as the undulations of the water moved it back and forth, up and down, grating one thick platelet against another. Other strange sounds emanated from the rasping, shifting ice; violin-like whining; electronic miaows; gurgles and farts. We watched for ages the slow, almost imperceptible rise and fall of the ice as the subdued waves rolled sluggishly to shore below it. Slow, twisting, rim-worn slabs of ice tipped and canted, forcing up a soup-like mixture of ground ice and seawater between them that sloshed lazily across their surfaces to disappear between the graunching cracks. Hauke lay on his stomach and captured the ice and its often rude noises on film. The shoreline itself was a massive, squared-off shelf of ice skirting the land, at times almost six feet (two metres) high, where the stormy seas had crashed ashore and frozen into solid blue-white walls. The low cliff faces beyond were overhung with vast, white curtains of hard snow, looped and knotted by the turbulent winds and screening the occasional sea-scooped cavern in the fractured rock. Kittiwakes in their hundreds cruised effortlessly on the updraught, flicking black-tipped grey wings, eyeing us from their yellow-beaked faces as they returned from feeding in a gull-filled lead, a channel of open water in the ice, about one and half kilometres offshore.

Our walk along the encrusted shore was blocked by a wall of ice on land and ice blocks playing bumper cars in the groaning sea, so we backtracked part of the way until we could clamber up to the top of the low, rough-iced cliff.

Scratching through the snow with their hooves, a group of eight or nine beige-brown reindeer were nibbling on the moss near the hut, so we circled downwind of them and positioned ourselves so that we could film them with the fjord as a backdrop. They were quite fat for this time of year, so had

49

overwintered well. Permission is given conditionally by the Governor of Spitsbergen, who also heads up the police department, to hunt them for a short period once a year, and they do taste exceedingly good however you cook them.

Regaining the hut, we banished the cold with coffee and some crisp chocolate. We reviewed in the camera screen the scenes we had taken, trying to see what we could do better, trying to remember what we had done to get some shots looking right. I soon learned it was essential to use a tripod or some form of stable support to film from, like a rock, otherwise we were just wasting our time, film stock and precious battery power. A hand-held camera worked OK for filming the birds, but if the bubble in the spirit level on the tripod wasn't perfectly centred when you were panning the horizon, it tilted the picture up at an alarming angle as you swung the camera round. Not very professional, and we aimed to do the best job we could with the filming. Hauke was hoping a television company would make a film of the expedition (as before) using our footage, plus he would use it to illustrate any future lectures he would give and, most important of all, to document his research.

We took our ease for the rest of the evening, reading books and writing letters by the mellow glow of the oil lamps, sweet-scented tobacco smoke drifting up to the ceiling as Hauke smoked his pipe. Red wine was kept warm by the fire. I'd had a lovely time so far, here in the hut at Revneset. It was very primitive living: the toilet was a quick sprint around to the wooden cubicle at the back of the hut, after checking for bears; no electricity, not that I was missing it; no phones; no TV; no running water, just melted snow for washing and cooking and making the tea. It was so relaxing, enjoyable, stressless. I thought I would have no trouble getting used to it. We were alone together, with nothing to disturb our peace, just like we would be in Kinnvika.

*   *   *

Sunday breakfast was something special. Hauke made a super effort with eggs and bacon, orange juice, and—wow!—a bottle of champagne. How's that for living in luxury? Before we got the frying pan on the heat, Hauke told me I had to open the bottle, but I would need to do it outside. Eh? So, on with all the outdoor clothing.

'You've forgotten something,' said Hauke.

'What?'

'Your rifle.'

'But I can't see any bears.'

'It's not for the bears. Follow me,' he said, picking up the video camera and setting off for the river valley. What was he up to?

Hauke set the champagne down on a thick bank of wind-driven snow.

'You said you could shoot. Let's see it,' he said. 'Shoot the cork out of the bottle!'

When I stopped laughing and I got my breathing under control, Hauke started up the camera, focusing on the green, black-labelled bottle with the gold foil top. I held my breath, aimed and fired. A dirty laugh escaped my lips. With the first shot I'd removed the cork, much to my surprise as well as Hauke's. Trouble was I'd removed the contents as well, as the bottle had shattered with the shock and now lay in a green streak up the champagne-flavoured snow

51

bank. Poo. What a waste—but what a laugh!

We gathered up the glass shards and took them back to the hut, dumping them in the rubbish bin. No champagne breakfast today, but the eggs and bacon tasted pretty good, even so. Another test passed. Sort of.

By early afternoon we had restocked the wood pile indoors from the supply of sawn-up driftwood stacked at the rear of the hut, and let the fire go out so we could re-lay it for the next visit, matches being left handy, ready to find in the dark or in an emergency. Standard practice in hunters' huts, and life-saving. We packed up, and after a final check that all was safe and secure, we hefted our rucksacks and rifles and set off in bright sunshine back to the naust. We again stopped for a breather, coffee and cognac on the same abandoned, barge-like boat, which appeared in remarkably good condition, though I wouldn't have wanted to go anywhere in it.

Dark was creeping up on us as we tried to see the best place to recross the valley towards town. The ice was thick and crusty at what seemed to be the tidal limits across the width of the river, so we took a chance and picked a careful way along the icy piecrust, avoiding the thinner ice of the fjord proper. It felt, in the end, safer than where we had crossed when we set out, and whether that was true or not, it had saved us about an hour of walking.

As we tiredly breasted the final slope into town, we decided to go our separate ways. Though it was unspoken, we both felt the need in each other to have a bit of time on our own, and to take a long, hot shower and absorb our feelings about the weekend. A bit of personal space after the physical closeness of the weekend. But not for too long. Neither of us felt like cooking for ourselves, or for each other, so we decided to meet again in the evening for a beer and a pizza. Hauke had said when we first met that we'd either dislike each other, become firm friends, or romantically fall in love and live happy ever after. Whatever happened, we both agreed—if Kinnvika was going to be half as good as this weekend, we were in for a great time.

CHAPTER THREE

PREPARATIONS

Hauke had so much to do. He had to think about his research and experiments, what equipment he would need to complete them, what he would need to buy new or could borrow from the university. He had to prepare his own personal gear—clothing, books to read, music to listen to—then pack it and ship it to Spitsbergen. He had to organise the departure dates; the transportation of everything to Kinnvika and the collection of it all at the end of the year; find out about the hut we'd be staying in and how we would heat it; where to store everything prior to shipping; ensure we had safety equipment; find dogs, order their food and borrow a sledge for them to use; prepare lectures for a trip on the *MS Berlin* that we would both be making just before the big adventure got under way; cameras, film and batteries, radios. A thousand and one things to think about, plan for.

All I had to do was to organise the provisions list for the year.

How do you know what you eat in a year? How much pasta, how much cheese, how much chocolate, how much muesli? How many loaves of bread do you eat, how many kilos of vegetables? How much toilet paper do you use? I had absolutely no idea. How would I work it out?

I began with breakfast. It seemed the easiest thing to start with as it was a constant amount every day. Muesli. Every time I had it for breakfast, I would pour my usual amount into a bowl and then weigh it, but why did an ordinary bowlful suddenly stop looking like an ordinary bowlful? Was it more than usual? Less? Did it contain less fruit than yesterday, so therefore lighter? Did it matter? I took an average over a week or two, and then calculated what we would likely munch our way through over the year, plus a bit in reserve. It would have to be enough. Pasta and rice was calculated using recipe books which gave quantities of so many grams per person per meal. All I had to do was estimate the number of times we would eat it per week and so work out the final total. Potatoes would be another staple, and we'd take packets of dried potato to supplement them towards the end of the expedition.

I wandered around the food hall of Svalbardbutikken with a notebook, writing down a list of things I thought we would take, trying to remember the high cost of everything up here and shop accordingly. Spitsbergen levies a lower rate of tax and many Norwegians find the cost of luxury items, particularly alcohol and cigarettes, cheaper than on the mainland, but for food and household goods, by the time you factor in the exorbitant freight costs imposed by shipping and flight companies, you end up paying pretty much mainland prices in the shops. And Norway is extremely expensive. I was conscious of trying to take the right kind of foods to give us a healthy diet, and where possible, I went for the store's own brands to save money. Other basic foodstuffs included flour; dried milk powder; coffee; tinned fruit, vegetables and meat; dried meat and fish—Kinnvika is in the North East Svalbard Nature Reserve, so we were not allowed to shoot reindeer or catch fresh fish; cheese;

sugar; dried fruit; eggs; margarine; salt; herbs and spices; cooking oil. Everything would have to survive being deep frozen. A few luxury items would have to be included such as biscuits, chocolate, crisps and sherry, a few treats, but it was essential to get the basics right. I would have to make my own bread—not something I'd done since I was at school, over thirty years ago—and I didn't even know if there was an oven in the hut I could bake in. I couldn't think of anything to eat that I absolutely couldn't do without, but Hauke had to have his honey and chocolate powder. They were top of the essentials list and if we ran out it was Hauke's fault as he worked out the quantities. He had honey and chocolate powder with his breakfast, in his coffee and in his tea (no—no chocolate in the tea), even on the end of salt sticks. These were a bit like Twiglets but not so horrible—long, thin and brown with lumpy bits of salt on them.

We both liked our red wine too and estimated we would need 200 litres to keep us going, which seemed an enormous amount but worked out at less than a bottle a day, or two small glasses each. Better to have too much than not enough, and we did plan on having a happy, relaxed time in the evenings while we were in Kinnvika. We'd taken a fancy to having champagne breakfasts too so, at Hauke's suggestion, we took enough to have a bottle every Sunday morning. We had to leave our 'alcohol cards' with Svalbardbutikken, as all beer and hard spirits has to be registered at the time of purchase, and only a limited amount was permitted each year, probably in an attempt to control alcoholism. I think they stretched the limits a little for us. When the regulations were introduced many years ago, no one drank much wine—certainly not the majority of working-class Norwegians, so it is exempt, luckily, from the rules. We ordered loads of toilet paper, probably far too much, but not something we felt like running out of. At times it seemed more like planning for a party than an expedition. Who was paying for all of this I wasn't sure. It certainly wasn't me. I assumed it was Hauke, as I couldn't imagine his university paying for anything but essential items.

Eventually, between us, we came up with a completed list of everything we thought we would need. I still had plenty of time to buy forgotten items or those that we weren't bulk buying and could box separately. We would have to take four weeks' worth of provisions with us when we first went to Kinnvika, and then the rest would be delivered later on, so we put in two separate orders to Svalbardbutikken, and they would ensure that they were ready in time. Hauke had spoken to the policeman that had responsibility for overseeing expeditions and he said they would take us by ship to Kinnvika, and drop us off by Zodiac (a rigid inflatable boat, or RIB) with our initial supplies and essential scientific equipment. They would sail back again around four weeks later with the rest of our tons of food and equipment and airlift it ashore by helicopter.

Coal was available free, probably a leftover perk from the days of Longyearbyen being a coalmining 'company town'. It just had to be collected. While I was working and there was still enough snow on the ground, Hauke made several trips with his snow scooter and sledge-trailer to the coal store near the airport and dug out a couple of tons of coal, packed it into doubled black bin bags and then into strong cardboard boxes to make it manageable. We borrowed pallets and some fold-flat, slot-together pallet 'walls' for them from Svalbardbutikken and stacked the coal boxes carefully, covered them with a secure lid and left them where they could be easily transported by forklift trailer to the ship.

For extra heating, Hauke decided to buy an additional diesel-powered heater of the type he used in *Mesuf*, his yacht. All he needed was fuel. He discovered that Kinnvika was used as an emergency fuel depot in case helicopters were working in the area or had to undertake a rescue mission for fishing vessels or cruise ships in distress. The highly refined fuel had a limited shelf life, so we agreed to purchase some of the out-of-date fuel still stored there, and run the stove on that. Driftwood for the woodburning heater was available all along the beach, just like everywhere else on Spitsbergen. We'd be warm.

So that was food and fuel under control. Next was defence. Just a tad important.

Berit and Karl Våtvik were known to both of us. They owned the *Silje Marie* which was parked next to Hauke's naust and I had repaired dog harnesses and clothing for them in the sewing room. They ran the Villmarkssenter (The Wilderness Centre), on the edge of town. The Centre was basically a huge, wooden tent-like structure (with a giant cooking pot suspended in the middle from the ceiling) and surrounded by kennels housing dozens of dogs that they used for sledging tours out into the wilds of Spitsbergen, though in summer the dogs towed a stripped-down VW Beetle, and they agreed to lend us a couple of suitable dogs, currently out on loan

58

with a group of British gap-year students on an extended expedition to Spitsbergen organised by the British Schools Expedition. They would also order up the dog food and lend harnesses and a lightweight sledge. Hauke and I were both keen to meet the dogs, but we wouldn't be able to see them until a couple of weeks before we left, so hopefully we would like them. I was so looking forward to having dogs around again. They would be great fun, friends, and a nice warm cuddle. I just hoped they were as good against bears as Bjosse and Svarten had been in Mushamna. Hauke had hoped to take both with him this time, but Bjosse had died and Svarten was already booked to overwinter with Eero Lindberg in the hut at Mushamna.

We would be taking a small, rubber inflatable boat with us to Kinnvika so we could explore further afield, but it was essential to wear survival suits in case of falling overboard, as you wouldn't last more than a few minutes in the near-freezing water. The zip in one was broken—it was already a bit old, bought second-hand from one of the local outdoor adventure companies—and it would cost a fortune to get it replaced as the suit was tested for watertightness at the same time, so we decided to replace it with an ordinary, extra strong zip. The suit would see little use in Kinnvika as the boating season was so short, and we would only go out in very calm conditions, so we thought we would take a chance on it. That sorted, it was down to the firearms department of Ingeniør G. Paulsen, the snow scooter specialists, to sort out suitable ammunition with Jakob, a big, burly, friendly Norwegian. I knew his Dutch wife Constance quite well. We talked about Hauke one day when we met in town. She'd got him down to a T.

'He's a really nice guy, but boy, does he talk! How do you get a word in edgeways?'

When I first came to Spitsbergen I had obtained my weapon licence from the police with Jakob's help, and I had it and my rifle within 24 hours, which he thought was a record. Normally I bought only practice ammunition from him, but now we were here to buy the serious stuff; heavy duty, soft-nosed bullets that would hopefully fell a polar bear if necessary. Unfortunately Hauke's rifle and mine were of slightly different calibre, so we had to get two different sets and not mix them up. Hauke was taking his old wartime Mauser rifle in reserve, and my bullets could be used in that as well. We bought extra packs of practice ammo which we would use to scare away bears. Some hunters took a variety of different bullets to use, even rubber ones, but Hauke said 'Keep it simple, stupid,' as then there's less to go wrong. Additionally Hauke bought for me a metal item that looked just like a biro, but on the end one screwed on what looked like a party popper. It was an explosive device that could be fired towards bears at close range, about twenty-five metres away, and which let off a loud explosion to frighten off the bear. They didn't look much, but were often very effective, and easy to keep in your pocket at all times as a first line of defence. We bought packs of spare cartridges for the 'warning pens' and hoped we had everything we needed.

Whilst there we bought long lengths of chain to stop the dogs chasing the reindeer, assorted ropes and nails, methylated spirit to run my Trangia cooker and start up Hauke's Primus stove, and he treated himself to a new sealskin hat.

The important jobs taken care of, it was off to our

respective home countries; Hauke to prepare his experiments, and me to fetch some handicraft items with which to keep myself busy over the next year, and for both of us to see our families for the last time until the following year.

*   *   *

Kinnvika. I was paranoid about having nothing to do there. Apart from taking on the cooking and cleaning, which seemed logical to me as Hauke would be busy with his research, how was I going to occupy my days? In summer we would probably be outside much more, but in the long winter of total darkness, what would I do to fill the hours? I loved reading, but I couldn't sit on my bum all day and just do that. I would have to do something constructive. Be active. Keep my mind busy.

Up in the box room at my parents' there were, funnily enough, boxes. Lots of them, banana boxes mostly. All filled to bursting with fabric. New fabric, old fabric, recycled fabric, dress fabric, craft fabric, horrible fabric, pretty fabric, coordinating fabric, I'll-never-ever-use-that fabric, I've-had-that-fabric-since-I-was-ten-years-old fabric. Where fabric was concerned I had sticky fingers. I bought it like other people bought clothes they never wore. Buying fabric wasn't therapeutic, just irresistible. I did use it, but not as fast as I bought it. There were always projects I was going to do, bags to make, shirts to sew, soft toys to create, quilts to fabricate. Well, now was the time I could rummage through it all and pick out my favourite pieces, box it up with a carton of assorted sewing threads and send it off to Spitsbergen.

Although I had my little Singer sewing machine at home in Longyearbyen, it was electric and not much use in Kinnvika, so I pinched Mum's old hand machine and hoped the airport staff wouldn't check the weight of it.

I'd ordered a mass of wool on Spitsbergen, too. I planned on knitting an intricate Norwegian jumper for Hauke's Christmas present. He'd have to watch me making it, but I would pretend it was for me. When that was done, I'd start on one for myself.

I rifled through more boxes and dug out my embroidery silks, carefully stored in an ancient, four-layered chocolate box. Some of them I'd picked up at car boot sales and were older than me. In Longyearbyen I had photographed the homes of three of my friends and was going to make cross-stitch pictures of them as Christmas gifts. Just for once I felt as if I was really planning ahead. I grabbed some white Aida cross-stitch fabric and a couple of big cross-stitch kits and stuffed them in the pile of things to take, along with some squared paper and a bunch of felt-tip pens. In my boxes of books I found one on silk painting, and added it to the pile. I'd ordered a small roll of silk and some basic paints, and never having tried my hand at it before, I thought I would take the instructions. A couple of sketch books and various grades of pencils topped off the stack.

Boredom? No chance.

*   *   *

While in England, I raided the local supermarket for things I couldn't buy in Longyearbyen, such as Bournvita, fig roll biscuits, blancmange and custard powder, Branston pickle, lots of real English tea. And Tampax. Periods weren't going to stop just because I'd decided to drop out of civilised life for a year. I kind of overdid those a bit, but just like toilet rolls, you didn't want to run out; at a push, you could substitute the latter for the former, but not the other way round. I got a few strange looks as I wheeled the trolley up and down the aisles with a year's supply.

One of the things Hauke and I were a little concerned about was scurvy, though with a sensible diet we weren't likely to succumb to it. More importantly, as we would be using melted snow for water, we would be lacking in minerals, something Hauke knew all about. On *Mesuf* he had developed problems with his hair and fingernails, and worked out what was causing the problem. Bjosse and Svarten were doing fine with their specially balanced dried dog food, whereas Hauke was living a lot on seal meat. After swapping dinners, Hauke soon picked up health again, though he did need a lot of pepper to make it palatable. I popped back to the supermarket and bought extra pepper. Well, you never knew, did you. I bought a lot of vitamin C tablets and found a good supply of one-a-day multivitamins with minerals: a bit hard to swallow, but better than my hair falling out. I also stocked up on ibuprofen tablets. I was somewhat prone to headaches, most often caused, I thought, by eating cheap chocolate, monosodium glutamate and drinking fizzy drinks with aspartame. The headaches were occasionally quite severe; I would lie in bed tossing and turning, trying to find somewhere my head felt comfortable, have hot flushes, throw up and then shiver with cold afterwards. Once I'd got an ibuprofen down my neck and got off to sleep for a couple of hours I would be fine. I wouldn't wish them on my worst enemy.

Last stop was the Army Surplus store in Portsmouth where I bought a couple of warm shirts, combat trousers and two pairs of quilted trouser liners. The rest of my extra clothing I would buy back in Longyearbyen where they had 'the right stuff'.

*   *   *

I have no idea what my family thought about my latest escapade; we didn't talk about it much, like most things. They thought I was mad enough when I first left for Spitsbergen, but this was really something else again. Maybe they weren't all that surprised, just a bit worried about me living amongst the bears, and of course all they knew about Hauke was what I had told them and what they could see in some photographs and the copy of the book he had written and given to me about his Mushamna expedition, *Leben im Eis*—not that any of us could read it, since it was in German.

It was hard enough trying to give an impression of what Longyearbyen was like. It's difficult to describe what the low temperatures feel like, the lie of the land, the 24-hour daylight or darkness, the people, the charm of the small, grubby, not very pretty town. 'A God-forsaken hole' as one English cruise-ship tourist put it. How could I explain about Kinnvika when I couldn't really imagine what it was like myself?

Many of my friends were interested in the project, and one, Alan, lent me an ancient, galvanised oven, like an oversized biscuit tin, that I could heat up on the woodburning stove or Primus and bake my bread and cakes in. I wasn't sure how well it would work but was willing to give it a try. Meanwhile it was filled with sewing threads, scissors and other bits and bobs to save on space.

Finally, after parting with lots of money at the post office, my anti-boredom boxes were on their way to Spitsbergen, and with the good wishes of everyone and many a 'Take care', I followed them north, clutching mum's Singer sewing machine.

∗   ∗   ∗

More boxes. Life seemed to be nothing but packing. I was finally leaving my bedsit and moving down to the naust while Hauke was still away. It wasn't too much to put away, but it took a while as I was trying to separate stuff going to Kinnvika and stuff that was staying down at the naust. As I finished packing a couple of boxes I would pick them up in Isbjørnbutikken's van after fetching the bread rolls and drop them off at the naust as I drove past on the way to picking up ice cream. As I sealed the final box, I took my last look at television for the foreseeable future: the Formula 1 Grand Prix in Monaco. David Coulthard won, so this little Scottish lady (one-eighth) was well pleased. I switched off, hoisted it up against my chest and staggered down the stairs, parking it outside the door of a Russian couple living there. It had been free to me, so I was more than happy to pass it on, and was touched to get a bottle of Russian champagne as a thank you.

Then it was just a case of scrubbing out the flat to leave it as I found it. Many people paid the Thai women who run such a service to clean it for them, which is very cheap, but I was trying to keep costs down, had time to kill. It was really more a matter of personal pride, too. It was hard work to get it gleaming as a new pin, but satisfying to leave it sparkling. The harder I scrubbed, the more the sad memories seemed to fade, the more dispassionately I could view my life. Life had begun again for me here. The past was settling into its proper place. I had turned a corner, relaxed, started tuning in to the real me, listening to what I wanted to do. Ready to look the world in the eye again.

The sun-flushed shiny surfaces were like the blank pages of a diary, waiting to absorb new experiences and adventures, new lives, new loves. I gathered up my mops and cloths and brushes, locked the door and strode down the hill to the naust.

My old book was closed. Almost.

*   *   *

In Kinnvika I was determined to keep a diary, recording everything that happened. It wasn't something I had ever done before, beyond a few unremarkable entries in a page-a-day diary. I thought that I ought to get in some practice before we set off, so I bought a spotless white A4 folder and whacked in a load of plain paper. I started it the day I moved into the naust, an auspicious day, I thought. I wrote a lot of rubbish about the comings and goings of the cruise traffic at the quay which I could see from the naust window, lots about packing and boxes, nothing of any weight, no mind-boggling thoughts or revelations, but at least I was getting into a routine. I found if I left it open, I would fill it in during the day, rather than last thing at night when I could hardly remember what I'd been up to. We'd be taking a laptop computer, but you couldn't beat paper, and electricity might be strictly rationed—we were taking a little generator mostly to run the microscope and charge up batteries for the video camera. So I bought five reams of paper for Kinnvika. Should be enough.

*   *   *

Money, money, money. It was burning a hole in my pocket. Expedition money. A very generous contribution from Hauke. Time to hit the town and buy sexy woolly underwear.

It was actually a one-stop shopping trip to Sport1, where I could buy everything I needed. First of all the undies. Absolutely essential to buy wool long johns and a long-sleeved, roll-neck vest. The best came in a fetching shade of French blue. Wool was warm, comfortable to wear and absorbed a lot of moisture, whether rain, snow, seawater or sweat, whilst retaining heat. It was advisable not to wash it too often and to dry it flat. Perfect washing instructions for Kinnvika. Wool socks I had a superabundance of, but my boots were worn out, patched and no longer watertight. The choice of boot was quite wide, but I preferred to choose from those made especially for women as they fitted much better. I had tried on several brands before, popping across the corridor to Sport1 when I was working in Motekroken, and borrowing a pair at a time to test them. I decided on a pair of sturdy Alfa Bever Pro in the end, taking a chance on the longer, shin-length rather than the ankle boots. There was plenty of room, even with thick socks, for my toes to wiggle, so that was excellent. Squashed toes were cold toes.

I didn't have a very warm jacket, having relied previously on thick wool jumpers (I just love jumpers) and a windproof jacket. I opted for a bright red down jacket. I made sure it was big enough to accommodate additional clothing underneath and that the hood was roomy with enough space to be able to wear a thick hat under it. I bought a pair of windproof and waterproof high-waisted overtrousers with braces and a further lightweight, windproof jacket (bigger this time and in pale blue) in case I should damage or lose my old red one.

I already had good sheepskin-lined leather gloves that I used on my snow scooter and a windproof neoprene face mask, thin windproof mittens, and several warm hats and scarves. Gloves with fingers were of little use, being too cold and not suitable for extremely low temperatures. My mum had knitted me the strangest pair of little woollen gloves with the thumbs sticking out at the sides as that was the only knitting pattern she could find. I couldn't imagine ever wearing them. Extra-warm boots Hauke had already bought me before leaving Spitsbergen, and with fat felt liners and very thick soles, they were guaranteed to keep your feet toasty down to $-72°C$.

So I was kitted out. Off to the doctor, then, for medication for the trip. I came away with a broad spectrum of antibiotics to cover a wide range of infections, strong pain relievers and antiseptic eye ointment which I was told I could also use on infected wounds. I ordered up a year's supply of the pill at the same time, and apart from buying some anti-diarrhoea tablets, Lypsyl and dry skin cream, along with Hauke's comprehensive first aid kit and my pack of plasters, we would be able to doctor ourselves if need be.

*   *   *

Hauke had been asked to lecture about his experiences in Mushamna on board the *MS Berlin*, which was cruising from Cuxhaven in Germany up to Spitsbergen and back. He'd accepted as I was invited too and we would also be allowed to disembark in Longyearbyen, and it gave us a short, relaxing holiday before the start of our big adventure. There wasn't much more that I could do before I flew down to Hamburg to meet him. I made some alcoholic marmalade, and bought the yeast for the bread mixes that we had forgotten to order. I made an 'expedition badge' from a ready-made cloth badge bearing a map of Spitsbergen, onto which I embroidered 'Kinnvika 2002–03', and sewed it onto my red jacket. And I bought an ink pad for my own personal expedition rubber stamp that Hauke had had made and sent to me in the post as a surprise. He phoned me to check that everything was under control, and told me not to oversleep and miss my flight from Longyearbyen. I wouldn't dare.

*   *   *

With a big bunch of miniature amber roses, Hauke met me at Hamburg airport, whisking me off on a bus to the main station. We just had time to collect his enormous rucksack from left luggage before piling onto the train for Cuxhaven where we were to spend the night before boarding the *MS Berlin*. After pulling out two paper cups, Hauke produced a bottle of champagne to celebrate the beginning of the start of the expedition.

On a walk around the quayside, we met a nice middle-aged couple, he being tall, she short, who enquired if Hauke was Professor Trinks of Spitsbergen fame. He was. Was he going on the *Berlin*? He was. We had to laugh, as the man was jumping up and down on the quay, pumping his arms in the air and shouting, 'Yes! Yes! Yes!' I think he was a bit pleased. He and his wife had followed Hauke's adventures with great enthusiasm and couldn't believe he was going to be one of the lecturers on the ship. We said goodbye and agreed to meet up on board. We nicknamed them 'the fan club'.

*   *   *

It was a terrific trip north, calling in at several places along the Norwegian coastline, with time for browsing in book- and junkshops, enjoying the warm sun, and stuffing ourselves with strawberries, before heading for Spitsbergen. The lectures and film Hauke showed were well received, but we did rather shock them. At the end of his last one, Hauke introduced me to his audience. I turned up wearing a glamorous bright orange and cerise dress, with matching silk shawl and high heels, which he declared didn't look very suitable for a hut in Kinnvika. So, much to everyone's surprise, I stripped off everything with a seductive wiggle, tossing it all to Hauke until I stood there in a very brief sports top and shorts. From behind the film screen, Hauke dug out overtrousers and jumper, jacket and hat. He threw them to me one at a time and I quickly pulled them on. That looked much better. I waved a bare foot in the air. He threw me some boots. Arm in arm, we said goodbye, and walked out.

*　　*　　*

As we stood on Bykaia, Longyearbyen's town quay, waving off the *Berlin*, clutching four bottles of rum from the captain and a bottle of champagne 'to celebrate arriving in Kinnvika' from one of our lady dinner companions, we met our Dutch friend Mark, who had recently sailed his beautiful red yacht, *Jonathan* (as in Livingston Seagull), all the way to Longyearbyen from the Netherlands. He'd built it himself and the craftsmanship really showed. He was to overwinter in it in Signehamna, a well-protected small bay towards the western side of Spitsbergen, lying at under 80 degrees north, together with his compatriot and girlfriend, Marina van Dijk, Longyearbyen's resident gold- and silversmith. I had first met her through the sewing room and it was she who had made my polar bear necklace for Hauke. Later, over dinner on board, Mark picked Hauke's brains about the ice and the best way to secure the boat in it. We hoped to keep in touch with each other by short-wave radio throughout the year.

I had left my two jobs at Isbjørnbutikken and Motekroken before flying to Hamburg, but I was still working at Randi's. In the mornings Hauke and I kept on top of all the final jobs.

With two weeks to go before the off, there was no sign of the dogs we had been promised. Berit

71

showed us some alternatives in the kennels, which we liked, but she told us she was sure they'd arrive on time. 'Don't worry. It'll be all right.'

We went to the offices of *Svalbardposten* to give an interview about the upcoming expedition and had our photographs taken back in the naust, where we pretended to be checking a list of things to take. It was mundane stuff to Hauke, having given hundreds of such interviews before, but I was having great fun, enjoying the attention of being a 'celebrity', having my five minutes of fame.

Up at the Governor's office, we got confirmation of our leaving date; Sunday 21 July 2002, 8 p.m. sharp, with an expected arrival time in Kinnvika of 8 a.m. on the twenty-fourth. All the boxes for the initial supply drop (labelled 'KV1') were to be delivered to the quay on the Friday before we left. All our boxes for the second, and main, supply drop (labelled 'KV2') had to be stacked securely on pallets on Tuesday evening so that they could be transferred to the Governor's warehouse the next morning.

One evening I borrowed the van from Isbjørnbutikken, we loaded it up with all our KV2 stuff, and attempted to fit it all onto six pallets, which were already half full with the coal. After much cursing and back strain, we just had one big box left which wouldn't go on, no matter how we tried. I read the label on the outside. It was just sewing stuff and some curtains. If I was staying in a hut for a whole year, I at least wanted to make it look nice, so Randi had given me some old ones of hers. We stuffed the contents of the box into several different black bin bags and wedged them into any spaces we could find. Next time, I thought, I must remember to use a lot of small boxes as space fillers. We nailed on the lightweight metal lids and arranged for them to be transported down to the quay. Another job done. Another step closer to the big day.

Time was running really fast now. Kinnvika filled our thoughts the whole time; everything we did revolved around Kinnvika. Everyone we talked to talked about Kinnvika. It was amazing how they seemed to root for us, wishing us a lot of luck and a great time. Not so much for the expedition, the science, but for us personally, I think. It was quite touching how they hoped our relationship would work out well. It wasn't said as such, but you could feel it in the air, see it in their smiles, hear it in their voices. One of my pensioner friends, Anne, had taken one look at us and declared, beaming: 'What a fine pair. You look really good together. Wonderful.' A bit embarrassing, really, but it made me smile, feel good inside. Glow.

*   *   *

The polar bear was hanging upside down from a thick metal bar attached to a pulley in the roof. The back paws had been removed, and a man and woman in white coveralls were carefully paring off the long-haired skin, working their way down towards the head resting on the floor. Some of its innards, spread out on a tarpaulin, looked like thick green sausages, and stank. Samples had been taken and bagged up for research. A small crowd had gathered at the door of the draughty hall to watch the whole process, fascinated. It was the first bear some had seen; it was my third, having finally seen two on a trip out with Hauke and his son in late spring. This was a female bear, about ten years old and in average condition. The fat layer was three centimetres thick, so in the middle range of fat values for bears, creamy-white and waxy in appearance. We were mesmerised as the two people worked their way down the torso, the bear being hoisted higher and higher until they began the delicate operation of removing the skin from around the ears, eyes, nose and mouth.

The bear had been airlifted into town by helicopter from Akseløya where it had been shot, killed by a single bullet. Felled in self-defence. A young woman had been helping out collecting eiderdown from the ducks' nests. (Eider ducks are happy to nest near human, and therefore somewhat protected, habitation, in the hope that bears, Arctic foxes and gulls are less likely to come raiding eggs and young if people are around. A large, and commercial, colony had thus developed over the years close to an otherwise very remote house. The inexperienced young woman suddenly found herself in close proximity to the bear which had arrived unobserved (it was maybe a hundred metres away), and she was very frightened, and shot at it straight away, killing it instantly with a single, very lucky shot. The police always investigate such shootings as bears are strictly protected, and a hefty fine is imposed for any unlawful killings. The bears are brought in for scientific, as well as legal, investigation, and we were witnessing the first stages in this absorbing, though gory, process. With just a few days left before our departure to Kinnvika, it gave me pause for thought.

*   *   *

We jumped into the inflatable boat and purred slowly across the rippling water to Revneset to escape the pressure of our final days in town. It seemed a strange thing to do as we were about to leave all our friends and disappear for a year, but the tension and stress was building and we felt the need to escape and wind down, have some peace and quiet and time to ourselves. The weather was beautiful, windless, sunny and hot, very unlike July on Spitsbergen. After a super-fast skinny-dip in the ice-cold sea, we lazed around near the hut, drinking wine, or lay naked on the springy saxifrage, the sweet honey fragrance of the flowers heavy in the air. It was 12°C in the shade, but out in the direct sun it felt more like double that, perfect for an evening barbecue to keep the mosquitoes away.

With the wind increasing on Sunday, we left early and stopped off at Hiorthhamn, climbing a low hill to look at an old propeller from a German plane shot down by the Norwegians in 1942. It was made of a strange-looking material, a bit like aluminium, possibly magnesium, and was delaminating into soft flakes. It had four or five holes at the ends of the twisted blades, and it had sheered off at the hub. The four-man crew were all killed, but the Norwegians refused to bury them, so an Englishman had sneaked across the fjord from Longyearbyen and buried them at night.

*　　　*　　　*

On the Tuesday before we left for Kinnvika, I walked down to Bykaia to use the shower and toilet there as the naust had neither. I met Elke, a German student who was currently doubling as the harbour master, talking to three men and a woman who I learned were from the British Schools Expedition. Having introduced myself to the Brits, I casually asked about 'our' expedition dogs.

'They're really nice,' they said.

'When are they coming back?' The 64,000-dollar question. Were we going to get them or not?

'Tomorrow, I think.'

Much to the surprise of the others, I jumped up and down, waving my arms in the air shouting 'Yes! They're coming with us on Sunday! Whooppeeeee!' Calming down, I enquired, 'Are they good bear-watchers?'

'Don't really know. We've only seen four bears, and one of those they never even noticed.'

Fingers crossed, then.

*   *   *

Berit and Karl, the dogs' owners, invited us to a 'working' dinner with them at the Villmarkssenter. All the other (paying) dinner guests were from Taiwan, and tucking into delicious Berit-made food; kebabs with potato salad and wok'd tomatoes, coconut and orange cakes and coffee. We all went to the dog kennels next door and ooh'd and aah'd over the 80 dogs there. Once the guests had left for their hotel in town, Berit drove us back to her home where we collected 100 kilograms of dried dog food, which we then dropped off at the naust. We continued on to Bykaia as Berit told us the English students had just arrived back.

The dogs were huge; their father was a Greenland husky, their mother a malamute. Their heads were big and broad, their feet outsized, tails long and fluffy, and dark eyes in intelligent faces. Sako and Balto. Sako, named after a rifle manufacturer, was the biggest of the brothers, jet black with a white front and legs, and the tiniest of white tips to his tail. Balto was white and marled grey in colour, and named after the hero of the Nome dog-sledge team. Both were so friendly, really strong and very cuddly. Karl turned up in his ancient and battered Landcruiser pickup, and their ears pricked up at the noise, recognising it even after having been away for several months.

We left dogs and students in a tangle of ropes, kit bags and tents, and wandered slowly home, happy that the last piece of the jigsaw puzzle had just fallen into place.

*   *   *

I finished working at Randi's on Wednesday, and went home to cook dinner. It was boring and bland but we livened it up with a liberal dose of pepper. After, we double-checked that everything we needed for the trip was ready to go, even though we knew it was, then picked up the van in preparation for an early start in the morning.

It was a miserable day, rain falling from dull grey clouds as we piled everything onto pallets, wrapping them up in swathes of cling film to keep everything dry and together. We eased the inflatable boat onto another pallet, along with the outboard motor, and strapped it down. The last pallet held the food ordered from Svalbardbutikken, enough to keep us going for six weeks before the rest of our supplies came in September.

*   *   *

Our last days in town. We sent off letters to friends and family and sat in Kafé Busen with a coffee and cake, reading about ourselves in *Svalbardposten*. I was feeling really strange, wanting to see everybody, say goodbye, but also wanting to run off to the naust and hide. My stomach seethed with clouds of butterflies, my fingers trembled. I laughed, I smiled, I stared off into space. I hated the waiting, I wanted to go. Now.

*   *   *

Randi came down to the naust with a leaving present for me. I had been wondering what she was making as she kept saying to me, 'I haven't finished it yet.' I thought it was a pile of CDs she was putting together for me. Miles out. It was practical and . . . beautiful. She had made me a knife. It felt good in the hand, light and well balanced. She had used a light, close-grained juniper wood for the handle, and set in a single-edged blade. She had made the scabbard too, stained a rich chestnut colour and hand-sewn to fit the knife perfectly. It was stamped on the back: Takk Marie. RSP 2002. Thank you Marie. RSP were her initials. She told me I must use it. 'Don't keep it just for decoration.' We gave each other an emotional hug. There wasn't much to say. We didn't have to.

*   *   *

After Hauke had been off to exercise the dogs and give them a bit of training—and goodness, did they need it—we went to dinner at the Radisson, sitting at the best table they had which gave us a panoramic view over the fjord. We were both feeling a little subdued, but Anthony, our friendly English chef, brightened us. He was on duty in the kitchen and came out to us to tell us what we would be eating: smoked char with salad to begin, followed by lamb wrapped in bacon, with asparagus and mushrooms. For dessert we had gooey, sticky chocolate pudding, accompanied by lilac-coloured ice cream and two sweet sauces, one red, the other green. They may not have looked so good but tasted wonderful. The whole meal was delicious. My old friend and neighbour Marianne came in to give us a present and wish us well, and later we met more friends in PubEN. It was a lovely last night, and we crawled under the quilt, exhausted and a bit pissed, at 3 a.m.

*   *   *

Sunday 21 July. Departure day. A flurry of dutiful phone calls home, last minute conversations, last chances to say 'Look after yourself'. No one mentioned the bears.

Hauke fetched the dogs in the early afternoon and tied them up to *Silje Marie*'s cradle. We had an hour to spare and dozed off under a polar-bear-patterned blanket, lost in our own thoughts. I was, despite the nerves, looking forward to spending the year with Hauke. We'd been talking about our feelings and expectations concerning Kinnvika and ourselves and the future. Although I still couldn't explain exactly how I felt, it had been good for me to attempt to put my thoughts into words. Hauke was very patient, and I liked talking to him. He understood that I found it hard to discuss my innermost feelings, probably because I didn't try to analyse them myself enough, and he gave me time and nudged me along. By getting me to talk, not only he but I too would get to learn more about myself. It helped to strengthen our relationship and perhaps he also had an idea that it might help to circumvent any personal problems in Kinnvika. This strange, solitary way of life we were about to embark on was hardly going to be 'real life', but it would seem real enough to us.

*　　*　　*

Why is there never a taxi when you need one? We tried both companies, nothing. We tried again. Someone answered and all we could hear was static. Smoke came out of Hauke's ears. We should have booked earlier, maybe, but normally there's no problem. Plan B. Carry everything. Two trips. Balancing as much as we could on my bicycle, we took the short walk to the quay, holdall handles looped around our shoulders. At least the Governor's red ship, the *Polarsyssel*, was there, waiting for us, humming. No one else was about, so we dumped the gear at the bottom of the gangplank and headed back to the naust for the last time.

We wheeled the bicycle inside, piled the remaining bags and the rifles on the doorstep and locked the door. Closed until next year. Hauke helped me on with my rucksack then untied the bouncing, twisting mass of dogs, jumping about like a pair of kangaroos. It wasn't the time for play. Tempers were frayed. Leads were crossed. Discipline administered. I hoisted the last holdall while Hauke fought to get the dogs moving. It was like trying to control a couple of runaway steam trains. The pair of them were incredibly strong, and trying to hang on to both at once when they were pulling in opposite directions was almost enough to pull your arms out of their sockets. Hauke dug his heels in as he walked, applying the brakes, leaning sharply backwards, hanging on for dear life. As we got onto the main road, a taxi pulled up. A bit bloody late, I thought. The side door slid open and out popped Mark and Marina. They were just off to an important meeting and couldn't wave us off, but we said we looked forward to talking on the radio over the next year.

When we reached the ship Hauke tied the dogs to the port railings, which didn't please them too much, while I transferred the bags from the quayside to the deck. Eero Lindberg, who would be overwintering in a hut in Mushamna, had arrived in the meantime with his dogs and was placidly watching the proceedings. Stein Aasheim, a well-known adventurer in Norway, arrived with his young daughter. They and the rest of their family were overwintering at Austfjordneset. They bundled their little huskies into the rows of kennels on deck and tied their blond Labrador to the starboard rail.

Friends gathered around the foot of the gangplank. No sign of Edwin, which was perhaps for the best. Everyone was taking photos, hugging, filming. Then, on the dot of eight o'clock, ropes were cast off and we slipped our moorings as grey-black smoke puffed out the slender stack. We drew away and headed down Adventfjord. I waved and waved, watching as one by one the friends hopped back into their cars and drove home. Finally, only the slim, black-clad figure of Randi was left. A final, sky-reaching wave, and she was gone.

The others had gone below in search of cabins. Hauke disappeared too, both of us in need of some time alone. I stood, hands stuffed into my pockets, hair blowing and tangling in the breeze, the Norwegian flag streaming out over the stern, stretching back to Longyearbyen as it shrank and faded into the hillside. I felt numb, empty, unable to leave off looking back. A new chapter. I hoped it would be a good tale, not too much sadness. I wanted the new me in there, not the old one, not someone else's. The real me. I wanted to set myself free, to stretch myself, assert myself, expand my horizons. I couldn't change my past, but I could change my future just by being myself.

I shivered in the cold wind as we sailed out into the choppy, froth-topped pewter sea of Isfjord. I was leaving again. Seemed that that was all I had been doing lately. Left my husband, left my job, left my bedsit, left my parents, left my friends, left England, left Edwin; left another bedsit, left another job, left another town. When would it end?

Feeling drained and unenthusiastic, I tickled the dogs' ears, feeling the warmth of their soft hair on my fingers. I left them too, and went in search of coffee.

CHAPTER FOUR

BREAK OUT

I had no idea where I was going, but I wasn't supposed to be wearing any shoes. I leaned back on the cold metal door, bracing myself against the roll of the ship as I tugged at the flat laces of my shoes. Setting them to one side, I zigzagged down the stairwell, following my nose towards the kitchen and dining room.

Hauke was there, sitting at the end of one of the two long tables bolted to the floor, talking to a couple of crewmen. I poured myself a coffee from a glass jug on the percolator and slipped onto the bench on the opposite side of the table, thawing my hands around the mug, letting the Norwegian conversation flow over me as I stared into the black liquid. It slid down, heating the inside of my empty stomach, sloshing around with the roll of the ship. We'd forgotten all about eating and hadn't allowed for it in our 'last minute' plans. I felt I could eat a biscuit or two, something sweet, sugary, but there was only the coffee. Its aroma wound itself around the damp muskiness of warming wool and the thick, stale, oily smells from the kitchen opposite.

Ships, the smell of food and being inside didn't sit well with me; I found it an uncomfortable, queasy mixture. I slid off the bench and into the kitchen, rinsed my mug and returned it to the chattering rack by the percolator.

'Where's the cabin?' I asked Hauke. 'I think I'll lie down for a while.'

It was down another flight of stairs, carpeted in a worn shade of ginger. I found myself in a short, narrow corridor to nowhere, brown doors on either side. I wobbled over to the last one on the left where a yellow Post-it was stuck high up in the middle. Holding down the curl, I read it.

'Hauke & Marie.'

I lightly tapped on the door (just in case) and then pushed it open. Hauke's bags were pushed tight into a corner and his jacket had bagged the lower of the two narrow, varnished bunks built into one side of the tiny cabin. A round porthole opposite the door looked out over the steel grey of the rolling sea which I could see spitting thick white foam, like frothed toothpaste, onto the shore running parallel to us.

I dumped my day-sack on a tiny chair and rested my forehead against the thick glass of the porthole, concentrating on the land beyond, willing it to keep still. When it didn't, I straightened up, stripped off and climbed up to the top bunk, slipping under the two-tone yellow stripes of the thin duvet. I lay on my back, the quilt tucked around my neck to keep out imaginary draughts, and concentrated on a smudge of black on the ceiling, trying to calm the gentle swirling in my stomach, tensing and breathing deeper as the cyclical rhythm threatened to get out of control, relaxing again as the urge to leap out of bed and be sick receded. I tried to console myself that Lord Nelson had always been seasick until he'd found his sealegs again, and when, as a 16-year-old, I went on the Sail Training Association (now the Tall Ships Youth Trust) ship *Sir Winston Churchill*, it made us queasy-feeling girls feel better to see the Number Two throwing up over the side.

The regular rumble of the ship's engines drowned out the constant barking of Balto and Sako up on deck. The other dogs had long since settled down, nose to tail, to sleep the voyage away. I sniffed my grubby fingers, smelling doggy smells, and thrust them back under the quilt, tucking my hands under my thighs to keep them warm. The galley smells were fainter here, but an odour of diesel, motor oil and grease pervaded the cabin from the engine room below me, blending with a light scent of chemical lavender from the fresh linen.

I rolled over onto my stomach to look at the western coastline of Spitsbergen, snow-shrouded and cold. Thin grey clouds had settled over the mountain tops like a creeping gloom. The arthritic fingers of glaciers poking out between the knuckles of rock were usually sparkling, diamond white or sapphire blue, but now lay melancholy and fractured, the colour bleached from them, matching my mood. I felt strangely empty, as if all the excitement and fervour of the last few days had exhausted me, bubbled away like flat champagne. I felt lonely, in limbo. Neither here nor there, between jobs, between adventures, between emotions. A cold, leaden weight settled within my chest, making me tremble and teary. I wanted my moose to cuddle, but he was squashed up in a rucksack in the hold, out of reach. I was alone. Wanted to be alone. I gripped the top edge of the quilt and held it close.

I felt the cabin door ease open and Hauke come quietly in. I knew he'd come to check up on me, but I didn't want him there, didn't want consoling. Didn't want a friendly hug. I lay perfectly still, tense, eyes closed, pretending to sleep, trying not to let the tears escape as he peeked over the edge of the

85

bunk. Creeping away, he turned out the light and left, closing the door with a soft click behind him, leaving me more empty than before. Tears dribbled down my cheek, dripping off my nose and spreading onto the pillow. I turned over onto my side towards the wall, wiping my eyes on a corner of the duvet cover, and curled up, rocking gently backwards and forwards to the motion of the ship. Rocking, rocking, drowsy, drifting, dreaming . . .

*   *   *

Sweat soaked my back as I stretched forward and heaved, stretched forward and heaved. My hands were slippery, my face, arms and thighs glowed red with perspiration, burning with heat and pain.

'On the legs! On the legs! Keep it there! Keep it there!'

Sucking in great lungfuls of salty air, I pushed as hard as I could against the foot rest, shoving my seat back along the runner, pulling on the long wooden oar, twisting it deftly up and out of the water before sending my hands away and sliding forward again with bent knees, to dip the oar, push hard on the legs and start a new stroke. We rowed hard and fast, cutting the waves, dashed by the salty spray, desperate to win our home event, keeping time together, heads up, as the cox called the strokes, urging us on with a roar. Poor stroke, rowing inches from him, getting the full blast, but setting the pace for me and the two other girls sitting in between us—the powerhouse of our slender wooden boat.

'Ju-ni-ors! Ju-ni-ors! D'you want-to-be, Ju-ni-ors!' urged the cox, in rhythm with the ebb and flow of our movements.

'On the legs! On the legs!' He glanced back over our gurgling wake to what we could already see, a growing gap between us and the next coxed four, the other teams falling astern. It was a great feeling to be leading, seeing everyone behind you, and we worked harder, harder, in the long, lazy swells of the Solent, just outside the Lymington River. A huge cheer washed over us from our clubmates as the finishing horn sounded the moment we crossed the line, shattered and ecstatic. We were novices no longer. Real Juniors. Yeah! Yeah! Yeah! It was the biggest day of my rowing career. Fantastic! Wonderful! Brilliant!

We paddled slowly back under the wilting heat of the sun to the shingle beach, hopping out gratefully into the cooling sea, waves breaking across our waists, rinsing the sweat from our backs. We made a good team. We'd trained hard for this and reaped the reward. We had done it! We'd won! The men did the honours of upending the boat and replacing it on its cross-legged trestles as we staggered after them, hugging each other in triumph as best we could as we carried the four oars between us. What a day!

And where was my husband Colin on this momentous occasion? No idea. I'd been so proud when he had turned up on his big yellow motorbike an hour before the race, chatting to everyone—wives and husbands of the competitors, children, girlfriends, boyfriends, friends and supporters. And then he'd jumped back onto his bike and ridden off after 20 minutes leaving me deflated and sad. He couldn't be bothered to stay and cheer me on. I was so upset, I couldn't think what to do, what to say. I was sure everyone had seen him leave, so I got stuck into selling sticky buns and sandwiches in the refreshment tent. I know he wasn't interested in rowing, but just this once he could have stayed. He could have watched us win.

Little things.

I supposed he was off enjoying himself, and I was determined to do the same. There were other events to watch, other teams to cheer to victory, other teams to commiserate with, raffle tickets to sell, trophies to be collected, tents to be struck, litter to be collected, boats to be trailered back and returned to their racks at our rickety old clubhouse, showers to be taken, a couple of beers to be drunk. On the whole it had been a superb day. As dusk crept over the quayside and the bobbing gin palaces in the marina, I took my leave of the hardened drinkers and fired up my little Moto Guzzi. In the warm evening I left the visor of my helmet open, enjoying the sultry breeze on my rosy cheeks as I rode slowly and reluctantly home through the twisting, tree-lined roads, wondering just where my relationship with Colin was heading.

A twist of smoke spiralled lazily upwards from a cigarette as Colin sat at the kitchen table, watching the TV on the dresser.

'How'd it go?' he asked, as I closed the door behind me, his eyes swivelling back to the telly.

'We won,' I said. 'Beat them by a mile. It was really good.' I paused momentarily. 'Where were you? I thought you were going to stay and watch us. You missed a good race.'

'Oh, it was too hot to sit around in my bike gear, so I went off for a long ride. I went for miles.' He took a long drag of his cigarette, stubbed it out in the ashtray, exhaled a stream of smoke across the table. 'Not long been back myself.'

'I'm glad you had a good run out, then,' I said, as

88

Colin stood up, scraping his chair back across the tiled floor. 'Must have been nice in weather like this.'

'Yeah, it was. Think I'll do a bit more on that gearbox,' he said, reaching for the door. 'I should finish it in a couple of days,' and out he went to the garage.

I flicked off the telly. Nice to see you, I thought, as I flopped into my rocking chair in the corner. Thanks for the interest.

We had started off so well, meeting at an MG Car Club 'Natter and Noggin' in a pub. I had made myself a new year's resolution to get out more in 1986, meet more people, try and get a boyfriend as I hadn't had one for so long, and the first time I made the effort I met Colin. He was popular with his friends, being great to have around in a crisis, and could fix just about anything. We had great fun together, going to watch vintage car races, dining out, taking a touring holiday to Scandinavia (the best holiday I'd ever had up until then), and for romantic weekends in the New Forest. After nine months, we found a beautiful 200-year-old house on the edge of the New Forest, close to the sea; white-painted and red-tiled, still retaining its huge open fireplace, original window shutters, and a hearth in the main bedroom where the windows came down to the floor; in the bathroom a skylight overhead allowed you to gaze up at the stars in the night sky as you wrinkled in the tub. The soft, green garden was all curving grass and accidental chamomile lawns (we weren't much in the way of gardeners—and anyway, it was lovely and springy underfoot), with a flowering cherry tree encircled by a romantic, low, wooden seat; a six-car garage opened onto a

89

gravelled driveway leading to a white five-barred gate. We bought it and moved in together. Six months later we got married, going off to the service in our own pre-war MG that Colin had restored. I gave up work at the local post office and worked alongside Colin, fabricating the hoods, trim and seat covers for the cars he restored. When he decided to concentrate on repairing mechanical components rather than complete cars, I found myself another job working in the reference library at the National Motor Museum, a short country drive across the New Forest to Beaulieu. It was a job I loved, researching everything from cars to people to clothing and events.

Colin had bought himself a 1960s BSA motorbike, perhaps trying to recapture the tearaway days of his youth. Although I enjoyed riding pillion, I was determined to learn to ride myself, and eventually passed my test, going off on rallies and runs together with a local enthusiasts club that we had joined. We kept adding to our stable of bikes, new ones and old ones, big ones to suit Colin's tall, bulky frame, small ones for my short legs. I enjoyed the bike scene and the people in it, but I began to wonder about what I was doing when I acquired, at Colin's suggestion, a third Moto Guzzi. It seemed that every time a small, interesting motorbike came along, I had to buy it. Was I doing this for me, or just to keep Colin happy? I didn't mind sharing his hobbies, but I began to realise that I no longer took part in any of my old outdoor activities. Why not?

I'd always been an outdoors person. I blame my mum. With Buster, the silky-haired mongrel dog keeping guard, she used to park me as a baby on the doorstep, our pre-fabricated post-war emergency bungalow, in just about all weathers. Except in fog, there I would be, the hood of my pram protecting me from the prevailing wind, from frost and snow, from the rain and sun, a gauze screen keeping out the local cats. As I grew up I excelled at sport and loved being out in the fresh air, going for long walks, cycle rides and camping expeditions. I'd given up all those activities when I got married, even though it was something I'd always told my friends not to do. Colin was no great fan of physical activity—he needed something with an engine to get him from A to B—but that had not been a problem in our relationship before. It had made a welcome change to do something different with him, to expand my knowledge, to take in new horizons, but now I felt I needed more. So I took up evening classes in German and yoga. I took up rowing. Was I rebelling against a stronger personality? Was I scared of losing the real me?

But all this was a symptom of an underlying problem in our relationship. By 1999 we seemed to have drifted apart, we'd stopped doing things together. We didn't seem to gel like we had when we were first married. We didn't share things any more and had stopped going out for the occasional dinner or trip to the cinema. I went rowing instead of out on bike rides. Interest in each other was waning. Conversation was drying up when we should have been talking more, attempting to sort out our problems before they got any worse. There was nothing really wrong between us, nothing important. It was something that had crept up on us. We weren't shouting at each other, we weren't fighting. We were still friendly with each other, friends and neighbours still called round for tea, though perhaps not as much as they used to. The longer we lived together, the worse it became. We both lost ourselves in the TV, even watching the same programme in different rooms. Stupid. I felt sad and depressed about the way things were going. I couldn't believe that Colin was happy with the way things were going either, but neither of us made any effort to stop it, to halt the slide. I wanted our marriage to work, but had it deteriorated too far? Was it beyond repair? Did I want to repair it?

The more I thought about it and the longer it went on, the more miserable I became. I started to feel part of the furniture, like a saggy old armchair too familiar to throw out. I dreaded the idea of going home after work and cooking and eating in near silence, so I ended up buying more and more takeaways to get the ordeal over as soon as possible. I felt trapped in a way of life I didn't want to belong to any more. I wanted to escape.

Yet I had it all. I had a good husband and nice neighbours and friends. I had no money worries, enjoyed my job. Did I want to give all this up? And go where? What would I do? How would I tell Colin if I decided to leave? I had no idea. I felt guilty even thinking about it. I hugged a knee, creaking the rocker back and forth, flexing my foot on the chill floor, up and down . . .

*   *   *

I opened my eyes. Hauke was gently tugging at my ankle.

'Wake up, Marie. Wake up. Breakfast is being served. Aren't you hungry? Come on. Come and eat.'

I screwed up my eyes and rubbed them with flat hands, yawning. I was hungry, starving, in fact, and feeling much better. The queasiness in my stomach had given way to hunger rumbles. I remembered what Hauke had told me once: 'A good sailor always eats when he feels well.'

'Give me five minutes,' I said, pitching back the stripy quilt and swinging my legs over the side, remembering not to bang my head on the low ceiling. 'I could eat a scabby horse.'

*   *   *

It was a long voyage, expected to take three days, and Kinnvika was the last port of call. Much of our time was spent in the lounge, drinking coffee and conversing with off-duty crewmen when they weren't watching the latest films on the video player. Currently it was a Harry Potter film. I was feeling a bit fidgety and not inclined to watch the film. Hauke was off talking to the captain, trying to find out when we would be arriving and what the procedure for unloading would be. I got into conversation with a tall, slim crewman who spoke good English. He had been all the way around the island group on numerous occasions with the *Polarsyssel* and seen quite a few bears in his time. Seeing the big colony of walrus on the low lying island, Moffen, also lying just above 80 degrees north, had been a highlight. He got the chance to see all the remote, seldom visited coastal areas, though he didn't always get the opportunity to go ashore. He asked if I'd like a look up on the bridge, and offered to show me around.

We had to go down to the hold below the

helicopter deck first of all while he checked that everything was ready for the expected early start the next morning. It was a cavernous area, cold, draughty and rattling. Along the outer wall, enormous skips were full to overflowing with the finds from a recent beach clean-up. Ragged remnants of blue trawl nets filled one; round, colourful, plastic floats threatened to overflow the rim of another like a children's play pit; an assortment of plastic ropes, bottles, tubes and carrier bags peeked out from the top of a third, flopping lazily about as the ship coursed through the rough water hissing below us. Ten skips had already been filled and disposed of after the annual voluntary spring-clean on one of the beaches around the shores of Spitsbergen, and these were the last three waiting to go for recycling.

Alongside grey-painted lockers, orange survival suits swayed lazily with the swell, their attached reddish rubber boots waltzing to the rhythm of the rolling waves. Life jackets hung on heavy-duty pegs and rubber and canvas work-gloves lay in a confused tangle in a wire mesh basket like mismatched socks in a drawer. Lying lonely on the dimpled, grey floor, our pallets lay temporarily abandoned, strapped to the floor with retaining clips, waiting for us to slice off the see-through plastic on our arrival in Kinnvika. Our rubber boat looked tiny and inadequate in the vast space. Above our heads, the heavy-duty, sliding metal doors giving access to the hold were locked fast, one of the policemen's lightweight inflatable boats sitting on them deck-side, its huge twin engines out-powering our very modest single one.

I followed the crewman up a steel stairway to the

bridge, warm and stifling after the sharp, cold air of the hold. A wide spread of toughened glass looked out across the deck where ropes were coiled tidily, cranes stowed and fixed securely and spray slashed upwards as the bow cut the wave tops. Hauke was here with the captain, talking over his days in Mushamna with *Mesuf*. We smiled at each other as my friendly crewman showed me the radar, the image of the nearby coastline glowing green against a dull background as it made its 360-degree sweep around the boat. Red and emerald lights winked or glowed steadily between the gauges and dials of the control panel below the window; a tiny, almost inconsequential, wooden steering wheel twitched left and right. Another green-faced display reeled off the latitude and longitude from the Global Positioning Service satellites, and I stood fascinated as it read well over 80 degrees north, not the furthest north the ship had ever been, but certainly the furthest that I had—and it wouldn't slip below 80 until after it had dropped me and Hauke and the dogs off in Kinnvika.

As the crewman pointed out the places he'd been to on a map on the wall, I thought how much he reminded me of Edwin when I was 16 and first met him. His thin, long face and sandy hair had changed over the years, darkened and receded, but he'd put on no weight over the 18 years since I'd last seen him (though we'd sporadically kept in touch by phone), and he'd lost some breadth across the shoulders if anything, less muscle, but still had the same cute, pinchable backside. We'd gone out with each other three or four times in the past, never quite seeming to get the right formula to make it work permanently, though I could never work out why. It hadn't worked this last time on Spitsbergen, but I'd forgive him that, for giving me the encouragement and faith in myself to break out of my marriage.

I had been so unhappy at home, knowing I was going to have to leave Colin if I wanted to retain any measure of sanity and self-esteem, to be me, but I needed to pluck up the courage to make the break, and I hadn't been able to find it. I'd been weak and timid. Frightened of grasping the nettle and taking the consequences. At work one lunchtime, feeling wretched, I had fed Edwin's name into an Internet search engine. I had lost touch for some time, but knew in a roundabout way that he had moved to Norway. I pressed the button. I knew I shouldn't have but it was too late. Milliseconds later, there he was. There was no mistaking it was him, complete with e-mail address. I shut down the computer, aghast. What was I playing at? But it nagged at me like an invisible splinter in my finger. I couldn't leave it alone, I worried it. I needed him to help ease the pain. He'd always been good to me in the past, given good advice, been my friend, and I needed him now. I brought up his name again and wrote him a note, signing it with a familiar nickname, almost wishing to remain anonymous. I waited nervously for a reply. Would I even get one? Would he help me sort out the mess I was in? I waited. Waited.

Then, making me feel anxious and panicky, or was it relief, he replied a few days later, and so began a slow rebuilding of our old relationship. He kept me sane through the dark days of indecision. He told me that I should be true to myself, do what I wanted. In effect be selfish. Leave Colin and face the consequences on my own. He only told me what I already knew, but I accepted it from him. It made more sense, somehow. I promised him that I would tell Colin I was going to leave, but only I could find the courage to do it. I was so scared, too cowardly, and that made me feel worse. I was feeling so guilty about ending our relationship. It was me finishing it all. I was the one walking out after 14 years. I cried more and more into my pillow at night, I squashed my moose tighter.

Then, it was as if the can exploded. I tried to open it just a little but the air rushed in and it blew up in my face. Edwin was coming to England on holiday and was coming to see me. I wanted to see him, but there was no way I would do it while I was still living with Colin. Call me old-fashioned if you like, but I'd always been faithful, and I planned on staying that way. It wasn't in me to be otherwise, to cheat like that. I had to tell Colin. But I couldn't do it. I just couldn't.

I got back from rowing on the Lymington River. Colin was waiting for me, prowling around the kitchen, inhaling deeply from the unending, throat-scratching cheap cigarette.

'You're late again! Where've you been?'

'You know where I've been. Rowing. I usually come in at this time. You know that.'

'Are you seeing someone from the club? You're never here!'

'Of course not. If I'm not rowing, I'm here. When do I get time to see someone?'

Maybe not having much to do with each other any more was a bit like not being home. It just seemed as if I'd been away more.

He confronted me about the way I was behaving at home, about our relationship. What was going on?

'Nothing,' I answered, glad that the moment had

97

come. 'Nothing's going on. It's just not working and I can't go on living like this. I feel horrible. I can't do this any more. I want to leave.'

There it was. Said. Out in the open. Forced out. I felt immediately better. Should have done it before. All those months . . . Colin asked me what I was going to do.

'Move out, I suppose. Get a bedsit or something. Don't know. Haven't really thought about it.' He didn't try to stop me.

I didn't want to give up my job and move back to my parents', so a bedsit really was the only option for me. I couldn't afford anything else and I sold my motorbikes to help fund the move. I hoped to be able to afford something more suitable once our divorce settlement was arranged. I had no wish for him to sell the house on my account, and my first aim and priority was to look after myself and not rely on anyone else for help. It was that independent streak of mine.

I scoured the adverts in the local newspapers and shop windows and almost every day after work I went to look at the rooms on offer. They were awful places, and I couldn't face accepting any of them, but I began to feel that I had no choice; they were all alike—dark, dingy rooms in dysfunctional houses.

It was my neighbour, Julie, who suggested Dave's place. It wasn't far away and handy for work and she thought it was still vacant. She gave me his number.

I gave Dave a call, nervously pressing the keys of my mobile. Yes, it was still free, come and take a look. Dave was a work colleague of Julie's husband, Si, and I had known him for many years. He and his wife had converted a rambling Victorian house into a family home with a flat on the ground floor and a bedsit on the first floor. The bedsit was a large room facing onto the road with lots of natural light. It came with its own separate bathroom (and even a washing machine if I gave him 25 quid for it), so we did the deal there and then and I moved in as soon as I could.

I had made the break. It felt good. A huge weight lifted from my shoulders. I had done the right thing. I was so much happier, relieved, alone but independent. I didn't own it but somehow that didn't seem to matter for now. I had escaped the sadness, the disappointment, the pressure of living what seemed like a lie. I was free to be me.

*   *   *

Edwin came.

I felt it was OK to see him now I'd moved out. I didn't see it as cheating. We soon slipped into our old friendly ways, enjoying each other's company as much as we'd ever done. We even managed to squeeze in a camping and walking holiday. Over a couple of weeks we talked about his life on Spitsbergen where he was a tour guide and organised all the equipment for the company he worked for. He told me all about life in Longyearbyen, the people, what they did, the climate, the nature, leaving me with a couple of brochures full of glossy pictures of happy people smiling at the camera for the tourists. Eventually Edwin suggested I come and stay with him on Spitsbergen for a year while I settled down a bit and got myself back on an even keel. It would be a new adventure for me, a complete change of direction, and maybe we could even rekindle our long-lost romance. If all went wrong I would have had an experience I would never forget, I would learn a new language, meet new people, change my job, go snow-mobiling, cross-country skiing, so many exciting things. What an opportunity. But it was a big move and, following hot on the heels of having just left Colin, made me think hard. Out of the frying pan, into the fire? I looked at *The Times' Atlas* in my local library to find out exactly where Spitsbergen was. 'Oh, shit!' I exclaimed, seeing how close it was to the North Pole. I must be mad.

*   *   *

'You're right here,' said the crewman, dabbing his finger on the map. I re-focused my attention as I stared at the map on the wall, following his finger as it traced the route down Hinlopen Strait and into island-dotted Murchisonfjord where Kinnvika lay, an insignificant speck on its northern side and surrounded by cold, white, never-ending glacier. I smiled brightly at the crewman, trying to look more cheerful, braver than I felt.

'Thanks for the tour,' I said, suddenly feeling like being alone. 'It was nice of you to spare the time.'

'A pleasure,' he said, taking the hint and disappearing back down the stairs.

Hauke had gone outside meanwhile, and I looked out to the stern of the still-bucking ship towards the helicopter deck where he was busy shovelling dog shit over the side. My relationship with Edwin had fizzled out after just a few short weeks and I had found it exceptionally hard to come to terms with. We'd both been looking forward to being together on Spitsbergen, had sent each other dozens of sweet, romantic e-mails since I'd left Colin, built up hopes, pictured the dream. Too much, too soon? Or just never gave ourselves a chance? Never had a chance? Whatever, it didn't work and two broken relationships in such a short time were almost more than I could bear, and I'd become distraught with the accumulated stress. My new good friends in Longyearbyen had helped pull me round and get my life back together again, but I really didn't want another fractured relationship so soon. I crossed my fingers and hoped that at least Hauke and I would remain amicable throughout the year. As the *Polarsyssel* steamed on, I realised with a sudden clarity, how lonely and helpless I'd feel if things didn't go well in Kinnvika. I didn't need another disaster.

Despite the uncomfortable chop of the waves we had made good time around the northern coast of mainland Spitsbergen and were arriving a whole day ahead of schedule, so were tucking into a hearty breakfast at the ungodly hour of six-thirty. I really fancied some bacon and eggs, with lots of fried potatoes, but they weren't on the menu today, so instead I had boiled eggs and salmon, bread and cheese, washed down with the inevitable strong black coffee, my stomach back in business. Hauke and I spoke little together, as if we were saving up conversation, both feeling the last minutes of civilisation ticking away. The last chance to talk to other people. The cook came over with a bulging carrier bag.

'A little something to keep you going,' he explained. Fresh, home-made bread. I was surprised and appreciated his forethought. It would last us a week. One less thing to worry about. I took it down to my cabin after finishing breakfast and wedged it under the flap of my day-sack.

I sat on the little chair for a while, glad to be alone, gazing out of the porthole, watching small translucent fragments of wave-sculpted blue and white ice drift past us as we headed down Hinlopen. Did life really start in such an environment as this? It seemed hard to believe.

I jumped as Hauke burst through the door with a crash.

'Grab your stuff and come up on deck. We're almost there. Hurry. Come on.'

As I felt the vibration of the ship hum a slower beat, my heart drummed rapidly and a surge of adrenalin kicked in at Hauke's words. I scooped up my bags, gave a long 'have I forgotten anything' look around the room, and followed Hauke up the stairway to the deck.

Sako and Balto were jumping up and down on their twisted-short ropes, still barking, as I dumped the bags in a sheltered corner of the deck. I walked over towards Hauke, the deck tilting as we turned left into Murchisonfjord, trying to catch a first glimpse of Kinnvika. A scattered group of light brown wooden buildings lay ahead of us, barely visible against the surrounding fawn rocks sweeping up to a low ridge behind. A flat area of crumbled biscuit rock crept down to the beach, and dipped into the gentler waters of the bay. To the right, a 'dip and scarp' mountain blocked our view of the glacier; to the left, a long, flat finger of land stretched towards us, beckoning us in. We eased to a stop as the anchors were freed and bit into the seabed. It couldn't have been more bleak, more barren. Not a living thing could be seen. Nothing. Deserted. Desolate.

It was like arriving on the moon.

102

CHAPTER FIVE

ARRIVAL

The winch man, pushing and pulling levers on his console, eased up the inflatable rubber boat suspended from the crane and swung it out over the port side. One of the police officers, Andreas, already inside, roped it to the railings to stop it swinging out in the wind. He waited while Hauke untied Balto and Sako, and with a hefty shove on their reluctant bums, bundled them into the boat and securely tied them in. Hauke climbed aboard after them and, with a whirr of cables, dropped out of sight to the sea surface below. Realising what was happening, I grabbed my bags and shot down the stairs to the hold where a huge steel door had been opened in the side of the hull. I could see Hauke and the dogs rising and falling in the swell, blue wisps of exhaust smoke rolling away from the hefty twin outboards, mumbling throatily. I was helped in to the RIB, closely followed by fast-flying rucksacks and a crewman, and with a back-bending lurch that almost flipped me out, we sped off in the direction of Kinnvika.

I grinned at Hauke as he turned to me with a 'this is it!' sort of look, the headwind flapping the deep collar of his ancient waxed jacket. The dogs enjoyed the ride, noses in the air, ears twitching. We drew closer, bouncing across the wavelets in the calm bay, and my heart raced as fast as the engine revs while I stared with unbelieving eyes at the empty landscape and the long line of huts slowly disappearing from view as we neared the shelving beach. Running the hull up onto the stones as far as he dared, Andreas hopped out and hauled the painter, tying it round a salt-bleached log half buried in the pebbles. Hauke leaped ashore, and, after throwing out the bags, I unhitched the dogs, tossing the ends of their leads for him to grab; they were glad to get their paws back on land. I jumped off the bow and planted my feet onto Nordaustlandet for the first time. We'd arrived.

Scrabbling up the shingly, two-metre-high bank, hanging on to Sako as best I could, I looked back at the *Polarsyssel* gleaming red in the warm sunshine as another RIB snuggled up to its side, loading up with some of our packages to come ashore. I followed Hauke and Andreas, passing a string of rust-coloured barrels roped together (the helicopter's emergency fuel depot), as they strode out over the flat area between the beach and the huts. I tripped along behind them, wondering how long my new boots (and the dogs' paws) were going to last on the razor-edged red rocks as we neared the huts. They were all shapes and sizes with felted, pitched roofs, the windowless ones apparently the scientific huts and not our living quarters. As the rock surface smoothed into flaky, pale orange, we approached a tiny building on the far side of the complex. It couldn't be that one, could it? It was so tiny. You're kidding, right? It didn't look much bigger than a rabbit hutch!

'It's a big hut,' remarked Hauke, looking back over his shoulder at me. 'Looks in very good condition.'

It is? I wondered. It still looked like a rabbit hutch

to me. Built of wood that was now almost grey, vertically panelled, with the gaps between covered by nailed-on battens to help keep out the draughts, it didn't look big. The slightly overhanging roof was covered in grey-green felt and an elbowing chimney poked out near the apex of the roof. The wooden shutters over the windows were bolted tight shut, so we'd have to find the right-sized socket in Hauke's toolkit before we could open them. A wooden table hugged one long wall facing us, and a neat stack of logs was piled near the entrance. Thick cables from the corners of the eaves were ominously fixed firmly to the ground to stop it blowing away in strong winds. We found a big iron ring, a leftover from the original expedition, shackled to a plate of yellow rock near the hut, and we fixed the dogs' leads to that so they wouldn't run off, leaving us free to go inside.

Andreas fumbled in a pocket and pulled out a small key as he ascended a couple of pallet steps to the door. It twisted easily in the lock and the door swung silently back on its hinges, letting in a little fresh air and sunlight. I followed the two men into an outer vestibule, the width of the hut, furnished with a storage rack and an old, rickety table and some shelves over coat hooks. A central door led into the hut proper, but it was impossible to see much inside with the windows bolted fast. It smelled musty but dry, and felt tiny and claustrophobic as the three of us stood together in the middle of the room next to a table and chairs that I could dimly make out. Hauke expressed his pleasure with the hut. I despaired. A whole year in here together? I couldn't imagine it. How was I going to survive in here with Hauke, the two of us behaving like a pair

105

of self-assessing laboratory rats? I was about to find out. Bit late now to start worrying about it.

We shuffled back outside into the glare of the bright, clear sunlight, the formalities of officially handing over the hut completed. Then it was back to the beach to lug up all the equipment we had brought with us. Men from the ship were already helping out, carrying boxes and containers as they were shuttled in by a small fleet of RIBs. It was tricky work walking back and forth on the ankle-jarring rocks, trying not to drop a heavy, cumbersome parcel. Once everything had come ashore, everyone gathered in front of the hut door and took photographs of us before giving us chest-squashing hugs. We walked with them back to the beach and waved them off as they raced back to the ship, engines buzzing like angry bees. They would be around for the rest of the day, flitting here and there, checking that everything in the area was OK, doing whatever jobs they had lined up for the day, the *Polarsyssel* sitting like a broody red hen waiting for her chicks to return to their nest.

Hauke and I carried up the heavy boxes between us, sweating and stripping down to rolled-up shirt sleeves with the exertion and the unusually warm day. We used the pulka, Hauke's plastic, covered sledge, to haul the heavy lorry batteries up to the hut, the knife-like rock making deep scratches in the white underside. All around the hut, everything lay scattered in untidy piles for us to sort through and distribute between our little hut and the much, much bigger one a few metres away—you couldn't even really call it a hut when it was 30 metres long. (It had once housed 13 scientists in centrally heated comfort, but now it was stripped out and bare. In 1958/9, the four overwinterers had 160 barrels of

106

fuel to use for heating and running the station—a shortfall of 220 barrels due to bad weather preventing the remainder being offloaded from their supply ship, and they almost ran out. We had eight.)

But first a little rest. A little celebration.

Hauke rummaged in his Tardis-like rucksack and produced a bottle of champagne, the one given to us by our lady dinner companion on the *MS Berlin*. We went around to the front of our hut, and sat in the sunshine on a couple of fat logs, two white whalebone ribs arching over our heads. Hauke launched the cork skywards, poured the effervescent golden liquid into a couple of cups we'd found inside the hut and toasted our adventure. Now I'd arrived, I didn't feel quite so apprehensive, but I'd been too busy for any serious thoughts. Bears hadn't even crossed my mind, I realised, as Hauke reminded me to keep an eye open for them. They weren't likely to come by with so much noise about, but you never knew. We made bets on when the first one would appear. Whoever lost would have to buy the first beers back in Longyearbyen.

With the glow of alcohol fizzing through our veins, it was back to work, sifting through the scatter of containers. Hauke looked after the scientific stuff and essential equipment, carting it all up to the big main building, while I looked after the household boxes, food, kitchenalia and bedding, taking most of it inside the hut.

It was a slow job, back aching with all the bending and lifting, but essential to get everything under cover before we had a bear visit. After about half an hour Hauke shouted out to me. A bear? No, he'd found the socket set, so now we could open the shutters and get a real look at our new home.

107

There were four shutters covering the four windows, one on each wall, the hasps solidly closed with long bolts top and bottom. Hauke had to stand on a chair to reach the top ones, replacing the bolts after he'd pulled back each shutter so we wouldn't lose them. We were patient, waiting until all were tied back before taking our first real look around the hut together.

The main room had a single, central window, facing out onto the bay. The room was square and panelled in age-darkened pine. Dusty, white mould crept across the naked bodies of girlie pictures pasted up on the ceiling, turning the paper into fragile flakes that crumbled to the floor. Fine black mould hung like unwashed black hair, limp and tangled. It made my skin crawl. It would have to go. Very soon. I didn't fancy sleeping under that lot as it floated down on me in the middle of the night. Worse than spiders. Eugh!

Along the left wall, two low beds with foam mattresses lay end to end with a pair of shelves running above them. From under the window a reasonably sized table, narrow but longish, divided the room into two. A third bed was to the right of the table, shelves above, then a small, blue cupboard. A Jøtul woodburning stove stood small and black in the corner, framed by dry wood and kindling, a wooden clothes-drying rack suspended above. On either side of the door were shelves and a large cupboard high up on the wall. Four cream metal chairs with red plastic seats completed the furnishings. I wondered if they were contemporary with the hut.

'It's good, isn't it?' said Hauke, turning round and round, pleased.

'Is it?' I said.

'Of course it is. I've stayed in some old huts where you were lucky if you had a door. You were just glad to get out of the weather.'

'If you say so. I'm sure I'll get used to it.' I suddenly missed my bedsit back in Longyearbyen. Its warmth and comfort, its light, its cleanliness and fresh smell, its cooker, its shower, its neighbours. Its security. But I didn't want to go back. In spite of all the drawbacks, I still wanted to stay; see it through to the end. As agreed. I could, and would, do it.

We went out, back to shifting and sorting, rummaging and readying. Meeting between the huts, we stopped to catch our breath. The sun had swung lower in its arc, casting shadows in front of us as we looked out over the wide, little bay towards the *Polarsyssel*. All the rubber boats had been winched aboard, and we could see an increase in the density of smoke trailing out of the chimney. They were preparing to leave. We ambled down to the beach, side by side, quiet. The air took on a chill I hadn't felt before, a deepening of atmospheric pressure, a greying of the sky as thin cloud drifted in on the early evening breeze. We could hear the winch, even at the distance of a kilometre, as it hauled up the anchor chain. Almost imperceptibly, she started to ease out of the bay and point her bow towards Hinlopen Strait once more. As she gathered speed, she saluted us, whistling toot toot, tooo-t-toot, toot toot, as she slipped around the rocky digit of land, leaving us alone. We waved long, lazy arcs above our heads until she was out of sight, and turned back to the hut.

I was glad she had gone. She had been a comfort and an annoyance as she sat in the bay, waiting for her day-tripping, scattered crew to return. It felt as if she was postponing the start of our adventure. I wanted her to stay and be gone. Now, as the fans of her wake spread and sloshed ashore, I was glad she had gone. I didn't feel lonely. I had Hauke. I didn't feel excited, but experienced a feeling of deep satisfaction. Odd. For once in my life I felt grown up; no longer a child. This was no game. It was for real. My life. As I walked back up towards the hut, it was strange, but the most natural thing in the world. I was happy in a low-key, contented sort of way.

I felt I had come home.

CHAPTER SIX

ACCLIMATISATION

It looked bigger now. A bit. Certainly a lot tidier since all the boxes had been unpacked. After a week, the saucepans, pots and pans, mugs, the Primus stove and all our food was neatly stacked on the shelves in the 'kitchen' or entrance hall, leaving a bit of workspace under the back window for Hauke's microscope. Assorted outerwear hung on the clothes pegs, boots and shoes underneath. Hauke's rifle hung on a nail just inside the door; mine in the living room. Under my bed, the one on the left, I'd stowed all my clothing and some of my handicraft items; a few books and odd paraphernalia on the shelves over it. I had scrubbed the furniture and swept the floor, and got the ceiling as mould-free as I could get it, at the expense of one or two naked breasts. The original triple-glazed windows were now sparkling and still fairly draught-free after almost 50 years. Where the wind scythed through, mainly where the prefabricated sections of the hut joined together, the cracks were stuffed with toilet paper—not pretty, but effective, and we had lots of it. A small water container, lidded and with a drainage tap, was kept topped up in the kitchen from the water in a pond 25 metres away.

Over the first few days, whilst I was playing housewife, Hauke was hard at work, nailing up the solar panels high on two sides of the hut and running cables through an air vent down to two lorry batteries under his bed. Up went the aerial for the radio, stretching from the roof to an old flag pole. The remote weather station was screwed to a post and fixed to the hut high above roof height, and the receiving station attached to the wall in the living room. The paraffin heater was installed and its chimney T'd into that of the woodburner. Finally the first data logger—a small plastic box about the size of a packet of cigarettes which would automatically record selected data, such as temperature, over a year—was taped to a bamboo stick and set 100 metres from the hut. 'Now the science begins!' Hauke declared happily.

Apart from a few 'side-issue' experiments on behalf of one or two scientific colleagues back in Germany, including collecting samples of red algae from the snow and searching for enzymes to use in the cleaning industry—a first, simple experiment involved leaving a tea-stained teacup in our pond to see if anything in the water would 'clean' it— Hauke's main aim was to answer his own questions raised during his expedition in Mushamna: to confirm his theory that life on earth started in sea ice. He would study the sea ice in greater detail and observe what transpired within its microscopic channels and cells. He'd study the chemical reactions taking place; how light affected it; what effects melting and refreezing would have; what were the optimal temperatures for activity in the ice; and much, much more: all those processes that theoretically led to the first life on earth. Without knowing the proper construction and content of sea ice, it would be impossible to recreate it accurately in the laboratory and further his ideas. He would also measure the quantity of CO_2 in the ice and the air with a wand-like instrument; and collect data on weather, wildlife, plants and whatever else had occurred to his amazing mind. Aside from working in difficult, extremely cold conditions, it was a huge workload for one man.

Three days after arriving, science of a different sort was going on in the kitchen. Bread-making. All the fresh air and exercise was making us very hungry, and our lovely ships' bread had rapidly disappeared. Using the bread mix was simple (each pack made two loaves), and kneading it was good for getting rid of aggression or tension (which might be useful later on), but my first attempt at cooking it was a nightmare. It seemed to take forever. First, the paraffin stove went out while I was trying to prove the dough and I had to get Hauke to fix it, then I tried cooking it in Alan's 60-year-old oven but couldn't maintain the heat for long enough to cook the bread, so I sat the bread on top of the woodburner, the paraffin heater and the Primus stove in turn. It was either too cool and the middle didn't cook, or too hot and it burnt the bread. After four hours I had my two loaves, but beautifully cooked they were not.

I had a lot of free time while Hauke set up his laboratory in a small room in the main hut, so decided to see just how big my rabbit hutch was. With the aid of my tape measure and a chair, I found the external measurements to be 6.35 by 4.26 metres, with a height of 2.45 metres to the bottom of the roof. Inside, the main room was four metres square and two metres high, with the little kitchen two metres wide. So it was a big hutch. For rabbits.

The other buildings were spread out loosely across the flat plain of Kinnvika so that, during the

International Geophysical Year of 1957/58, the various scientific instruments inside would not interfere with each other. In front of us, annoyingly blocking part of our view over the bay, was the motor house, which had generated electricity for the complex in the early days and also housed a workshop and storage area. To the rear, the main building had long been stripped of all its useful fittings, and was eerily empty. Its individual bedrooms were very tiny, but there was a communal living space, kitchen and dining room, plus a few other rooms which we took over for storage and a laboratory. The big, old, grey-painted boiler that kept the hut warm was still in situ. Up in the roof there was a small stock of flour and crispbread, still edible after 45 years.

Nearby was a large, square, pyramid-roofed building, originally the 'cosmic house' (which housed equipment to help study geomagnetism, aurora and cosmic rays—the effects of electrically charged particles colliding with the earth's magnetic field), which we set up as our 'sports hall' where we could play table tennis on two doors, handles still attached, balanced on four chairs. A further building was the balloon house, where weather balloons had been launched at midnight and midday through the sliding roof; beyond was the 'absolute house', a non-magnetic building that was used for making geomagnetic observations and constructed with copper nails and fittings. An additional hut was maintained as emergency accommodation and contained a bed and a small table and chair. On the walls, visitors had signed and dated themselves in. One or two were well-known Arctic researchers, another was one of Hauke's old friends, Stefan, the only person known to have kayaked all the way to Nordaustlandet and returned to tell the tale.

Our village covered a distance of about 200 metres east to west and overlooking everything was the slight hump of Kinnberget, not much of a mountain at 124 metres, but we were keen to get to the top to get an overview of the landscape. As soon as we could spare the time and the weather remained clear, we took a dog each on a long lead and set off to explore it.

Trying to keep the two bounding masses of beasts under control after they'd been lazing around for so long was as hard for me as climbing up the steep, fragmentary slopes of pale, yellowish rock. Pink saxifrage and a few pale cream or yellow Svalbard poppies were still thrusting out blooms between the sharp slivers of stone, interspersed with other low-growing plants we had yet to identify. I felt hot and breathless, calf muscles complaining, unused to much hill-climbing recently, and I was glad of the strong if erratic tow from Sako. Hauke was shooting up the hill far faster than me and looked a bit impatient as I stopped for frequent rests. Speeding up over the final few metres, we gained the summit, marked by a cairn balanced above a sheer drop on the far side. We hopped out of the way as the dogs pissed all over the cairn and sniffed the air. I stood close to Hauke, gazing out over the flat terrain glowing warmly in the soft afternoon sunshine.

Looking due west, Kinnvika Bay swept gracefully below us in a long arc of water reflecting the silver-blue of the sky. Slightly north of west, an elbow of land nudged out where the huts lay remote and insignificant, blending into the pale rocky ground. The land beyond our huts stretched away and left to encircle the bay on the far westerly side with its twin fingers of land lying one behind the other. We turned towards the south-west, where long, scrawny islands resembled a half-submerged geriatric hand; in between, the sea lay quiet, its blue skin stretching far into the distance until it blended with a thin rim of whispy white cloud on the horizon, or it joined up with the pointed- and flat-topped mountains lying brown-black and deceptively low on the mainland. We looked further south, to our left, beneath the wings of innumerable kittiwakes flying back and forth to their nests on the high cliffs, to where a spray of rough, small islands shimmering and guarding the entrance to Murchisonfjord and more islands beyond. To the south-east of Kinnberget, looming up from the far easterly shores of Murchisonfjord, red-rocked Celciusberget rose to a height of 350 metres, somewhat dwarfing our modest lookout point. A long line of solid white cloud stretched out either side beyond Celciusberget, hanging sharp-edged like a frozen sheet on a washing line.

'That's not cloud,' Hauke pointed out. 'It's the glacier, Vestfonna, that you can see.'

As we swung around to the north to look back at Kinnvika, all we could see was rock of many different colours: grey, yellow, orange, red, green, cream, brown; all frost-cracked and bare, with the occasional patch of lingering snow. Between the two 'bergs', rugged, high, flat-topped bluffs of red rock streaked with cream, lay like great slabs of beef on a butcher's block, sparkling streams trickling down their sides to the blue-green lakes dotted at their feet. Great flat expanses of rocky land filled the space between the mountains and the sea, wave-worn and ridged where, over millennia, the land-lying ice had melted and the land had gradually lifted with the decrease in weight, leaving clearly discernible formations delineating the ancient uplifted beaches. North of Kinnvika, a bony-backed ridge divided the flat land from the sea, creating a great circular inland lagoon, Claravågen, home to a small colony of lazy-flapping glaucous gulls.

I'd never seen anywhere so empty, so naked. Stripped of its clothing. Stripped back to its essential elements. Nothing was covered up. No secrets. It was a hard, aloof, indifferent land perhaps, had no pretensions. It was all there was. All it could be.

The sun had coloured the rocks around the hut beautiful shades of peach, doing nothing to dispel the feeling of separation from the rest of the world, but intimating warmth. An invitation to a new, basic life. Shared with nature. Shared with Hauke. In England I'd felt trapped in a big world, like a bird in a golden cage. I had so much—was it too much? Was it too little? Too much in the material sense, too little of life's basics. Friendship. Companionship. Conversation. Contact. Love. Hope. Would the wide open spaces, the wind, the sea, the long dark nights, the discomfort, the aloneness, fill the empty caverns I felt inside me? I wanted it to take away the loneliness, to fill the void. To heal.

There is always something magical about standing on top of a hill or mountain; exhilarating; satisfying; a deep-breath-taking, eye-closing sense of renewal, a tangible smell of energy absorbed, as if the wind took away your cares and refreshed and stimulated the mind. Wound up your spring. Charged your batteries. I could feel my nerve endings start to tingle, felt a twitch between my shoulder blades, a subdued shudder up my spine. I filled my lungs with the pure, scentless air, pulling it deep down into my grateful chest, holding it for a few moments, then exhaling slowly, very slowly, pulling in my stomach to expel the last of the air, waiting, then drawing in the next deep, cold lungful, drawing it down to my toes, feeling them buzz with the effort. I knew I'd be returning here to the top of Kinnberget. It was looking after me.

*   *   *

We seemed to be lucky with the weather. It was sunny most days, unusually warm and clear, good to be out of doors so often. I was fetching more logs for the fire when Hauke whistled to me from the doorway of the main hut.

'What's up?' I called.

'Bear alarm!'

'Where?' I shouted back. I followed Hauke's extended arm pointing towards the beach at the corner of the bay below Kinnberget, away to our left. 'Oh, bloody hell,' I thought. 'Here we go.'

I dumped the logs back on the stack and whizzed indoors for rifle, binoculars and camera as Hauke casually walked over. The dogs were half asleep and hadn't sniffed anything.

'There's plenty of time,' he said calmly. 'Don't get in a panic.'

It was all right for him, he'd seen loads of 'em. With my rifle parked up against the outer wall by the door, I slung the long-lensed camera about my neck and focused the binocs on the bear, which was approaching almost at a trot, angling inland and towards the huts. I could hardly see him for shaking so much. My heart was racing, chest thumping, kneecaps jumping. The bear was sniffing around and, oddly, kept looking down at its left front leg. Hauke set the video camera up on the tripod and started filming. I didn't move from the rifle. On my camera, even using a 200-millimetre lens, the bear hardly filled the middle of the screen, but it was more than close enough for me, probably 800 metres away. Hauke moved closer to the bear to get better film. I stayed put. The bear, rapidly covering the ground with its long strides, didn't like the look of us and changed direction, keeping well away and skirting the area between our hut and the foot of Kinnberget where the glacial melt water bogged the land and squishy green moss grew. Keeping parallel to the main hut, he hastened towards the low ridge behind us. Balto and Sako finally woke up and barked, straining against their strong leads, leaping about, wanting some fun. Again Hauke moved position, advancing towards the bear, effectively threatening him. The bear started to run, shot up the ridge with ease and disappeared over the top and was gone. He was in such a hurry we called him Speedy Gonzales. It was all over in three minutes but I was shaking like a leaf for ages afterwards. I'd taken a couple of photographs which I knew would be rubbish, but it was my first Kinnvika bear, and I just had to record it. Shakes or not. Hauke reckoned Speedy Gonzales was off up to the north coast to hunt seals, and now he was off to do some research down by the beach, just where we'd first seen the bear. To me, it seemed a stupid thing to do, but I knew that was illogical. Balto and Sako stood scenting the air for a while and then flopped back down again. I had a cup of tea with a tot of rum, then carried on fetching in the wood.

*　　*　　*

When our first reindeer came by, it excited the dogs no end. Unfortunately for the dogs, they were firmly fixed on their long lines, so no matter how much they looked longingly at the deer, they had no chance to chase after them. It seemed to be two fat adults and a dark-coloured baby who was full of the joys of life. Tucked below the ridge was a wide patch of snow that was refusing to melt away under the sun, and the baby found it fascinating, skipping about on it, racing back and forth, jumping about and twisting in the air, stopping to catch his breath before dashing off again. The adults were more interested in eating, stocking up on the meagre ration of moss and flowers, taking one bite here, another there, never eating everything to ensure a supply for next year. Despite the paucity of plant life, the reindeer seemed well fed, though not as rotund as some we had seen out on Revneset. After a few weeks, we noticed how the same small groups of reindeer would come round again, time after time. Some came by every week, some every ten days or so, some took much longer to call back. They all seemed to have their own favourite tour of the area, reminding me that New Forest ponies have exactly the same habit, remaining and wandering around in their own neighbourhood. The reindeer would come quite close, just like in town, which exasperated the dogs no end, and they barked and jumped and tried to get at them every time. They needed some training.

And boy, did they get it.

What they didn't know was that Hauke used to

120

train police dogs, so he had his training skills well honed and stood no nonsense. Hauke had been nice to them in Longyearbyen, under the eyes of the locals, but now they were going to get a shock. Short and sharp. And even I didn't like it.

Hauke mostly took the dogs out alone at first; it saved me getting wound up and him cross with me because I didn't like his methods. If the dogs put one paw wrong whilst on their very short leads, they got the side of Hauke's boot on their backside, sometimes so hard it knocked them over. Hauke was going to be top dog. No ifs, buts or maybes. They had to learn, and fast, that they were the underdogs—hopefully below me too, though at present they still took me wherever they wanted. But I too was learning. Creeping up the chain of command.

No commands were used, nothing to confuse a sit with a lie down, a come here with a stay. Just 'Hey!'

'They've got brains, make them use them,' said Hauke. And they did. Within ten days Balto was allowed to run free, while Sako, much the stronger-willed of the two, remained on a short line close to Hauke. It worked, both happily accepting their roles. Balto always came back to us when we shouted 'Hey!' Sako was happy being guard dog, and when we took him for a walk he no longer pulled like a truck, but left the line slack and comfortable. I couldn't believe how fast Hauke had worked the miracle. I'd seen the English students galloping behind the dogs and hanging onto their leads for dear life. They wouldn't believe the difference either. But how much nicer the dogs were to have around. How much more comfortable out on a walk. Hats off to Hauke. When the time came to let them

121

both run free, Hauke tied long lengths of heavy, blue rope, found on the beach, to their leads which slowed them down and tired them out. After a few short weeks, both were under complete control and were allowed to go free on walks, though we held them on a lead when reindeer were near. You could see the temptation in their quivering bodies and bright eyes. We took no chances.

When not out for training or accompanying us on exploratory walks, the dogs were clipped to their long lines fixed to the heavy ring, and lazed about or curled up and slept, paws twitching, obviously dreaming of deer, not rabbits like good English dogs. They lived outside all the time, well insulated with their thick fur and almost immune to the cold temperatures. They seemed to drink very little and were fed once a day, in the morning, with the dried dog food soaked in warm water.

*   *   *

The finger of land enclosing our bay was called Austre Twillingneset, roughly translated as The East Twin Nose, because behind it, joined together like fingers to a hand, was Vestre Twillingneset, or The West Twin Nose. Here we found a hunter's hut, last used in the 1970s when polar bear hunting was banned. Above the lintel we could read Ruud's Hytte, Ruud's Hut. The square wooden structure was nailed over with assorted roofing felt and the door barricaded against bears. The chimney had long since rusted through and fallen to the ground, allowing snow and rain in to rust the woodburning stove; a couple of books, utensils, a lamp and a rough bed lay untidily inside. I borrowed the plastic flowers hanging up in the corner. I'm sure I had some just the same as a child, each one free with a packet of Daz washing powder. Our hut was luxurious in comparison, and at least twice the size, but even this was ten times better than another hut further down the beach, set behind a small lagoon. It was almost invisible, being semi sunk into the rocky ground. It had an A-frame at the front, boarded in and with a small door. From the top of the A-frame a long, thick log stretched backwards and rested on the ground and lots of thin pieces of sea-bleached branches and planks filled in the sides, resting on the long pole. Over all this, a thick layer of creamy, fine, sharp rocks had been piled, leaving the ends of the poles poking through, like interlaced fingers. Inside, the floor was lowered and it was surprisingly cosy, if cramped. It made a fine emergency shelter, but I wouldn't want to spend a year in it.

Two kilometres to the north of Kinnvika lay a small lake called Drikkesvatnet, Drinking Water, used by the Swedish expedition members from 1957. They used a 'Weasel', a caterpillar-tracked vehicle a bit like a snowcat, to collect the water and bring it back to their scientific station. Here we found an expanse of pink snow, coloured by algae flourishing in the cold and sunny conditions. Hauke always had some sterile collecting pots in his pocket, and we carefully took samples. Back at the hut, we examined it under the microscope, but it just looked like a mass of little, red-edged black dots. Hauke also showed me under the microscope the crispy orange lichen found on the rocks, looking, much to my surprise, like brown snot. I shuddered as I thought of squishy brown slugs. The water from our pond was more exciting. In it was slimy green hair full of dashing-about bugs, a thin, red, squirming leech and something that looked like an aquatic caterpillar. I'm glad we drank the water boiled.

*   *   *

The short, ice-free summer allowed us to use the inflatable boat to explore further afield. Although the dogs liked being out on the water, there was no way we could take them plus rifles and the filming and scientific equipment. The boat was just too small. They had to remain in Kinnvika.

On a flat, calm day we motored slowly up to Claravågen, to investigate the ancient lines of the raised beaches more closely. Passing through the narrow entrance to the almost completely enclosed bay, glaucous gull youngsters crouched grey and slightly fluffy on the rocks, parents dive-bombing us until we were no longer a threat. Scattering a dozen female eider ducks, we landed on the northern beach, a high and narrow collar of land dividing Claravågen from the smaller, and completely enclosed, Junodvatnet to the north. It was amazing how clear the individual raised beaches, or strandlines, were, each concentric ring curving gently around the bay, a new one being formed below the previous one as the ice retreated and a small shift upwards in the level of the land resulted. Some joined and separated again, but I managed to count 63 separate levels. In 10,000 years, the land had lifted about 55 metres. Here we found more pink algae in the occasional patch of snow, so we took additional samples, then explored along the beach where thousands of little tadpole-like creatures were swimming about in the shallow water. Hauke found part of an old cork lifebelt, still covered in snow-white canvas and sealed with red wax. The best I could do was half a dozen reels of Sellotape and the torso of a plastic doll with one arm and an opposite leg. A lot of driftwood lined the shore, which must have taken hundreds of years to accumulate as the opening into the lagoon was only about 50 metres wide. And shoes. Wherever we went we found shoes, mostly stained green by the salty water. Why were there so many?

Puttering back to Kinnvika on 2 August, we were surprised to find a small white cruise ship, operating out of Longyearbyen, anchored in the bay. We had done our best to avoid tourists so far. Very few tourist ships came by, operating from July to September, and sometimes not getting this far around Spitsbergen if ice conditions were bad. Usually we sneaked out the back door of Kinnvika and went for walks until they had gone, but we couldn't avoid these ones. Luckily for us they were ferrying passengers back to the mother ship, just one more boatload left on the beach. They were obviously more pleased to see us than the other way round. But, as it happened, among them was one of the expedition members who had stayed here between 1958 and 1959, Lars E. Andersson, and another man, who I believe was called Lasse. That was quite a treat for us, and we had almost missed seeing them. We talked rapidly about shared experiences while tourists took our photos and the last RIB came back, tactfully slowly, to fetch them away.

We managed to avoid most of the other large groups of visitors throughout the short season, and so missed our old friend Jason, the Arctic filmmaker, ten days later. He was lecturing on board a ship making its way towards Iceland, Greenland and Canada. He had left us a note, addressed to the 'young lovers', along with a goody bag of fresh fruit and vegetables. Yummy.

Late in the afternoon the next day, a chunky cabin-cruiser came rumbling into the bay, carrying a whole bunch of men from Longyearbyen, two of whom were teachers at the school. We made a fair exchange, a bottle or two of cognac for a huge bag of fresh fish which they had caught en route to visiting us—they knew that as we lived in a nature reserve we were not allowed to catch our own. Filleted, we packed it into a big plastic box and salted it with seawater. It was enough to see us over the winter. Even more yummy.

It was one o'clock in the morning, a couple of hours after our fishing friends had returned to their boat, and sunlight streamed in through the window. I could hear Sako barking, and struggling awake, rushed off to look out the kitchen window towards the dogs. A huge white bear was standing by Balto, sniffing, checking him out. I nipped back to Hauke, shaking him awake.

'There's a bear outside,' I said nervously, starting to tremble again.

'Where?' whispered Hauke, probably expecting me to say 'On the beach'.

'He's right outside, standing over Balto.'

Hauke was up in a flash, pulling his jacket over his blue long johns, grabbing the video camera. I hurriedly dressed too, pulling on a fleece jacket over my pyjamas, shoving on my slippers.

Looking out the window, I saw that the bear had moved off but was making feint attacks on the dogs,

126

they were barking like mad and trying to chase him away as best they could, being fixed to their lines. The next hour was pretty exciting, with the bear dodging the dogs' snapping teeth and refusing to be shooed away with our warning pens. He was thin and hungry, long-legged, and soaking wet. Retreating to the back of the main hut, he shook himself, haloed beautifully in a shiver of golden drops lit by the midnight sun behind. Hauke left the video on its tripod, went after him. I shelved my camera and shouldered my rifle, knees twitching. Halfway between me and the bear, Hauke started to throw stones, forcing it away, backwards. He jumped up and down, waving his arms in the air. Threw more rocks. The bear turned and started to move off as the flurry of stones became too much. Hauke stopped and started to run back towards me. The bear turned, and saw Hauke trip and fall over, sprawled on the gravel. The bear ran towards him. Hauke jumped up, faced the bear, ten metres away. It stopped, paused, one front paw resting on its claws. Hauke walked slowly backwards. I covered him with the rifle. He made it back.

'Be careful, Hauke. You are pissed!' I hissed at him, pissed too. Our fishing friends weren't the only ones that had been drinking cognac.

Hauke took up his rifle, still on the nail behind the door, and set off again after the bear. A few close, carefully aimed shots near its rear end had it thinking twice about staying, and it moved away up onto the ridge behind the main hut, the dogs keeping watch as best they could. We went back to bed, only to be woken up by the bear coming back and the dogs barking again. Once more Hauke shooed the bear away, firing close to it as he walked

127

determinedly towards it, imposing his will, as I stood watching from the doorway, tired and nervous. But the bear wouldn't give in, wouldn't go away. As soon as we began to relax back into bed, drifting off to sleep, the bear would come back again, setting off the dogs and making us rush outside. We repeated this on and off throughout the night. The bear didn't seem to be intent on attacking the dogs, or us; as the night wore on it appeared to be more curious than anything else. Eventually it lay down near the main hut and went to sleep. It seemed we had a stalemate. We gave up the game, and the dogs, Hauke and myself, went back to sleep, ignoring the furry problem as best we could.

The bear stayed around for a few days and became our house bear. We decided to call him Lady Franklin (for no other reason than that we liked such an aristocratic name) after the wife of the famous English Arctic explorer, Sir John Franklin, who disappeared on a search for the Northwest Passage. We were never quite sure whether it was a male or female bear, though it was probably a male, so it interchangeably got called 'he', 'she' or 'it'. Using its name was simpler. We tolerated each other, observed each other.

When it began to feel confident and came for another close visit, Sako was so cross, he strained at his lead, kept leaping forward, almost throttling himself. Balto wanted to get at it too, but Sako grabbed his line in his mouth and pulled him back. 'That's my bear!' Hauke filmed the interaction between bear and dog. I stood guard with the rifle over Hauke, the bear close, too close. Suddenly I saw a dash of black as Sako lunged at the bear, attacking, going for the throat. I screamed, and

128

Hauke shouted at him, calling him Svarten by mistake. Getting no response from Sako, Hauke filmed, while I stood, transfixed, screaming at Sako to come back. Sako was having fun, wagging his tail, running around the bear, nipping in to bite its neck. The bear jumped around and around, got wise, grabbed him with a huge paw, wrestled him to the ground, bit his back. I hefted the rifle, pointed into the air, chambered a round and fired. We all jumped at the unexpected noise. Sako was free. He'd soon learnt you didn't attack a bear in the same way as another dog, so he snapped at the bear's heels, chasing it down to the beach and out onto some ice that had drifted into the bay. The bear was safe. Sako was unhappy on the ice, came back. Eventually. The bear was gone.

*　　*　　*

A touch of autumn had crept into the air with a change in wind direction. The sky had greyed over and brought the ice up from the south, bringing it into Kinnvika or swishing it back and forth across the entrance to the bay on the tide. Ice from the south? We reckoned it had floated south from the ice pack all the way round the eastern coast of Nordaustlandet, swung westwards and then come up Hinlopen Strait. Old sea ice was just what we needed. Research! Science! Out with the boat!

The only trouble was, once we got out of the bay and in amongst the ice, I had to steer, control the engine, and get us close to the ice but not cut the boat on the razor-sharp edges of the floes. Stress! Stress! Stress! I kept cutting the engine out as I decreased the throttle, drifted off and lost steerage when I used too little, wasn't close enough, was too close. Yaargh! I got the hang of it in the end, and Hauke was able to film and take lots of ice samples. It would be simple enough over the winter to obtain fresh sea ice, but ice more than a year old was what Hauke had hoped for by coming to Kinnvika. He'd be able to make comparisons between the two. Once the work was done, we could relax and enjoy swooping in among the opalescent blues and greens of the ice. Seawater sloshed up the concave undersides of the ice and splished down from the greeny curves above. Bergy bits, mini icebergs up to three metres across, revolved slowly, parading intricate lace trim on turquoise knickers like a catwalk model.

We took a break on a small, circular island, exploring a little, watching the Arctic terns buzzing about our heads. But Hauke found bear tracks on the beach and felt uncomfortable. A mother and near-adult cub. 'Let's go,' he suggested, trusting his instincts. I agreed.

He steered us homewards as I peered ahead. Was that a rock, a lump of wood, or a bear on our beach? Oh no. It was Lady Franklin, lying at the top of the shingle, waiting for us. If you think it's a bear, it is a bear! We pootled up in the boat, engine idling, drifting along on the current, filming the bear as it paralleled our course on land. Seeing enough, the bear moved inland, towards the huts. We beached the boat, made it fast and waddled up to the hut in our survival suits, keeping an eye on Lady Franklin. He was just curious, inquisitive, wanted to know what we'd been up to. The dogs were OK. There didn't appear to have been any trouble. They were now fixed to long chains so they couldn't have escaped. We all relaxed and resumed our normal procedures.

At one-thirty, Hauke woke me up. I couldn't hear dogs barking, so I wondered what was happening. It was Lady Franklin back again, but the dogs were sound asleep. He was rummaging in our bonfire pit, but there was nothing to interest him there. It was well burnt. What to do? We kept quiet, seeing what would develop. Lady Franklin knew we were watching, but wasn't bothered. After ten to fifteen minutes the bear's smell finally penetrated the dogs' dreams and they jumped up and barked, a bit surprised that the bear had got so close unnoticed. Lady Franklin looked at them, decided he'd had enough of them, and wandered off in the direction of the ridge. Hauke wondered whether to fire off a warning shot, but decided not to as the bear was still moving away. And he continued to walk away, a bit faster than his usual slow gait, up the lower slopes of the ridge, on and upwards, taking the route that had been taken by the other bears we'd seen, heading northwards. Were we seeing what we thought we were seeing? Suddenly, after thinking about it once or twice, he breasted the ridge and was gone. Just like that. No drama, he just quietly went, after eight days, almost to the minute.

I looked at Hauke. He looked at me. We agreed. Lady Franklin had gone. We were ninety per cent sure, anyway. We went back to bed and slept like logs.

CHAPTER SEVEN

SORTING OUT

Ice had packed into the bay like a mass of water lilies blown to the end of a garden pond, wedging bunches of white and turquoise 'flowers' amongst the blue-white ice leaves that were tilted and crushed by the press of wind and tide. Some were stranded on the shore by the receding tide, giving Hauke the opportunity to take samples to analyse and scrutinise in his laboratory. After stowing the video camera and appropriate scientific equipment into his backpack, he set off down to the beach with the dogs in tow, leaving me to my household chores.

I tidied up a bit, not too much. Housework wasn't my favourite occupation. It never had been. The good job I'd made of the bedsit belied the fact. I seemed to live in permanent untidiness, even though I much preferred it neat and organised. Living alone, I had a tendency to disappear under mountains of junk and clutter. I could spend all day straightening stuff out, putting everything away, cleaning up, and then immediately manage to turn the place back into a bomb site. In the hut, I tried to be tidy because I had to be. There was no space available to allow me to be messy.

I gathered up the bag of muesli, the milk powder and the squishy packet of apricot compote, returned them to the kitchen and wiped down the table. To keep our table space evenly divided, Hauke had carefully drawn a blue biro line down the centre of the wooden surface. His side. My side. I wasn't too sure about this at first—it seemed a bit draconian—but it worked well. I could be as disorganised as I liked on my side of the table (Hauke had said so), but woe betide me if I encroached on his. To ensure perfect harmony, the communal tea and hot water flasks and the nibbles were positioned on the blue line within easy reach for both of us.

As I used it for kneading the bread, the end of the table got a regular, good scrubbing with hot, soapy water which is more than the rest of the hut got after its initial clean when we moved in. Here on Spitsbergen in the 1930s, a German woman, Christiane Ritter, overwintered with her husband and another trapper. (Now that must have been interesting!) I read in her book, *A Woman in the Polar Night*, that whenever she got cross or out of sorts, she would scrub the hut within an inch of its life. That seemed like too much hard work and hassle. A good sweep out a couple of times a week and clean work surfaces were good enough for me.

I didn't need to wash the bed linen too often, because the pure quality of the air kept us, and it, pretty clean. It was also quite difficult to wash a thick, cotton sheet in a rather small washing up bowl or bucket—there never seemed to be enough space for sheet and water together. I shook out my quilt and folded up my pyjamas, shoving them under the plumped up pillow. Most of my clothes remained up in the main hut and those that were worn all the time were stuffed into shallow boxes under my bed, out of sight. Hauke had little room for his clothes and personal effects because of the batteries under his bed and the radio equipment on the shelf above it, though it didn't bother him as it would have bothered me. But then, I always need more space. Books, sewing machines and fabric always expand to fill the available nooks and crannies.

*　　*　　*

In the kitchen, I washed up the breakfast things in a minimal quantity of frothy hot water. As I threw out the dirty water well out to the side of the hut, I noticed a bear walking around on the ice in our little bay. I wondered if Hauke had seen it, but I couldn't see hide nor hair of him or the dogs anywhere. I suddenly felt very lonely and vulnerable, a bit nervous, but at least I wasn't shaking as I had seeing my first bear here. That was an improvement. I told myself to keep calm. Nothing had happened so far. Remember what Hauke said, don't leave decision-making until the last moment, plan ahead and make life easier for yourself. I knew I wouldn't panic. I never had before, and I wasn't going to start now. At least I hoped so. I took a couple of deep breaths and assessed the situation.

The bear seemed more interested in staying on the ice than coming to visit me, so I had time to think about what to do. If the bear came up to the hut, I could either attempt to scare it away or shut myself up inside depending on whether I thought he was a nice bear or an aggressive one. I had the dog bowls to bang together, the warning pen, my rifle indoors and the spare one in the outside loo. There was plenty of ammo—though I was determined not to kill a bear unless I absolutely had to. We had agreed on that point. Meanwhile, from the safety of the hut, I had time to observe my furry friend carefully through my binocs. I wrapped myself up warm, looped the strap of my rifle over my head and shoulder and climbed up the ladder onto the roof to watch. With the additional height, I saw not one, but three bears, the most I had seen together. I didn't have the nerve to get closer to that many bears, so I stayed on my lofty perch and was content just to watch in safety.

Out on the ice I could see the remains of a seal, polar bears' favourite food, its ragged, red and upturned rib cage all that was left to witness its demise. There must have been a few morsels left to eat as the bears took it in turns to investigate the carcass before toddling off to lie on the ice and digest their meal. Two of the bears were fairly large and white while the third was enormous and a grubby yellow colour and kept hiding amongst the jumbled ice chunks. It seemed to sit down on its rump and lean back against a frozen mass, looking as snug as if it was sitting in an armchair. And then I saw why. What I had thought was a huge male was in fact a remarkably large female, suckling a little, yellow cub. I'd been unable to see it before as it was kept well away from the other bears. A baby bear is a tasty bear. A good snack for a male.

I watched for a couple of hours, counting and re-counting the bears as they moved around on the drift ice. Could I now see seven bears? No—it was eight! Eight! Brilliant. And I even felt quite relaxed sitting up on the roof as there was no sign of them coming my way. I kept an eye open for any other bears sneaking up on me from other directions, as they can pick up the scent of a kill from miles away. As it was, it was Hauke and the dogs who came up to the hut unobserved, making me jump.

'Have you seen the bears?' I called down to him.

135

'What bears?' replied Hauke, somewhat surprised. 'I've been over to Hinlopen Strait and haven't seen one.'

'That's not surprising,' I said, 'they're all here! Eight of them!'

'How many?' laughed Hauke, amazed. 'Where?'

'Come up and I'll show you.'

A few minutes later we had secured the dogs and, grinning at each other, scampered off to the beach to film our bunch of bears.

*   *   *

Although the bay remained full of ice, the temperature continued warm, above freezing for much of the time, and after a period of dismal grey fog, it cleared up leaving sparkling blue skies again. I thought I could hear thunder rumbling and echoing all around me, but I'd got it all wrong again. Hauke told me not to be so daft, of course it wasn't thunder, just the distant glaciers calving in the heat. The roaring noise was the fall and crash of gigantic, many-tonned slivers of ice parting company with the main glacier and collapsing into the sea, creating a mini tidal wave. Awesome natural power. We could often hear the roar of the ice out on Hinlopen Strait, as it pushed and shoved with the tidal flow, pieces squeaking, groaning, grating like rusty bumper cars, knocking bits off each other, leaving a trail of icy debris in their wakes. There was no chance to go out in the inflatable with such difficult conditions out on the water, so it remained, firmly tied to half-buried logs on the pebbly beach. It seemed too early to pack it away for the winter.

One day towards the end of August, I was about to

cook some peppery scrambled eggs for breakfast when the dogs woofed their bear alarm. Down on the beach was a mother bear, quite small, with a fluffy dandelion clock of a baby trotting along happily behind her. Mum stopped at the boat and tested it just in case it was a funny shaped grey seal. We were not amused, and Hauke fired a warning shot over their heads. I told Hauke to be careful as they were both moving pretty quickly towards us.

'They're OK,' he said. 'Mums with babies aren't a problem.'

Oh, no?

Just as the two reached the motor house, Mum scorched ahead leaving baby well behind her, switched direction suddenly and charged the dogs. I had grabbed the dog bowls, and now banged them for all I was worth. Mum stopped just short of the dogs straining on their lines, their noses within millimetres of each other, and about ten metres away from me. Hauke dashed around to my side of the hut and fired a shot over all our heads. After a moment's thought, Mum decided the odds were too high and scarpered, chasing after baby who was already halfway back to the beach.

I'd only had the dog bowls for protection. It hadn't been dangerous, but maybe we'd just been lucky so far. Sako, after his bear fight, just had a couple of puncture wounds on his back. Our boat hadn't been so lucky. We had a small repair kit with us, containing assorted round patches to deal with minor punctures, but nothing to cope with the raking claws and sharp teeth of what we later called our Teenage Mum. Even without the ice, our boating days were over. Unless . . .

We rummaged about in the other huts and

137

collected up odd bits of wood and an abandoned door. But building a boat is man's work—at least that was my excuse. I got the impression that Hauke didn't want any help from me, so I left him to it. He'd been working so hard on his research that he deserved a little playful project of his own. He used the door as the flat bottom and old floorboards for the sides, bow and stern, making the latter strong enough to take the weight of our little outboard motor. There was a lot of tar left over from when the hut roofs had been re-felted, so when the boat was finished (after a bit more than Hauke's estimated couple of hours), we heated it up and coated the outside to try and make it watertight. When the tar had dried, we towed her down to the beach on a rickety ladder with a pair of ancient skis nailed under. We named her Lady Franklin, just like the bear, only this time it was more appropriate. (Lady Franklin had privately financed one of over a dozen ships that went on a fruitless search for her missing husband, Sir John.) As it wasn't Sunday, we launched her without champagne. Hauke, in his survival suit, climbed aboard and paddled around in the only small, ice-free area near the beach. It was decidedly unstable, and I wouldn't want to go anywhere in it, even in an emergency, with or without an engine. It had been a fun exercise, but it was back to square one in the transport department.

*   *   *

Winter was in the air. The first snow, five to ten centimetres, fell on 5 September, just one week after the last of the midnight sun. The sun now disappeared below the horizon, though at present not for very long before reappearing again. Our year's supply of provisions arrived, ferried over from the *Polarsyssel* by helicopter, and we had a mad scramble to get it all away before the bears came. Our letters and scientific samples were sent on their way to various destinations and we could both relax again. It had been nice for us, and the dogs, to see people, but we were glad to be alone again and get back into our routine.

From the new supplies, I made up an emergency rations box that would last us a couple of weeks, and put it to one side so that I wouldn't be tempted to use it. I sorted the bulk of the supplies in the main hut into three-month sections so that I could control the amount of food we were eating and not worry about running out. I kept all the dry and bulky stores like flour, muesli, tinned goods and pasta on pallets on the floor, and the smaller, more lightweight items on shelves above. The biscuits and chocolates were all lumped together in one big box and we helped ourselves to them whenever we liked. As I started each three-month pack, I would sub-divide it into thirds, load one lot onto the pulkas and tow it down to the hut. All the eggs were stored in the kitchen, high up where it was fractionally warmer, and the boxes were turned over every week so that they kept fresh longer, a tip that Karin had given me. The cabbage and potatoes were also stored in the kitchen until air temperatures outside remained below zero, when they were moved out to a box made from a low-walled pallet with an aluminium lid alongside the hut. As long as the frozen potatoes were plunged straight into boiling water for cooking, we never had any problem with them. If you thawed them out first all you'd get would be a black, squishy mess.

After a few weeks our pre-packed bacon had started going green with mould even though it was frozen solid. Hauke had the same thing happen in Mushamna and found it better to remove the packaging, scrape off the mould and leave it to dry in the air. It worked well with no recurrence of the fungus, much to my taste buds' pleasure. We normally had muesli for breakfast and Karin had told me to make up the powdered milk the day before I needed it as it seemed to taste better, but once the winter set in it would, of course, freeze overnight, so we switched to Plan B: two spoonfuls of powdered milk over the muesli, pour on hot water and stir. To this we added either tinned fruit or some of the packet fruit desserts (and chocolate powder and honey in Hauke's case), and, of course, washed it down with lots of tea or coffee. We kept one flask permanently filled with tea and a second with hot water, making sure they were full before we went out walking or working. When baking bread I'd sometimes add raisins to the dough or raid the muesli for nuts to add to the bread mix. After much trial and error, I had found it best to cook one loaf at a time inside the woodburner, sitting on a stone, ensuring that the heat wasn't too great. Most of the time it worked. At least it didn't take four hours to cook any more. I made crumpets using small tins (once containing pineapple rings) with the tops and bottoms removed as moulds, Hauke declaring they were the best he'd ever tasted. Not really a compliment as he'd never had them before. Ultra-thin and crispy Norwegian flat breads were delicious baked directly on the top of the paraffin heater, but the cakes baked in Alan's little oven weren't so successful. Nothing was wasted as we had two mobile dustbins in the dogs.

140

*   *   *

Sako and Balto were barking. We hurried out to see the dogs looking down to the bay. Hauke rushed us down to the beach to see why. There, just showing their glistening, finless backs out of the water, were beluga, or white whales; a small pod of them. It was hard to tell how many—I could only see three at once, but surely there were more. Their creamy white bodies stood out sharply against the graphite grey of the sea in the fading gloom of evening, as they gracefully broached the water in flat arches, swimming in the shallows around the edge of the bay, popping up between the ice, feeding off crabs or shrimps on the bottom.

As whales go they are not very big, up to five metres in length and weighing up to 1,500 kilograms. They are known as the 'sea canary' for all their whistling and squeaks, not that I heard a thing—they probably have too high a pitch. These wonderful, entirely Arctic or sub-Arctic creatures came back into the bay on two or three occasions, staying just a short time before disappearing as quickly as they'd come. I never, ever expected to whale watch from a beach.

*   *   *

After being almost hunted to extinction on Spitsbergen, walrus are making a slow, steady, well-protected comeback, but there aren't many more than a couple of thousand even now. They can often be seen hauled out on Moffen Island, off the north coast of Spitsbergen, but are still quite a rare sight.

So imagine our surprise at seeing a dead one washed up on the beach bordering Hinlopen Strait. We were all curious to get a close look, and Hauke was about to let the dogs run free when I saw it move.

'It's not dead!' I shouted, just in time. Sure enough, it was just fast asleep. From behind, it looked almost like a rounded, brown rock, shapeless and ugly. Not much better from the front; but what amazing tusks! We grabbed a few photos, but knew we should get some good video shots, so took the dogs home, left them tied up and returned to the walrus about an hour and a half later. He was still dozing, and hardly took any notice of us. His great bulk and weight (he was around three metres in length and perhaps weighed as much as 1,000 kilograms) meant that he wasn't particularly scared of polar bears—the biggest bear ever weighed on Spitsbergen was only 700 kilograms—but as a lone animal he would have disappeared back into the sea for safety if one approached. He certainly wasn't frightened of us.

He was lying on his side, his long, ridged, double spikes of ivory pointing skywards from under a bristly, off-white, short moustache. His nose was flat and sealed with flaps which only seemed to open when he breathed out, no doubt very useful when swimming to great depths in the sea; his round piggy eyes hardly opened, and it was a wonder he saw us at all. It was hard to tell just where his head ended and the rest of him began and his bewhiskered head was far smaller than I expected, almost stuck on as an afterthought, barely visible in the great rolls of fat covering the thick, pink-knobbled skin around his neck and chest. One front flipper was stretched out to the side of his blubbery body, the other hung lazily across his furrowed, pale brown belly, twitching occasionally. He rolled over onto his fat gut, tucking up his rear flippers under his body and propping himself up on a front one, watching us with a 'haven't you got enough photos yet?' kind of look.

No, no. Just a few more. Me with the walrus. Hauke with the walrus. 'Enough is enough!' thought the walrus and, with incredible swiftness for such a vast, fat lump, he lunged at Hauke who leaped out of the way with a squeal. OK, OK. We get the message. Time to go.

The dogs were pleased to see us as we got back to Kinnvika a couple of hours later, jumping about on their hind legs and boxing like a pair of kangaroos. Sako yelped in obvious pain so we ran the last few yards to him, while Balto fussed around him, concerned. Had he pulled a muscle, jarred a shoulder, landed on a sharp rock or been bitten accidentally? We checked him over but could find nothing wrong. It was a mystery. He walked properly, didn't limp or anything, just one of those things. We forgot about it.

*   *   *

I woke up feeling as if I hadn't slept all that well, and as if a black cloud had settled over me during the night, leaving me tired and listless; my mug of tea failed to help dispel the gloom. My shoulders were hunched as if I was cold and my head was humming with tension like electricity pylons after a shower of rain. I felt I was building up a head of steam and was about to explode. Scrambling around my mind was a mass of unnamed feelings trying to get out, battering the inside of my skull. I didn't

143

know where they had come from or what had built them up. I hadn't argued with Hauke and I wasn't bored with his company, but had I just seen too much of him for too long? Was the daily routine grinding me down? It can't have been that, life is a routine most of the time. We get up, eat, work and play at roughly the same times each day or week, wherever we are. People can be fairly predictable animals. The four walls of our hut seemed to close in, and it felt as small as in the first few days we were here. A touch of cabin fever perhaps? I looked out of the window and gazed at the rocky landscape, still coloured like a biscuit assortment, treeless, greenless, no vivid colours. I was getting used to seeing this strange landscape day by day, though I wouldn't have wanted to live in it forever; getting used to seeing it up close and discovering its hidden jewels and surprises. Spending another day in this landscape wasn't my problem. It was as though I was a bit claustrophobic here in the hut, but then it wasn't quite that either. I didn't know what it was. I just felt strange. Odd. I didn't know how to deal with it except I knew I had to get out, get away from Hauke, the dogs, the hut, everything.

I told Hauke I was going for a walk. It was the only way I could ease the tension, to relax, wind down. He wasn't happy about it as I'd never gone out alone before; I'd always had him and the dogs with me. No wonder I needed space!

'Take a dog with you,' he said sensibly.

I thought about it. No. It seemed too much hassle. No. I'd go completely alone. It was what I needed. I wouldn't go far, just down to the beach for a bit. I wouldn't stay out too long; but I had to be on my own. Hauke was acquiescent, accepting the way I felt, my way of dealing with it. It didn't mean he liked it.

As I made my way past the motor house and angled left towards the corner of the bay below Kinnberget, I had tingles across my shoulders and up my neck. It was strange having no one with me. The rifle slung over my shoulder was essential security, but my eyes were the most important defence system I had. I felt a bit like English soldiers patrolling in Northern Ireland in the 1970s, turning and turning about, checking my safety, checking for bears. A weird feeling. Scary. Foolhardy? Was I being masochistic? I didn't think so. Was I rebelling against Hauke's protection in some way? Maybe. Maybe not. I'd place a hefty bet, though, that he was keeping a discreet eye on me.

I took my time after all, ambling along the beach as lazy waves flopped weakly onto the shore. I picked up pebbles, cast them away, rummaged amongst the driftwood, loosing myself, shedding the built-up tension. Jellyfish-like creatures seemed to be dying in the edge of the tide, breaking up and shredding into slimy strips: clear, Zeppelin-shaped ones, now tattered, and small, opaque jellyfish drifting lifelessly to and fro, trailing tangled tentacles. I was watchful of bears and repeated to myself over and over, 'If you think it's a bear it is a bear. If you think it's a bear it is a bear.' But I saw none. Didn't even spot a reindeer. I meandered along the beach as far as I felt happy to go, then turned about and walked in the other direction.

The walk acted like a safety valve on a pressure cooker and by the time I got back up to the hut, I was feeling marginally better, a little less fragile, though still confused by my emotions. Perhaps I hadn't been coping with life in Kinnvika as well as I thought. Maybe I was just putting on my happy face for Hauke and pretending I was content. All my feelings about Spitsbergen were now bubbling up to the surface. There was little in my past to give me much of a clue about how to deal with these new life experiences, these mad adventures. It was all so out of the ordinary. So alien. So . . . I don't know, just crazy. But the walk had done me good. I felt I'd hit bottom and could now start to climb back up and find some sort of normality in this existence. I felt more positive again. And I still wanted to stay.

*   *   *

My daytime feelings may have been back in hand, but I had been having one or two odd dreams of late. I think I must have been subconsciously missing grass and trees, at any rate the colour green. Apparently I was a member of the Green Police. People were becoming very ill with not seeing any greenery over the winter. I went to a huge football stadium where people no longer went, and saw the groundsman had kept a small patch of turf free from snow so he could sit and look at it and feel better. It transpired that the pitch had underground heating, so I suggested he turn it on and melt the snow so that lots of people could look at the grass and feel better, too. Then I woke up and it was back to reality. Back to the hut. Back to endless snow.

Another night I was buying an old house, about a hundred years old, brick-built with yellow, stone corners, not beautiful but homely. After a tour inside it was clearly much larger than it first appeared. The right wing had, on the second floor, a huge enamel bath with fat pipes at the end, and it was set high off the ground so you had to climb steps to get in. Below, on the first floor, was a swimming pool— why it wasn't built on the ground floor I couldn't work out, but it seemed like too much weight in the wrong place. The room at the top of the left wing was, I knew, completely lined with shiny white bricks, not tiles, that covered the doors and windows too, even though I couldn't possibly get in to see. Outside in the garden were several holiday chalets which I could paint up in different colours and let out, but no one seemed to know of their existence before and were rather surprised to find them there. Bit odd. Perhaps I was missing people and feeling a bit claustrophobic after all.

*   *   *

I hadn't realised, but on 21 September, the whole world has a day and night of equal length. For us it meant the sure onset of winter. Temperatures dropped, and it became much more windy. At times we had to move the dogs from one side of the hut to the other to give them some shelter from the wind. With Hauke's weather station it was simple to follow the increase in wind speed from the monitor in the hut. It didn't have to be all that cold outside, but the wind-chill factor could make it quite ferocious; it could be −8°C but feel more like −30°C in a gale. From the comfort of the hut we would keep an eye on the maximum strength of a gust of wind, measured in metres per second: 12.8, 13.4, 14.7, 17.7, topping out at 20.2 metres per second. We were glad not to be dogs outside. The iron ring we originally fixed the dogs to was buried over a metre under the surface. I expected snow to pile up around the hut, but the wind kept the ground almost completely free of snow for a width of about one and a half metres around the hut, which made it comfortable for us to come and go. The light in the sky late afternoon grew beautiful at times, quite breathtaking in its variety of colour, from soft greens, lilacs and blues to the more unusual shades of amber and red, with the clouds blushing apricot and creamy peach. On other days the sky was suffused with lavender, puce and violet greys, all shades from the shimmering feathers of dove and pigeon.

At the end of September we made a survey of the driftwood and rubbish washed ashore on a nearby stretch of beach, letting the dogs potter about. We were amazed at the sheer quantity of wood, both natural and worked, and the amount of flotsam and jetsam lying about, half buried under storm-shifted pebbles. We decided it would be an interesting research project and something a bit different to include in our expedition report at the end of the year. We paced out a rough 500-metre stretch, which enclosed a small expanse of water, popular with the eider ducks, and chose different elements to count. We had decided on six categories, counting everything we saw with the exception of the very small fragments of wood. The results were as follows:

Item	Number of units
Wood: clearly natural/not worked	100
Wood: worked by man	600
Wood: hut or other building pieces	143
Wood: clearly from ships, boats	22
Modern rubbish, bottles, shoes etc.	240
Fishing by-products, nets, ropes, floats	130

The results were a bit surprising as we expected to find more natural driftwood than we did. The number of pieces from shipwrecks was small, but in size some were enormous and incredibly heavy, such as a rib from a substantial-sized ship, maybe an old whaler from the seventeenth century; we didn't have the expertise to be more accurate. The most numerous items were wooden barrel staves; all sizes and thicknesses, banded with rust. Some had flattened out over the centuries, others still retained their shapely curves. It reminded me of all the barrels I had seen crossing the road on wagons pulled by a little steam engine at the Bass brewery where my dad worked. It's all gone now; metal has replaced the wood, conveyor belts the railway. Progress.

The more we walked along the beaches in the area, the more interesting items we were finding strewn amongst the rocks and debris. Our eyes became accustomed to picking out unusual things from in between the dross, and we decided there would be enough things to make up a small museum. Our days of table tennis were over for the winter as it was now too dark inside the hut to see to play, so we turned it into Kinnvika's very own 'world's most northerly' museum.

We carefully documented where we found our items, photographing them in situ before relocating them to Kinnvika. They included enormous ribs, planks and timbers from ancient sailing ships, hundreds of years old; ski sticks; metal, cork or wooden fishing floats; wooden barrel components (staves, tops and bottoms); a wartime Mauser-made fuel barrel, possibly from the German weather station at Haudegen, a few kilometres north from us here on Nordaustlandet; oars; one side of a five-and-a-half-metre-long sledge rescued from an ice floe that had drifted into our bay; hunters' equipment; whale and bear bones; and lots of unidentified small but interesting items. The museum in Longyearbyen covered mostly coalmining and wildlife, and I didn't remember seeing anything about the history of Spitsbergen, its whaling heritage or its scientific expeditions. It would be nice if many of our pieces could be sent back for display when the museum moved to its new location in town. The quantity of wooden pieces found would surely make it a worthwhile project for students or scientists, especially those interested in old shipwrecks.

It was strenuous work collecting and transporting the items back to the hut from far away, but it was worth the effort. Hauke had his own ideas about how to display it all, so while I worked on the museum's information leaflet, Hauke set out all the items and wouldn't let me anywhere near the place until he'd finished. And, wow! What a job he'd made. It was amazing as I stepped through the door to see everything displayed with flare and originality. It was arranged chronologically, swinging around the square room from left to right, starting with all the barrel components. The staves were hanging in a roughly circular formation from the ceiling, the bases fixed to the walls like shelves; ropes were threaded through ships' timbers in a semblance of the way it would have appeared originally; oars of different shapes exploded like a bomb-burst from a corner; great chunks of ships' timbers adorned the rear wall, where our huge rib was securely fastened through an air vent to stop it dropping on someone's head. Some of the square-section timbers were

150

drilled through at regular intervals and dowels inserted into the holes. Was this to stop the wood splitting, I wondered? If it was, it worked a treat. Some pieces weathered the Arctic storms of time so well that when you set one piece upon another, the flat edges still fitted perfectly and no daylight could be seen between. Amazing after hundreds of years. The sledge runner (maybe from one of the expeditions of Norwegian Arctic explorer Fridtjof Nansen) just managed to squeeze in along the other side wall, hanging above what looked like a piece of lightweight boat, maybe from Adolf Erik Nordenskiöld's days (another polar explorer, born in Finland) and these were set above the mock hunters' hut display, complete with crockery, cutlery, lamp, book and the backbone of a bear. On our table tennis table, now hidden under a huge canvas cloth, were all the small finds, including bungs, shaped pieces of cork and wood, and carved handles. The whole was extremely effective in its layout. We called it the 'Strand Kant Museum' ('The Beach Edge Museum'), and opened it officially on Sunday 21 October to coincide with a champagne day. It deserved it.

Sako's leg seemed to play him up a bit now and then, making him squeal with pain and limp. Sometimes it didn't seem to bother him at all—it came and went. It made me wonder, when he was supposed to be pulling the sledge and didn't, whether he wasn't lazy or stupid but his leg was paining him. It was difficult to know if we should give him complete rest or light exercise to keep it supple and mobile. We wouldn't be able collect the driftwood from the beach so efficiently without his help pulling the sledge alongside Balto, so we hoped he would be better soon. Meanwhile, long walks would be out of the question.

We spent a long time constructing pyramids of logs on the beach around the bay, occasionally finding new items for the museum as we went. In winter, the logs would become covered in snow and frozen fast to the ground, and we needed to be able to see the wood supply clearly in the dark. We would load up the little, lightweight sledge and assist the dogs in towing it back up to our hut. There we offloaded it all near the sawhorse and returned for more loads. We accumulated enough logs to see us through the dark winter months and all that remained was to cut it up.

Hauke had brought a motor saw with him, but I couldn't bear to watch him cut up the logs, too nervous about the machine. A friend in Longyearbyen had almost had her leg chopped off by her husband in similar circumstances earlier in the year, so I was not keen to get too close to the ripping, rotating teeth. I'd rather stay indoors and not look. Hauke preferred it too as it made him less nervous. The saw made quick work of cutting up the logs into manageable lengths, and I volunteered to split them. It had been a few years since I had wielded an axe, and it took me a while to get into the swing of it again, but it was satisfying work, though back-breaking. I liked the rhythmic swing and chop, swing and chop, but not the bending down so much—that was the hard part. It was warm work, even on a very cold day, and soon had me stripping off layers of clothing until I was just working in a thin shirt. The chopped logs were stacked up three or four layers deep against the end wall of the hut, by the door, where they would be handy to fetch in the dark, or stored inside the hut in the kitchen, where they could dry out and be easy for throwing in the stove. When they had been cemented in place by falling snow, Balto loved to sit on them so he could be nosy and look in through the kitchen window to see what we were up to.

I liked these shared jobs that we did; it brought us closer together. I enjoyed the companionship of us working alongside each other, collecting the wood and loading up the sledge and transporting it back to the hut safely. It was an opportunity to work independently and together. It was the same when we were filming. Hauke normally decided how we would document our findings on film, how we would set up the scenes and capture them, and we shared the filming between us. If you are in charge of the camera you tend to be the boss, having control over what angle to use and how much zoom. It is easy to get trigger happy with the zoom button, and much better to leave it well alone during actual filming. Because I didn't understand German, I had problems at first when Hauke was doing explanatory pieces to camera or was describing his scientific work in detail, as I would chop him off suddenly just to change angle and he would get annoyed as he'd almost finished what he was saying and we'd have to do it all again. In the end, we worked on the simple method of me sticking my arm up in the air so he knew when I wanted a change.

He would also get really annoyed if I turned up for filming in my 'shitty-brown' jacket, which he said looked awful on film, and asked would I mind going back and changing into my red one. I did make the point that my brown jacket was warmer, but it was true that the red one looked much better on film. Just wear an extra jumper under it. Sometimes life is simpler if you make yourself aware of any likely problems and circumvent them before they happen. I wore the red jacket automatically for filming after that. The more we got to know each other the more we understood the way we dealt with problems and the less likely we were to quarrel. Tolerance was essential. We all of us have our bad habits, but if you allow other people's to annoy you, they may end up ruining an otherwise perfectly good relationship. I'm always twiddling with my hair, which annoys Hauke a lot (and my mum), and I'm perpetually untidy. I'd get impatient with Hauke when he wouldn't give me a chance to explain my point of view, over a filming project for instance. One problem I had with him in the beginning was that I felt he didn't give me time to think. The trouble was, I hadn't appreciated just how much he thinks. I just 'do', without thinking too much. He'd always think through a problem, and out of politeness would ask me for my views, and then he'd get annoyed when I didn't have one. I was learning a lot, not only about Hauke, but also about handling relationships and planning ahead. And like most men, when he wanted something doing, he wanted it doing there and then, even if I was in the middle of something that I couldn't drop that instant, like keeping an eye on the baking bread. But really, he was quite easy to live with, and I learnt years ago that it's much better to ignore bad habits and live with them. To learn the rules.

*   *   *

Hauke worked hard on his scientific projects, under extreme conditions, but there was little I could do to

154

help him with the actual experiments, and he wouldn't have wanted me to anyway. At least I could help carry equipment from A to B and keep an eye open for any possible danger, rifle at the ready, leaving him to concentrate on his work without worrying about his safety. Outside in the dark, I could hold lamps and torches for him while he worked with both hands free, so that he could get a job done more quickly and get back to the hut to thaw out. I didn't always understand when Hauke explained his scientific work. It made me feel a bit stupid at times, but I was beginning to learn about so many new scientific fields and processes: about the structure and composition of sea ice, what went on within its structure, at what temperatures it formed; about RNA (ribonucleic acid—the precursor of DNA) and the first life on earth; plant life; wildlife; how to record data logically; how to use the microscope and film through it. It was like being back in my physics and biology classes at school. And I loved it. I could share his enthusiasm for the fascinating samples seen under the microscope: feathery ice growing across a glass slide; snowflakes encrusted with hundreds of CO_2 bubbles; bacteria racing and bumping along tiny channels glowing fuchsia and lime green under polarised light; translucent brown micro-creatures waggling their multiple legs in the liquid within the ice; a fat, egg-shaped being that seemed to eject a bunch of short arms from within before sucking them back inside again; a tiny shrimp fluorescing electric blue. It was astounding. There truly was an 'incredibly huge amount of life' in the ice and it was impossible not to get excited about it. The sea ice wasn't just a lump of solid ice as I would have supposed, nothing like the ice in your freezer or on your pond. It was full of canals and tiny interconnecting channels with salty brine running through them; lots of individual ice cells—innumerable little laboratories—where initial life had a chance to start; there was energy stored in the ice, released when it melted; there were chemicals and amino acids contained in it too; a real possibility that life on earth first evolved in sea ice.

Hauke was attentive and took an interest in whatever I was doing too, whether my knitting or silk painting, what I was reading, or what I was concocting for dinner (naturally he had an interest in that). We were almost vegetarian, having only very small amounts of ham and salami allowed per day, with a third of a tin of vegetables, so I stretched it with pasta, rice or the potatoes, laced with chilli powder or dried peppers. Chocolate pudding, with or without rum, was a favourite, as was rice pudding, served with tinned fruit. When we were left fresh pears by Jason, our friend the film-maker, I poached them in red wine and cinnamon. Very tasty. The three-litre boxes of wine were stored in the main hut where they froze rock hard and took about three days to defrost standing by the side of the stoves, so I made sure I always had two or three boxes warming up slowly. Occasionally we shared the preparation of the meal, but it was mostly left to me to cook and Hauke insisted on doing the washing up, and after a few pointed comments I soon learned to leave as few pots for him to do as possible. One particular evening after Hauke had had a heavy research day, I thought I'd give him a break and started washing up, leaving him to continue writing up his notes for the day. Was that a mistake or what. Hauke took offence and went off on a tirade about

156

washing up being his job and to stop what I was doing and go sit down and not to take over and not to do it again and don't upset the routine and he would do his job when he had finished what he was doing and and and . . . And I only wanted to give him a rest as he looked so utterly exhausted, but I couldn't get a word in sideways to tell him that, at least not until later, when we calmed down again and all was back to normal. I decided to ask in future if he would like me to wash up for him. It's always stupid things that cause the problems. Yet if I'd been feeling under the weather, Hauke would offer to create one of his wonderful, tasty, almost instant soups for dinner, thick and filling. But he always asked first. And I always said yes please.

* * *

Hauke was still trying hard to get me to talk more to him about how I was feeling, but it was still difficult to articulate what I wanted to say or to talk about anything of a personal nature. He persevered and I could hear the difference in my conversation, but there was still a way to go before I freed up. I was glad he didn't give up trying as I still appreciated his efforts and knew I benefited from it. He was also trying to get me to argue with him too, to get my point of view across more effectively, not to give in to other people's arguments too easily, get to the point and not waffle. I kept trying, not always successfully, but at least he was giving me the opportunity to be more assertive and it was nice to have someone who actually listened to the answers.

*　　*　　*

With a change in wind direction and the help of the tide, much of the ice in our bay finally drifted off out into Hinlopen Strait and disappeared, leaving the sea iron grey once more. The twenty-second of October was the first day without the sun, and sunrise shades of softest dog rose to salmon were soon blending straight into sunset orange and coral reds with almost no break between. During the day the clouds often looked like Welsh slate, dark pencil grey shot through with subtle mauve and dull greens like sun playing on a rain-washed roof. The muted or striking interaction of colour and light was giving us a spectacular finale before it crept away and left us to the polar night and its own incredible light show. Air temperatures dropped considerably in October and were often hovering around −18°C.

For Hauke the most important temperature was that of the sea itself, and he eagerly anticipated the water temperature getting down towards −2°C when it would freeze. A narrow crust of ice was already forming around the rim of the bay where the tide rose and fell, and beyond it the water was turning soapy on the surface, like oil, a sure sign that a freeze was imminent. The soapy texture flattened the waves, ironed out the wave ridges. Then one morning early in November, having taken the dogs for their pre-breakfast walk, Hauke reported back to say that the sea was starting to freeze over. The soap had thickened up to five centimetres but it remained soft and pliable, flexing as the waves rolled under it. Near the beach it was freezing solidly, and extending further and further out into the bay with every day.

Hauke set a couple of electronic instruments into the ice where they would be left frozen in place over the winter, hoping he would be able to find and retrieve them again before the ice melted. The cold grasp of winter was truly clutching at the bay.

*   *   *

Sako was limping much more now and would often squeal with pain. We gave him some pain relief tablets and anti-inflammatory drugs, but they didn't seem to be doing anything for him. I'd often bandage his ankle to give him some additional support, but it would get wet when his body heat melted the encrusted snow and then it would freeze solid like a plaster cast, so we gave up on that idea. When the pain eased and he walked better, we would then take him for a longer walk, but again, not too far; and we didn't like to leave him at home on his own. Sometimes he went off his food and he was drinking a lot of water. We gave him a warm bed to sleep on but he pulled it to pieces in frustration. Sometimes he didn't like to be disturbed and gave a low, warning grumble if he didn't want a tickle, and would sit far back on the root of his tail with his teeth chattering as if he was freezing.

His leg had swollen up a lot, especially near the shoulder, and his knee got quite hot. Hauke had the brainwave to sit him under the infrared lamp for a while. It was one of Hauke's favourite ways to relieve pain as he didn't believe in taking medication if at all possible, relying on mind over matter and nature taking its course. You could say it was the only thing he was likely to use from his first aid box. Sako didn't take too kindly to being dragged nearer to the hut, but once we settled him and ran the generator up, he got used to it and liked it a lot. It seemed to help him, and we ended up doing it twice a day for about ten minutes at a time. Even Balto came and sat close by to catch some stray rays. We really didn't know what the problem was at all or how to deal with it. We'd have to contact owners Berit and Karl and see what they could suggest to help him. Fingers crossed.

CHAPTER EIGHT

TURNING POINTS

They looked rather stupid and made me feel a bit like Superman. They were supposed to be worn under my trousers, but there wasn't enough room so I wore them over the top. It was only –13°C outside, but the wind was howling like a banshee around my corner of the hut, dropping the inside temperature overnight down to –8°C. It climbed very slowly during the day, but I couldn't keep warm, hence the green, quilted combat trouser liners that were, to me, worth their weight in gold. Apart from the extra insulation, they were reasonably windproof and comfortable to wear, but looked silly because they ended just below my calf, so you saw a flare of trousers above my thick, grey felt slippers. I didn't really care what I looked like, though. I just wanted to be warm.

No sooner had I started to wear them than the temperature see-sawed, shooting up above freezing to 7°C. It was enough to make you forget where you were living. The ice on the bay was cracking up and melting on the surface, forming opaque, milky pools that swelled with the pouring rain and shivered in the screaming wind. Snow disappeared in the warmth, leaving bare brown patches like chocolate buttons on an iced birthday cake; defrosted dog shit was soft and slimy underfoot.

We often did many of the mundane jobs together, or at least partly so. I would select the monthly rations, Hauke would load up the pulka, we'd tow it to the hut together and I'd put it all away. We cleaned out our water tank together. Hauke alone decanted the paraffin from the 200-litre barrels (which we'd rolled up together from the fuel depot and stored in the motor house) into the 25-litre fuel cans, but I helped to carry these across to the hut as he would fill eight at a time. We both cut snow steps so we could get out of the hut. So many little things we shared without realising it. It was all logical, social, and plain common sense. I didn't feel exploited by being the cook and cleaner, the system was effectively flexible and I felt no loss of independence or freedom of choice. Work and free time wasn't divided equally down the middle as Hauke worked much longer hours than me—he had a real job to do after all—but that wasn't a problem between us. There was still a balance, a harmony in our separate activities.

In early December there was no moon to lighten the night, so it should have been the darkest time of our stay in Kinnvika; instead the sky was lit up with a strange red glow to the east. The cloudless sky was glowing a beautiful, intense scarlet as if an electric blanket was heating the heavens. Reflected light from the soft snow and glaciers acted like crystal mirrors to enhance the available light, casting pale shadows at our well-insulated feet. Hauke explained that it was all to do with the flat angle of the sun below the horizon and the weather being unusually warm and clear but laden with moisture; the water droplets scattered the sunlight, painting the canvas deep red above the shadowy, corrugated mountains. He gave me a demonstration of the effect by pouring hot tea into his mug then shining a torch through the

162

steam which I then looked at in a mirror. The reflection was incredibly bright and vanished as soon as he switched off the torch. Simple physics.

*   *   *

Whether it was cold or warm in the mornings, Hauke always got up first when the alarm went off. He got the fire going and put the kettle on, hopping back into bed while it boiled. Then he'd use the water for a wash for himself and his underwear and socks, then, whilst the water was heating again for tea, he got the dogs' breakfasts ready, warming up their bowls and defrosting the plate-rinsings from last night's dinner to make their food extra tasty. Once tea was ready and he'd made himself a steaming mug of coffee with chocolate, he would come and wake me up (as I usually slept through all these goings on), putting my mug of tea on the chair next to my bed and lighting a romantic candle on the table close by. Once I was half awake he'd go off with the dogs down to the beach for some fresh air and exercise, taking his coffee with him, leaving me to surface when I was ready. It gave us both time to be alone first thing in the morning and we could face the new day at our own speed. I would try to time being up and ready and going outside with Hauke's return, though I wasn't usually successful, so Hauke fed the dogs and did a few exercises to keep warm and fit whilst he was waiting for me to appear. I was a bit cruel to him sometimes, not intentionally, leaving him freezing outside in crippling temperatures and high winds. He wasn't amused at my tardiness, but wouldn't come inside until I was out.

Sometimes I got more than a candle and a cup of tea. When I was struck, usually in the early hours of the morning, with one of my horrible headaches (Hauke spotted straight away that they occurred just before a period), he would quietly wake me up and check that I was OK. I must have kept him awake with my tossing about and wriggling in bed, but he never complained, instead always left me with some small gift that I would find next to my tea. I never did learn where he kept them hidden. It could be a nice pot of face cream, or a silk scarf. One of my favourites was a collection of eight cards that Hauke had found in Sweden showing fashions at ten-yearly intervals, headed 'Soloman Davidsen 1841–1911'. The first print had two young girls in frilly dresses and lacy pantaloons, and progressed through fancy, flouncy crinolines to the last, which looked more like the slimline fashion from the 1920s than from 1911 as stated. It was so sweet to get these little tokens and cheered me up no end. I can't say I reciprocated in the same way. I hadn't thought to bring any little surprise presents to cheer him up when he was down. But at least I was nearly always good-humoured and optimistic and usually had a smile on my face which I think helped him a lot. I didn't get into a panic and worry about anything too much, and I certainly didn't whinge and moan about the uncomfortable situations we often found ourselves in. I was also glad he could use me as a sounding board for his ideas and theories, which helped clarify his thoughts. And when he asked for help with anything, I would willingly give it. If he was thinking about his scientific project, often lying on his bed for an hour or two to do it, I left him alone. I always wanted to look at what he was studying under the microscope, and had to resist the temptation to ask for a peek. He was usually freezing at these times and the sooner he was done the sooner he could warm up.

Sunday breakfasts were always special. Until it ran out, we had thick-cut streaky bacon and eggs, occasionally with fried, left-over potatoes, but always with a bottle of champagne. Occasionally we would finish the bottle before we had started to eat, so we were a little on the happy side. Our luxurious breakfast marked the crossing off of one more week in our stay in Kinnvika, and was a little boost to morale, especially welcome through the long, dark, polar nights when we felt the need to keep looking forward, to keep optimistic.

*   *   *

I found it pretty scary at times being outside in the dark, especially if I was alone on a moonless and cloudy day/night. No matter how much I tried not to think about them, bears were ever present in my mind, especially knowing the dogs weren't very observant. The 24-hour dark itself was strange, but for me, no problem to live with. It wasn't as if someone had come along and instantly turned off the sunlight at the flick of a switch, it had crept up on us slowly, given us time to adjust. In Longyearbyen the street lighting was on 24 hours a day over the winter time, so it was never truly dark in town. When I first arrived on Spitsbergen at the end of December 2000, I found it peculiar that there wasn't so much as a lightening of the sky at midday, and I had long wondered how people dealt with it. But it's just how it is. You get used to it. After a while the novelty

165

wears off and it's just accepted and daily life continues as normal, just in the dark. In Kinnvika the polar night was much more intense, more of it in a way. Longyearbyen is hemmed in all around by steep-sided mountains, but Kinnvika was perfectly positioned for wide open vistas and an enormous sky. Sometimes it was impossible to detect any change between the land and sky, and the amber light spilling out the windows illuminated only a narrow band around the hut. From a distance, the glow of the windows was truly romantic, heart-warming and welcoming, and was visible for miles. Cloudless nights were something else and the heavens shimmered with stars, blinking satellites and aurora. The darkness was less intense, more enjoyable. Moonlit nights were wonderful, particularly at the time of the full moon when everything was bathed in its silver light and we could see clearly. It seemed as if the only patches of darkness were the shadows cast by the moon. It was magical.

I never strayed far from the hut without Hauke or the dogs, as it was often impossible to see far when snow flashed past in the turbulent winds. But twice a day, just before breakfast and again in the afternoon, we would make ourselves go outside, whatever the weather, and exercise. We started jogging in early November when our walks were curtailed, getting a bit dizzy as we made circuits of the hut. Sometimes we would go round one way for ten laps, then about-face and go the opposite way. In the dark I would run with a torch and flash it about, running a bit quicker past the side of the hut opposite the dogs. The darkness itself didn't bother me, walking up dark lanes at night back in England didn't particularly unnerve me, but there, polar bears weren't likely to pop out from behind a hedge. It was being unable to see any distance that I didn't like. Not being able to look for a bear. We would stretch muscles, rotate arms, twist and turn, step up and down on chunky logs, touch toes, even do a few yoga exercises where possible. It was important to both of us to keep active physically and not to sit about and do nothing; it helped keep the mind active and buoyant and kept despondent thoughts at bay. Inside the hut we would often dance too, to whatever was on the CD player or the radio; on occasion we'd smooch to the news or the weather forecast, too. It was a great way for me to keep my feet warm, anyway; that was the only part of me that would feel the cold indoors as the floor was bare wood and offered little insulation from the freezing temperatures underneath. Wearing a warm hat indoors also helped to keep in the body's heat, though it didn't do much for my hair.

*   *   *

In the dark evenings of autumn and the 24-hour polar night (which in Longyearbyen had run from 26 October, the first day without the sun, until 16 February the following year), I did a lot of sitting about in the hut, but was always busy. I had been completing three cross-stitch pictures that I had started years ago in England, and now, as Christmas approached, I was making up four more for presents. Before leaving Longyearbyen, I had photographed the homes of three of my friends—Else, Anne-Mette and, of course, Randi—and bought the appropriate colour threads. Now I had made up charts for the houses on my squared paper and was stitching as fast as I could to get them finished before the traditional overwinterers' early Christmas helicopter came. Much of my time, apart from reading, had been taken up with knitting an intricately patterned jumper for Hauke for Christmas. He obviously could see me knitting it but I said it was for me. It became apparent that although I had started it early in October, there was no way I was going to get it finished in time, so I had secretly switched to Plan B and was also cross-stitching a picture of his naust back in town. As buildings went it wasn't very picturesque, so I added Berit and Karl's wooden boat, parked alongside the naust, for interest. Whenever Hauke left the hut for a few minutes, out would come the picture and I'd get a bit more done, which was why, over the last few weeks, he started getting a bit cross with me for not getting up and out early enough. I had been spending just a bit too long on his picture.

At the end of November we'd had a surprise helicopter visit, staying just long enough to drop off some mail and a box of fresh groceries from Randi, including some bananas which don't like the cold, turning black overnight, so I made up some delicious banana and walnut loaves with the ones we didn't eat straight away. Little children from Buriton School, near Petersfield in Hampshire, where my sister worked, had been doing a project on the Arctic and had sent a mass of super-glittery handmade cards which I strung up over my bed, showering it in silver sparkles. They'd asked a lot of interesting questions about our life up here: many of them thought we lived in an igloo and wanted to know how we'd built it; had we seen polar bears?; did we

168

have butterflies? Now I had a chance to send a reply with the Christmas helicopter, so from the beginning of December we got stuck in to writing letters home. They all tended to be long ones and consumed much time and effort. We'd taken a few pictures of ourselves on the digital camera and had printed some off as headed writing paper. After the first half-dozen times of recounting the same adventures, it was hard to keep them sounding fresh. I took to illustrating mine with my felt-tip pens, which luckily hadn't frozen, and drew seasonal motifs in the corners, taxing my brain to think of as many different ones as I could—trees, parcels, sherry, carol singers and mince pies.

In the main hut I delved down excitedly to the bottom of a cardboard box and produced decorations for the hut. Streamers criss-crossed the ceiling and tiny Christmas stockings trimmed the bookshelves; a Father Christmas on skis with his rucksack and a rabbit sat on the table (why a rabbit, I wondered?); miniature holly wreaths decorated the candlesticks and a cream-frocked angel floated gracefully in the window.

*   *   *

Sako was having a bad time of it. He had us up at 3 a.m. one morning squealing with the pain and had chewed through his line in several places. We brought him in but he wouldn't settle and we let him out again. Late that same afternoon I looked out the window into the oppressive blackness and saw that Balto had escaped from his line. I put on a thick jacket and went out and called him over from the main hut where he was running around. As he came back a large bear emerged from behind the building, so I loosed Balto again and nipped in to call Hauke and fetch a powerful lamp from the kitchen. Hauke had no need to fire the rifle; the glare from the spot lamp was enough to scare the bear away. We checked his prints in the snow and saw that he'd been close to the dogs, but Sako either didn't see the bear or didn't care, and had remained lying down at the end of his line.

Sako's leg continued to swell up and he found it hard to tuck it under his body to keep it warm. Now his toes were starting to enlarge and spread apart too. Hauke had contacted Berit, who said she was sending up some medicine with the Christmas helicopter; and also a vet in Tromsø, who thought from the symptoms we listed, that Sako had a lymph problem. The treatment was expensive and unlikely to be successful as the illness, a form of cancer, usually spread elsewhere and wasn't curable. Despite eating a lot, Sako was losing weight, and I could start to feel the ridge of his backbone sticking out as I stroked him. It didn't look good, but we would give Berit's medicine a try.

*   *   *

18 December 2002. At −26°C the paraffin heater didn't feel like starting; perhaps the fuel in the jerrycan high up on the outside wall was starting to freeze. Hauke got a roaring fire going in the Jøtul woodburner with a mixture of wood and coal, but it still took ages to get the hut feeling anything but chilly. We were up and about early, as the Christmas helicopter was coming, weather permitting. Although it was cold, visibility was good as it

wasn't snowing and there was little wind to swirl the settled snow. We had all our flasks filled with hot water and a pot of non-alcoholic gløgg—glühwein, or mulled wine—keeping warm on the stove. Biscuits were on plates on the table; the computer was set up ready to give the Governor a short presentation on the research and observations taken so far; our preliminary report lay waiting for him.

Such sweat and cross words had gone into the making of it, as the computer programmes on the PC were all in German, and neither of us had any idea how to use them. Hauke had never used a computer before, relying on pen and paper, and I was still very much a novice. I had used a computer at Beaulieu a bit with the aid of a dimbo's guide written by my secretary—it started by telling me where to switch it on. Hauke was used to working with a secretary that knew what she was doing. He dictated to me in English and I attempted to make it read a bit more logically as we went along. Still, by trial and error, we managed to create graphs of the various weather details we recorded: temperature, wind, air pressure, electric field strength, daylight, rain and snow, and additionally, seawater temperature and sea ice conditions. There had only been two other year-round weather observations made on Nordaustlandet before, at the German weather station at Haudegen in 1944/5 and here in Kinnvika in 1957/8 and again in 1958/9 when Lars E. Andersson had been here, so it would be interesting to compare them all. We also recorded the animals and plants we'd seen, visitors, our museum and our beach survey. The finished booklet looked very professional, I thought. Hauke was very pleased with it too.

The beds had been made straight and comfortable

for people to sit on and extra chairs were squeezed in at the end of the table. The outgoing post lay in a sack, label and string at the ready, just waiting for Hauke to pop in his ready-packed scientific samples which were staying frozen in the main hut until the last moment. Perhaps the helicopter wouldn't come today. Fine weather here didn't mean it was the same in Longyearbyen. Was that the whirr of blades we could hear? No, just the wind singing in the wires holding down the hut. False alarm. Then, again, was that the helicopter? Maybe. Sounded like it. We popped our heads round the door. Yep. Definitely a helicopter. We pulled on our warm clothes and went out to see where it was going to land. In a blaze of white light, the big, fat helicopter settled to the ground by the side of the motor house. As the blades wound down, a side door slid open and spilled its cargo of passengers, who all carried a package or box and trooped in a long line up to our hut like ants. We knew the priest, Svein Raddum, was amongst them, but with hoods up and pulled tight we had no chance to see who was who until they were all settled indoors. The kitchen space soon filled with parcels and boxes of presents and fresh food (none of which we'd ordered—it was all sent by our good friends in Longyearbyen, particularly Randi), and post spilled onto the floor and under the table.

One or two people went off on a tour of Kinnvika, whilst the Governor and the priest and a few others grabbed available seats. I served drinks to those who wanted them, surprised at the number drinking the gløgg and not tea or coffee—perhaps it made them feel more festive or it just made a nice change as we weren't their first port of call—so I topped it up a bit, then remembered, whilst Hauke did his welcome speech, to wind up the laptop and get the presentation going. Hauke started by thanking the Governor (a very friendly chap, a high-ranking police officer, ex-KRIPO) who was sitting at the top of the table flanked by the priest and helicopter crew, for giving his permission for us to stay in Kinnvika and for help with the transport of all the equipment, the dogs and ourselves. He gave a brief overview of the reasons for being here, to study the sea ice in great detail, the bacteria living within it and to investigate CO_2 levels in the ice and snow. He explained about the daily observations we were making and that they were all included in the preliminary report, which he now officially gave to him.

I had by then got the computer running and was able to illustrate it with some amazing pictures of the ice's microstructure as Hauke explained some of the more interesting details within the report's pages. I also snapped a photo of the two of them together which I immediately printed off and gave to the Governor. He studied the photo carefully, his glasses pushed up onto his forehead, and remarked that he hadn't realised he was losing so much hair. Everyone was fascinated with Hauke's short talk, and he once more thanked the Governor's department for all the help and assistance rendered to the expedition. A contract was produced, signed and countersigned for the loan of the hut, a bit late, I thought, and then Svein conducted a short Christmas service for us. He gave out a hymn sheet and after a short sermon on 'light in the dark', accompanied by the lighting of a huge green candle brought especially for us, we all sang 'Silent Night'. He then presented us with a traditional Christmas cake covered in tiny crackers and Norwegian flags, a gift from the church.

Anne-Mette's husband, Trond, had piloted the helicopter, and looked most suave with his short beard and one of her home-made glass beads attached to a long, thin plait of hair under his chin. (He shaves once a year, and has to let his young boys watch while he does it so they know it's still Daddy. They got very upset one year when they didn't recognise him.) Whilst he and his co-pilot moved the helicopter down to the fuel dump to top up the tanks, we took everyone else on a rapid torchlight tour of the museum. The Governor was surprised by the variety of material we had found and agreed that it would make a good research project. He would let us know if we could keep the museum permanently open, or if they would like some of the things for the museum back in town. Hauke said that if we heard nothing by the next post delivery, in about three months' time, then they could rest assured that everything would be returned whence it came.

We closed up the museum and trooped down to the helicopter. Hugs and fond wishes for Christmas were enthusiastically exchanged at almost −30°C. Then everyone squashed themselves back on board and we stood back as the rotating blades picked up speed, and, after three minutes, launched the helicopter into the twinkling night sky in a flurry of radiant snowflakes, dazzling us with the glare from the lights. It banked left and swooped out into the night, leaving us waving exuberantly and invisibly far below.

We took a few minutes to get our breath back and

174

calm down after the frenetic time with the visitors. We tidied up the room and washed up cups and mugs and glasses before sorting out the untidy mounds in the kitchen. I sorted out the fresh food we had been sent so that it wouldn't spoil in the deep-freeze temperatures, or ensured that items froze quickly where necessary. There was a big tub of Neapolitan ice cream from Hauke's god-daughter, Andrea, which we took special care of. We even had waffle cones to eat it with. Hauke sorted through the sackful of mail, dividing it up into wobbling piles of his and hers. We worked our way through the parcels and stacked them in two heaps, managing to make them roughly the same size and quantity by putting the joint packages on my pile. When we were more or less straight, we flopped down with a glass of reheated gløgg and attacked our letters and cards. I picked out a letter from my solicitor in England. It was my divorce papers. It felt like . . . what? Nothing? It was just another envelope and piece of paper. Thinking about where I was right at that moment, in a little hut near the North Pole, it seemed a bit surreal, almost a joke. Pointless. So I was back to being a single lady again. I laughed. I didn't feel any different. It was all over such a long time ago. I wouldn't ever forget the time Colin and I had had together—after all, we'd had a lot of fun, been to lots of new places, made new friends. I couldn't ignore the past, any more than I could ignore Hauke's—it had shaped and moulded the people we were today—but it was almost as if it had happened to another person. And perhaps, in a way, it had.

*   *   *

We resisted the urge to open all the presents at once, and would open them slowly over the next few days, but we did raid one enormous, and very heavy, hamper from Hauke's friend, Dietmar Wolter, in Germany. There was nothing in it that had been bought with any thought to weight or the postage costs involved, more for the taste sensations, especially the very nice wine and real champagne that had amazingly survived the journey. Ours was really only '*sekt*', sparkling wine.

One important packet that had been kept to one side was from Berit. Apart from a range of scrumptious home-made biscuits and hand-knitted mittens, there was the medicine for Sako. They were strong antibiotics. We sighed. Sako had been taking ours already.

*   *   *

Three days later we had another psychological boost to get us through the winter: the shortest day, or longest night, depending on how you looked at it. Tomorrow the sun would be that little bit closer, a little less distant. It made us feel the tiniest bit warmer. With the increase in wind overnight we had a wind-chill factor of −53°C. Brrr. Too cold for Sako's bad leg. We kept him in at night for a while, trying to ignore his whimpers and agitated behaviour, leaving Balto to sleep alone outside. But in the end Sako stayed outside most of the time, off his line in an attempt to make him more comfortable.

He was in on the night of the twenty-second,

when we were woken at 4 a.m. by an enormous explosion in the hut, both of us leaping out of bed and reaching for weapons. Sako, sleeping alone in the kitchen, didn't make a sound. Hauke carefully opened the kitchen door a fraction, heart beating wildly, then wrenched it open. Glass from triple glazing covered the floor and a cold wind seared our skin through the gaping hole. Hauke approached the black hole cautiously and peered out. Balto was standing close to the hut, grinning at us and wagging his tail in glee. Hauke went ballistic, calling him all sorts of impolite names. I reached for the dustpan and brush and a big bucket, started sweeping up the chaos. Outside, Balto was in danger of a severe whacking but sensibly kept out of reach. Hauke peered in through the smashed window, wondering how to block up the hole. He checked the snow outside, looking at how much glass needed to be picked up. What was that? Blood? And that was no dog's paw print by the window. It was a bear's. Bear alarm! Where'd it go? It seems that the tremendous crash of shattered glass combined with a gash to its paw had more than frightened the bear and we never saw it. It had fled in terror. Balto thought it was a hoot. We were not impressed with his non-existent bear alarm—he'd no doubt being playing with the bear—but we excused him. Hauke swung the outside shutters closed and fastened them, doing the same to the others, plunging us into a jail-like world. When we'd finally cleared up the mess we went back to bed, not knowing if the bear would be back and attempt to break in again. It severely unsettled both of us.

Next morning Hauke went up to the main hut hunting for sheets of hardboard and came back with some small ones, one large one, a box of nails and a fat wad of bubble wrap. In half an hour he had covered the hole from the outside with the large piece of board, then, from inside, nailed on the smaller pieces with the bubble wrap sandwiched between. It was better than the original, more windtight. We couldn't see out, but what could we see anyway in the polar night? We opened the other shutters but nailed up two lengths of old floorboard diagonally across each window so we could still look out. It wouldn't keep a bear out, but would at least give us a few seconds' extra warning.

*   *   *

We decided to celebrate Christmas German-style, so for me it came a day early, on Christmas Eve. There was tea in bed as usual after Hauke had got the fires going and fed the dogs. After an ordinary muesli breakfast with gallons of tea, together we got out the Christmas tablecloth, nice glasses for the wine, red candles, and a real English Christmas cake from my mum and dad (as well as the one from the church). We hung up sprigs of pine which were enclosed in one of the presents. We talked and reread our Christmas post and relaxed in the warm, heartening glow of Christmas. For lunch we had our first taste of goodies from the hamper, thin slices of fat salami and cheese with some of my fresh-baked bread, followed by delicious chocolates. We both opened a couple of presents in the afternoon, Hauke saving all the German newspapers used as packing so he had something interesting to read. When some soft music came on the radio, we stood up simultaneously and started to dance. We hardly moved, swaying slightly to and fro, snuggling into each other's shoulders, our feet hardly moving over the bare boards; just the two of us, alone on this special day. I gripped his pullover, clung on tight. Hauke pulled away, looking down at me as silent tears trickled down my face, dripping off my nose and chin. 'Are you unhappy?' enquired Hauke, softly, concerned. 'Are you missing your family?'

'No. I'm really happy,' I whispered. 'I'm having a really lovely Christmas.' At that moment I didn't want to be anywhere else in the world. I was at home. The tears were unexpected, but not out of place. It was perfect. We snuggled up on a bed, just lying there, being together. I played some CDs on the player. Mark Knopfler sang about something happening to make your whole life better.

It was windy outside again so we were happy to spend our time indoors. Our evening meal was a bit late getting started, and wasn't ready until 9 p.m. Hauke popped out to check up on the dogs and have a quick pee. He thought he could see some red lights on a fishing boat out on Hinlopen Strait, not the first time we had seen them there, but they didn't seem right. He soon realised it couldn't be a fishing boat as he could hardly even see the nearest hut in the foul weather. What was it? Sparks! Coming out of our chimney and flashing away into the night in the snarling gale. Great! Just what we needed with dinner ready. But there was nothing for it. I parked cooking pans on the table out of the way and took down all the washing drying above the heaters while Hauke shut down the air intake to the woodburner, turned off the paraffin heater and removed the jerrycan from the outer wall. We hadn't heard the fire in the chimney for the sound of the gale roaring

179

around the hut. We watched the fat, dull red glowing sparks popping out of the chimney and flying away on invisible, smoky wings. Slowly, slowly, they diminished in number and finally ceased altogether. We watched a little longer, just to be sure the fire in the chimney was out, then ate our somewhat cool and overcooked dinner. Afterwards Hauke climbed the ladder and unscrewed the cowl on the top of the chimney, bracing himself against the stack as the wind tried to blow him down. Inside, a finger-thick, black encrustation lined the pipe. Hauke said he'd thought about checking the chimney back in September but it had slipped his mind. How he wished he had.

He scrambled off the roof and emptied the hot ashes from the woodburner, thinking about how to clean the chimney. It was going to be difficult without brushes. Hauke was nearly blown off his feet as he crossed to the main hut where he found a four-metre length of thin timber which he then rammed up and down inside our chimney. The crud came away easily enough, the hard part was staying up on the roof. The racing wind sucked out ash and debris into the wild gale, blasting Hauke's face and getting into his eyes. It was painful for me when the odd speck got into my eyes; it must have been agony for Hauke, enduring it for almost ten minutes. He threw down the ramrod and set his feet back on the ground in relief. After wiping his reddened, smarting eyes, he cleared out the accumulated mess from inside the woodburner and left me to clear up everything else while he braved the tortuous winds again, screwed back the cowl and set up the fuel container. I got lots of hot water ready for him on the Primus stove, and once he'd got the paraffin heater up and running again, returning a modicum of heat to the now chilled room, he had a well-deserved wash. He looked like a real chimney sweep, black from head to foot. It wasn't a job that could have waited until morning; much better to do it straight away while the hut was vaguely warm. A job well done. Happy Christmas!

We had no further problems with the chimney, thank goodness. The wind whipped the heat from the hut as fast as we made it and the dogs were disappearing under a blanket of wind-driven snow. Poor Sako's foot was grossly swollen, with little spots of blood between the toes where the skin had split; the leg, thick and solid, felt quite cold. 'He's never going to get better,' I thought. Berit's antibiotics, although different from ours, hadn't made the slightest difference to him. Giving him extra food hadn't helped either. His hips had been the first things to lose their flesh, and now his ribs and backbone were even more pronounced through his thick fur. He was so bony. We'd left him off his lead to allow easier movement and a chance to get more comfortable, and sometimes we found him lying out of the wind by the steps of the main hut. We'd already agreed to keep him going until after Christmas, unless nature took its course, but then he'd have a good day, once even going with Hauke to the museum, hopping along on three legs, and then inviting himself in for a warm-up. He even wagged his tail a bit for the first time in ages. It was all so very sad, especially at this time of year. It was hard not to think about him all the time.

We opened a few presents from family and friends on Christmas Day (saving the others for the next few days); dried fish and magazines from our friends

Mark and Marina, frozen in on their yacht; cigars and tobacco for Hauke; two pairs each of hand-knitted wool socks and some delicious, melt-in-your-mouth home-made treats from the 'fan club'—the people we'd met on the *MS Berlin*; chocolate 'reindeer droppings'; perfumed massage oil; Kendal mint cake; books and sausage. We were having such a relaxing, cosy time in our little wind-blown hut. We spent a couple of hours in bed after lunch to keep a bit warmer, chatting to each other across the heavily laden table.

Hauke loved the picture I had made him and said he'd never noticed me hiding it quickly under my quilt when he came in unexpectedly. I took the opportunity to apologise to him for keeping him waiting on so many mornings. Apart from more socks—it was definitely a sock Christmas—I gave him a book about China discovering the world in 1421, and in return Hauke gave me the most beautiful string of pearls, the perfect length for me. On Boxing Day he made me wait out in the freezing kitchen for ten minutes while he got ready another present. When I was finally allowed back in, he'd set an old Swedish swivel dressing table mirror, white-painted, on the table, had it glowing with a dozen candles and the two little drawers of it stuffed full of luxurious chocolates. It was so pretty, I was lost for words. It made me want to cry all over again.

What were we going to do after this adventure was over? It was time restricted, we'd go our separate ways afterwards, but back to what? Back to Longyearbyen? Back to England? I didn't know what I would do. I felt extremely privileged to have met Hauke, to be asked to go with him to Kinnvika; to have so much fun too was always hoped for, but I never dreamed it would be such a pleasure, so satisfying. Was he the person I'd always been looking for? How could I tell? This was after all, an unreal, Arctic world.

*   *   *

It started off as a usual morning. I went out and tickled the dogs. Sako wasn't very interested, just lay there and licked at his swollen leg. At least he didn't growl as he'd done once before. There was blood on the snow, more than I'd seen before. I felt so completely hopeless. Ineffectual. But I knew there was nothing more I could do for him. I came in for breakfast, hot muesli as normal. Hauke went off to the loo while I washed up.

After he came back in I went to the kitchen and heard Balto squealing a bit, and told Hauke.

'I know,' he said. 'I've just shot the dog.'

I hadn't heard a thing because of the wind. I just gave him a big hug and whispered 'Thank you'. He was very upset, and I cried quite a bit. He apologised for not telling me about it, but there was no need. It was for the best. It was a hard job, and one I wouldn't have wanted to undertake (I'd asked myself several times if I would be able to shoot him if Hauke couldn't, hoped that I could), but Hauke's a good shot, and he said later he'd given him extra pain relief tablets last night and this morning. When he took him for his last short walk, he said he was very weak and was almost blown over by the wind. Now he was out of pain and didn't suffer any more.

After a shot of cognac, Hauke went to get the pulka and loaded up the dog, not wanting my help. Then after five minutes he came in to fetch me so we could take him up to what we called the Moon Mountains, where Sako had had his last real walk in fabulous, blue violet light under a cloudless, full-mooned sky. Sako was lying on his side on the pulka, very comfy, paws tucked up inside the sledge. I gave him a nice tickle and held his paws. Hauke got Balto, and I put the harness on him, not without some difficulty, as he kept leaning on me, and every time Hauke came by he backed away a bit; he knew without knowing. We hitched up the pulka and set off across the snow into the gale, heading for the rocks.

Hauke picked out a place for him, fairly high up the ridge in the lee of a big rock, with a beautiful view over Kinnvika and the bay, and Kinnberget behind. Hauke dug the snow and a few loose rocks away and we hauled the sledge up to the edge of the pit. We were both amazed at how heavy the sledge was. Despite Sako's very thin condition, he still must have weighed more than me at the end. Hauke tipped over the sledge and Sako lay in the hole as if he'd crept in himself and loosely curled up. Hauke made him more comfy, and I gave him a last tickle, feeling his sticky-out backbone, tweaking his ears and paws. Then we shovelled back the stones and snow, patted it down and headed back to the hut quickly, with no fuss and no torchlight. We clipped Balto back onto his line—the other had already been taken away—and Hauke gave him some nice food, a sort of wake for Sako. We left him to eat up and went indoors.

We talked about Sako, and knew it was the right thing to have done. Even in Longyearbyen there was no vet. Besides, no vet would have been able to help him. We had understood what the vet from Tromsø had been trying to tell us, and we were satisfied we had done our best under the extreme, harsh circumstances and given him every chance to help himself. We assumed he must have had this disease for some time. He'd worried at his claw for many months, and there were other little signs we'd noticed, ignored or forgotten about, not having understood their implications.

He left a big hole in our team, as he was such a lovely dog, and Hauke had trained him to be manageable, though he had still retained that stubborn, naughty streak, whizzing off given half a chance. He was a brave dog, perhaps too aggressive against bears, but was of no faint heart. Balto was different, and we wondered how he'd cope on his own with his first bear encounter. Would he bark or, as before, wag his tail and want to play, and would that be a great disadvantage to him?

We'd known the end had been coming for several weeks. We're used to taking our pets to have them put down; but doing it yourself is something else entirely. We liked to think that his last 18 months had been happy. A year with the students of the British Schools Expedition, who loved him to bits, and the last six months with us had undoubtedly been pretty exciting, too.

Bye, Sako. We'll miss you a lot.

CHAPTER NINE

RETURN OF THE LIGHT

'This is Kinnvika calling. Can you hear me? Godt Nytt År!'

No reply. We waited. Hauke tried again. Still nothing.

'Maybe we're a bit too early. I expect they're all still popping champagne. Give them a few more minutes,' I said, sipping at my cold glass, tiny golden bubbles dancing up my nose.

We'd been a bit premature, opening our champagne just after eleven thirty, and went out into the black night a minute or two before midnight. Deutsche Welle (the German equivalent of the BBC's World Service) was blaring out on the radio but didn't take much notice of the looming new year. There was no equivalent of listening to the chimes of Big Ben ringing in the new year and everyone cheering in London's Trafalgar Square. So we did our own strange countdown, counting two or three times until we decided it was now our official midnight on Nordaustlandet, and we cheered and toasted each other: *Skål! Prost!* Cheers! Balto thought it all great fun and soon had us all howling at the stars together in celebration.

We were ready for a grand link-up on air of all the research stations and overwinterers on Spitsbergen, organised by a chap called Erwin on remote Hopen Island, 35 kilometres long but just two kilometres wide and lying roughly 350 kilometres south-east of us.

The audible fizz in my glass was suddenly drowned out by Marek from Hornsund, the Polish research station set up in the same year as Kinnvika, but permanently manned. He managed to contact Marina on *Jonathan*, and they greeted each other in English. Then Svalsat, outside Longyearbyen, joined the airwaves briefly, followed by Svein on Bjørnøya, and then we managed to get a word in too. Hauke's old student Trond managed to join in the fun from Norway via a radiotelephone link-up—I believe he phoned on a landline to Svalbard Radio who then patched him through to our radio. Stein in Austfjordneset greeted everyone along with his 'three girls', his wife and two daughters, all of them shouting down the radio. He had a long chat with us, then just when we thought we'd got away with it, asked after Sako. We were hoping not to be asked about him, as it put a damper on things, but after a few condolences, the subject was quickly changed. And we all cheered up again. There was no word from the weather station on Jan Mayen Island far to the west, or from Eero in Mushamna. Perhaps atmospheric conditions were causing bad radio reception.

∗   ∗   ∗

A couple of weeks later, we still hadn't heard from Eero, and asked on air if anyone else had heard from him. All answered in the negative. We all agreed we'd leave it another few days and then get the policemen to check that all was OK. It was one of the reasons we all kept in touch with each other, though not everyone liked to. Perhaps, conversely, the contact made them feel even more remote and alone. But for us, every Monday and Thursday at 9 p.m. was an important time, keeping in touch with our fellow overwinterers—Mark and Marina, Eero, and Stein and his family—making sure they were all well and had everything under control. We'd share ideas and tips (such as how to get Eero's snow scooter going again after it conked out); discuss the ice, and naturally the weather; swap hunting stories; laugh and joke; find out who'd had a helicopter drop in on them; and hopefully give each other a lift, especially over the dark time. It transpired that Eero was fine, just having trouble with his sleep pattern. He'd been going to bed at 7 p.m. and waking up again at 2 a.m. He soon got himself back into a normal routine and our concerns were allayed.

Apart from the special new year link-up, we'd make an effort to call up on birthdays, trying to make the day a little more special for each other. We could also call family by telephone, via Svalbard Radio, but it being somewhat expensive, we kept it for special occasions only. Reception on air was sometimes awful, and we could hardly hear each other so would cut short the chat and save it for another day. Hauke's long aerial meant that we probably had better reception than the others, but local weather conditions made a difference as well. Often, after a week or so, or after an active period of Northern Lights, the crackle and static would clear and communications would resume in the clear, clean air.

Without street lighting to spoil it all, the night sky would glisten with myriad diamonds, glinting like shattered glass or scintillating deep red in the velvet cushion of the heavens; the Milky Way looped above like a softly contorted satin ribbon; satellites chased each other across the jet-black firmament, flashing on–off as they orbited the earth, dodging the planets and skimming the pole star in the Little Bear; incandescent meteorites scratched at the black vault. We'd first seen the aurora on 9 October, but it was very pale and uninspiring, and didn't tempt us to stay outside in the cold, yet now when we chanced to see a spectacular light show, it was always worthwhile to don our warm clothes and watch. Timing was all-important for seeing the Northern Lights as they would appear without warning and disappear as fast as they'd come. Concentrating around the poles, they are created when electrically charged particles from the sun and outer space collide with the earth's magnetic field and cause aurora in the atmosphere. I knew that different atmospheric conditions created different effects, though I'd assumed not all at the same time. Sometimes they looked like bleached, diaphanous torchlight, spread long and low across the horizon, with fountains of light shooting skywards, waving and wobbling in the air before dying again. We'd seen pale grey medusan snakes of light writhing and revolving above our heads, and great scrolls of malachite green undulating like giant palm trees across the sky. Coils and twists of silken emerald light danced high above our heads, partnered by purple and white-topped flames. A pulse of red light flowed the length of a gyrating spiral of green before dying away; a firework of luminescence exploded in the zenith like a dropped bag of flour, scattering trails like umbrella ribs above the huts.

Hauke told me the story of a hunter who said he could hear the aurora borealis, even though it was tens of kilometres away. Was this electrical activity really audible? Under investigation, it was revealed that all he could hear was the sound of his own blood in his ears. It was that quiet at times; I'd heard it myself. But in the middle of the polar night, the cold got to us as we stood and gazed upwards with aching necks, so it was fortunate that these magical displays were short-lived allowing us to scuttle back indoors to warm up before we froze our fingers off.

I was surprised at how well Balto was coping without his brother. He whined a bit for a few days but soon seemed to settle down again. Without any competition, he was getting a bit slow at eating his food, and even turned up his nose at some leftover rice pudding; until we took it away, of course, which quickly changed his attitude. We let him come indoors with us for the odd hour so he had company, as we weren't often outside in January.

Balto was either very curious or very vain, spending hours watching himself in my new mirror. If I was sitting at the table reading, he'd push his nose up under my arm and pretend to read too, and we stuck a pair of Hauke's reading glasses on his nose to make him look a bit more intelligent. When we were outside exercising, he would come and sit on my feet while I was twisting and turning, which kept my feet a bit warmer but didn't help much otherwise. When we did venture down to the beach for a short walk, mostly on well-moonlit 'days', he would whizz about and roll in the snow, bouncing around, racing off, tail high in the air, pleased to get off his line and stretch his legs.

*   *   *

It was hard to believe the difference a year had made

to me. I'd had a good new year last time, spending it with my Swedish friend Leif, a technician for Lufttransport, which runs light aircraft out of Longyearbyen, ferrying equipment, post, miners and scientists around. But I hadn't been so optimistic of the future then, didn't have that surge of life coursing through my veins—or was that the champagne? I hadn't been looking forward to the future alone, and couldn't get to grips with how I was feeling or what I wanted to do. Now, at least for the next eight months, I would be mentally and physically active, was enjoying myself thoroughly, despite losing Sako and the numerous dramas with the polar bears. I had begun to think about what I might do after Kinnvika. Perhaps I could buy my own place in England, somewhere more remote than I would previously have thought of, somewhere in the countryside or by the sea. I wondered what sort of job I would get, and would my Kinnvika qualifications help at all. There'd not be much call for bear protection in England (but it would look very interesting on my CV), though maybe I could lecture on a cruise ship like Hauke had done, do an illustrated talk or two. But before anything else, I would need to get myself a more permanent job. I was pretty flexible, just as long as the wages paid the bills. I had no more idea now of what I wanted as a career than when I had left school. But that's what allowed me the freedom to leave England for Longyearbyen, Longyearbyen for Kinnvika. I'd always wanted to be a needlework teacher, but in this modern world, there's not much call for those. While at school I'd even thought about being a costume designer for film or theatre or of joining the navy. What else could I do now?

191

But having a career wasn't everything. Being reasonably happy and contented was more important, and having someone to share it with would be nice too. Being here, out in the wilds of the world, you realised you didn't need too much of anything to survive. Having the latest, trendiest, biggest, smallest, best, newest, most fashionable things meant nothing here; that was all window dressing. Tarnishable gloss. Our stock phrase became 'less is more'. I hoped I could carry that philosophy over into the real world back in England. I would try, anyway. I'd look for my little nest.

Meanwhile, both Hauke and I had settled down again after the loss of Sako. The stress of the last few weeks had lifted and we felt a great weight slide from our shoulders. We still had the rest of the polar night to survive and looked forward to seeing the sun again in mid February, but we could face it with a better frame of mind, and we hoped the worst was over.

We sat a long time over breakfast, as we had done most of the time we were here, putting the world to rights, discussing politics, life up here, families, sailing, books and philosophy. A frequent topic was the origin of words, and with dictionaries sitting on our shelves in English, German, Norwegian and Spanish (which we planned to learn with the aid of some CDs, but never got past asking for the waiter), and Hauke's knowledge of Latin, French and Swedish, we had fun looking at the similarities and differences.

Quite often during breakfast, Hauke would latch onto a topic and I would sit absorbed, listening to his disquisition, hardly saying a word, and suddenly realise two hours had gone by. I came to call these episodes Hauke-vision, or Hauke-TV, and it was much more interesting than most of the rubbish on the box back home in England.

*   *   *

Having missed my Christmas deadline, I was spending as much time as possible (without going cross-eyed) getting Hauke's jumper finished, and had now progressed to the sleeves. I was determined he would have it for his very special birthday. He was going to be 60. I didn't have anything else to give him, and at least sitting with it on my knees as I was knitting gave me a bit of extra warmth and kept my hands from feeling the cold.

The weather had been pretty awful over Christmas, with the gale lasting right into the new year. The hut rattled and creaked as it was buffeted by the wind and screeched through the rusting wires that I hoped would keep the hut fixed to the ground. Sometimes, lying on my bed, I would hear a lull in the relentless wind, but it would suddenly pick up speed and roar across the open ground like a train, and wham! into the wooden walls, trying to shunt us off our rocky platform. We watched the monitor on the wall, the maximum gust passing 30 metres per second. Even in the winter of 1957/8, the scientists had complained that Kinnvika was one of the windiest sites anyone could have chosen. As fast as we tried to heat the hut with both stoves working hard, the wind sucked the warmth out the chimney and left us chilly and taking to our beds.

At −28°C and a wind of around ten metres per second, the wind-chill factor was −60°C. If it was −30°C or colder outside, my sheet and quilt would freeze to the outside wall and, under the bed, the nails in the wooden cladding near the floor were rimed in thick, fluffy frost. The wind found its way through the smallest cracks in the walls and window frames, and I discovered a cold draught clawing at my back where the walls had been joined together. Out with the toilet paper again! Wonderful stuff.

For safety reasons we turned off the paraffin heater every night, banking up the Jøtul before climbing into bed, so inside temperatures plummeted, on one occasion reaching −15°C. We were glad we had swapped quilts for extreme-cold sleeping bags at times like these, though sometimes mine kept me awake as it was too warm to use when the temperature inside the hut was not as cold as I expected. We yo-yoed between sleeping bag and quilt depending on the outside (and prospective inside) temperature.

The cold sapped the power in the batteries quickly so we had to use the generator more often. It worked extremely well in the dreadful cold, only complaining once when it was around −35°C outside. We thought that the air going into the engine was perhaps too cold, so we warmed up the air intake a fraction by loosely covering the generator with Hauke's scooter dress, and it ran without missing a beat as long as you kept the oil level at its optimum point.

It snowed frequently, the heaviest falls usually when the wind came from the north-west, but never in huge quantities such as Hauke had experienced in Mushamna (where he'd had to wade through thigh-deep drifts on his walks), and then the winds from the south and east would return and blow it all away again. It was always thinly spread on the ground making it easy for us to get about, though it piled up to above five feet (one and a half metres) near the back door of the hut, trapped by the sawhorse and wood, making it impossible to check for bears unless they were standing right on top of it. Collecting snow to use for water was not a problem as the wind compacted it and three bucket-loads of light, airy snow made one load of water. The trouble was that it melted in the tank during the day, but froze again at night, including in the tap, so Hauke had to prepare Thermosfuls of hot water before turning in so that we could have our tea and a wash on time next morning.

Water wasn't the only thing to freeze overnight. My toothpaste got so stiff that it was hard to squeeze it out of the tube. I always saved a drop of warm water from the kettle to rinse my mouth as the iced water from the tank was too cold to use alone. Periods went on as normal, regular as clockwork, so it was handy having the woodburner in which to dispose of everything. Just like Hauke, I did all my clothes washing in the same water I had washed myself in. I'd peg it on the line outside where it would instantly freeze solid. Leaving it out for a couple of days (hoping that the bears left it alone) allowed it to freeze-dry, so that when you brought it in and gave it a few minutes to go floppy, it was just damp and only needed finishing off on the drying racks above the stoves. Nothing ever got ironed, of course.

I indulged myself with two kettles of water for hair washing. It didn't need doing very often as the air was so clean, maybe once a fortnight, though even after three weeks it only felt a bit grubby. It was one kettle for the wash, one kettle to rinse out the remaining shampoo and do a bit of washing in. The poor washing-up bowl certainly had to work hard. My hair, although very long, has always dried quickly, and in Kinnvika it was no exception. I'd sit with it in a towel for an hour or two, by which time it was just damp, then it would dry quickly in the moistureless air. Only once or twice did I go bear-chasing with a fetching yellow towel wrapped around my dripping locks. It was enough to scare anything away.

Hauke grew a beard in Kinnvika as it was much warmer and less troublesome than shaving, and I had the job of keeping it all under control. He looked good with a short beard, but more and more wild the longer it got. He moaned about how short I would cut his hair, but I can only cut hair one length, snipping everything off just above finger width. It was tidy. What more did he want?

Going to the outside loo for a number two in the yowling, buffeting wind was an adventure in itself. After the light had disappeared, Hauke insisted on doing a 'loo patrol' with me. I waited until pretty desperate before telling him I had to go, at which point we both pulled on foul weather gear, then hurried to the loo 80 metres away, where I kicked away the snow blocking the door, got in, shut out the icy blast, got out of my scooter dress, trousers, woolly long johns and undies and perched on the wooden seat. Treating the whole thing like a military operation meant that Hauke, with his rifle and a torch, accompanied by Balto, could stand guard outside and not get frostbite having to wait too long. You certainly didn't take a newspaper with you. In summer if I needed a pee, I'd just pop outside, but in the polar night I was allowed a bucket indoors for my own personal use (strictly for a pee only, hence the loo patrols!) though Hauke did allow himself to use it at night-time if necessary.

One day, it was blowing ferociously outside, needle-sharp daggers of snow screaming off into the murk. The barometer had dropped like a stone overnight, from 1002 millibars down to 978 at 7 a.m., climbing again to 985 by 11 a.m. and steadying at 999 by the time we went to bed. Checking the wind gauge, we discovered that it was gusting a tiny fraction off hurricane force, and no matter how hard we wished it, it wouldn't go that extra half metre per second. Hauke decided he would go down to the loo alone, leaving Balto curled up outside and disappearing under a white blanket. He was gone ages, and I started to become concerned. I couldn't see anything but black and white outside, and anyway, I'd have been blown from Kinnvika to the North Pole in such wind, so I wasn't about to go looking for Hauke. After several long, agonising minutes, he came stamping through the door, fighting against the sucking vacuum to get it closed behind him. I was more than a bit pleased to see him back, though he looked a bit pale below his wind-roasted cheeks. Then he explained what had happened. Having made a dash for the loo in a slight lull, when he reappeared, wrestling to bar the door shut with the heavy balk of timber, he realised he was in white-out conditions and couldn't see anything at all. He was completely blind and could hardly stand up in the 70 miles-per-hour (115 kilometres-per-hour) wind. What should he do? Stay in the loo and freeze or try to get back? He decided to get home. The main hut, he knew, stretched out several metres either side of where the loo was

197

positioned, about 25 metres away, so making sure his back was first flat against the loo door, he dropped onto hands and knees and crawled forward into the storm. He said it was so scary as he crept up the incline, and he was immensely relieved when he bashed his head on the wooden exterior of the main hut. Hugging it close to his right, he contoured round to the front. Still there was nothing to see, and directly ahead, if he missed his aim, there was nothing but snow, ice and the deadly tempest. He took his chance, crawling away at a slight angle to the wind, using it like a compass, and with amazing accuracy got so near to the hut that he could just make out a faint glow of light in the kitchen window and came safely home.

'Next time,' I begged, 'use the bucket.'

*   *   *

By the middle of January, because of our open vista to the east, we began to see the first glimmers of cream and orange light, edged in palest blue, behind the still invisible mountains. The sea had frozen hard and thick enough for us to start taking short cuts across the bay to Twillingneset, so cutting the journey time on our resumed walks out to Ruud's Hytte on Hinlopen Strait. The full moon threw long and scrawny, pale grey shadows across the frost-encrusted snow, spangled with huge, rainbowed gemstones. As we walked, the snow creaked as if we were striding over polystyrene—enough to set your teeth on edge. Sometimes the ice roared like a jet taking off, or sounded like a tube train approaching a station, as it slowly heaved with the wind and tide. Where the ice met the beach it twanged like a slack rubber band. By the end of January, we could dimly make out icebergs trapped in the sea ice, but we had heard over the short-wave radio that most of Hinlopen Strait was ice free, most of it to be found around Bjørnøya where a lot of bears were hunting seals. The temperature fluctuated up and down like a yo-yo, and we could hear the boom of ice cracking in our Murchison Bay.

By the end of the first week of February, there was a definite difference in colour between the land, sea and sky, and at midday, the soft powder blue defeated the strength of the starlight. Light seemed to be racing back at an incredible speed. From the top of Kinnberget on a cloudless day, the horizon was rimmed in dark orange, fading to strong yellow above, bleaching out to duck-egg blue, turquoise and cornflower. Tourists would pay a small fortune for such a sight as we had. We were blown away by the sheer magical spectacle of it all. It warmed our hearts.

By the second week of February, Hauke could start to measure the amount of light we were getting on one of his gadgets, the first time since last year. He was surprised one evening to see the ice in our bay had completely disappeared and all was gently rippling water. We looked the next morning, and there was the ice again! Hauke thought there must have been a strong tide coming in with the wind and the intense pressure had forced the seawater up through the cracks in the ice and flooded the surface. We could see dark patches where it had pooled and re-frozen. Along the beach we found fragments of seaweed and other biological material washed ashore, so we took samples to look at under the microscope and found them to be full of bacteria, a sure sign there was life in ice and it still thrived in extremely cold temperatures.

Blue February light cast its soft, velvety hues across huts, sky and landscape as we harnessed Balto up to the pulka. He wasn't too happy as it was the first time we'd used it since Sako's burial. At the beach, while Hauke did a few experiments, we let him loose and he was happy to dash off across the ice following his nose and found us our first seal's breathing hole. It was little more than five centimetres across, but Hauke warned me to be careful as it opened out wide underneath like a bottle well and there was a danger of the rim collapsing and me falling in. On the way back we found a patch of snow sprinkled in cerise specks: our first snow algae of the year. It was a good feeling to find all these renewed signs of life, but we wouldn't feel that we had survived the dark time until the sun came back over the horizon. It wouldn't be long.

*   *   *

Tea in bed as usual, then outside leaving the breakfast bowls to warm up a bit and the coffee to percolate. Hauke didn't stay out long, nipping back in after a couple of minutes. I ran about, jogged on the spot, got some blood flowing through my muscles, windmilled my arms to keep warm. I waited outside for as long as I could, then made a lot of noise as I re-entered our little hut. Seemed OK to go in, then. As I pushed open the door, there was an explosion as I was shot at by a champagne cork.

'Happy birthday, old lady,' grinned Hauke, and poured out two frothing glassfuls of bubbly, passing me one as I took in the mass of burning candles and the pile of presents on my bed. After recovering from my minor heart attack, I gave him a big hug and goggled at the number of presents piled up on the table. What with all those Christmas presents from him, and now these, I wondered just what sort of impression I'd made on him in those early days of our meeting. It was a really lovely feeling. There was perfume and body lotion in ice-blue packaging, a silk scarf, more chocolate, and a lightweight, bright red (of course—good for filming) windproof jacket. Even my little video camera was tucked in amongst them, a reminder that it was really for me and not just on loan. So sweet. So romantic. There was a present from my parents and from my sister and her family too, which had been sent with the Christmas post. I had a lovely day, not doing too much as the weather was a bit unpleasant. The strong wind was back after a few days' wonderful respite. We snuggled up together, took a short walk, drank red wine. Although it was Sunday, Mark and Marina called me on the radio, though it took me a while to get used to using the handset. Although I knew how to use it, it was the first time I had, and I got things back to front in my excitement and nervousness, pressing the talk button when I wanted to listen. Marina and I had some girls' talk, discussing our knitting projects, and how well we were being looked after by 'our men'. Then Eero called in too; that was a surprise. What a nice day I had.

*   *   *

It was very difficult not to laugh and make farty sounds under the quilt. Hauke was out in the cold kitchen having a wash and I was trying to blow up balloons under the duvet without him seeing. I folded my knees and stored the balloons under them, trying to stop them escaping out the side as I squashed in more and more. If Hauke noticed anything funny going on, he was at least polite enough not to say anything, but I don't think he did. As soon as he went off with Balto for his walk, I leaped out of bed, tugged on some clothes and frantically tied bunches of '60 today' balloons together and pinned them up around the hut. I wrapped his present in recycled Christmas paper, finishing it off with a big gold ribbon and tucked a big 'I am 60' rosette under it.

When Hauke came back from his walk, he laughed when he saw what I'd been up to in his absence, and said he wouldn't open my present until later—he knew exactly what was in it from the size of it.

'I was always hoping it was for me,' he said, tucking it lovingly under his arm.

Our walk that day was very short and I could hardly make progress at all in the diabolical wind speed. It all but blew me away, and I started to laugh uncontrollably about it, which didn't help at all. Mid afternoon, I suggested a nice cup of tea and a bit of cake. Not something I normally offered as I'd given up cake-making as a bad job, and there were none in our stores. Hauke looked a bit quizzical, but agreed. My friend Marianne had sent us a home-made fruit cake for Christmas, but as we already had two others, I had doused it with whisky to preserve it, and now sneaked it out to the kitchen once the tea was made. I popped back into our living room, turned out the battery-operated electric light, then emerged from the kitchen singing 'Happy Birthday', with the cake blazing with candles. Mark and Marina called Hauke on the radio that evening, and while Marina was singing him a little song, I surreptitiously stuck two sparklers in the shape of a 6 and a 0 into a tealight in a glass holder, lit them up, and they hissed, dazzled and crackled for Hauke's last birthday surprise as we applauded Marina's song. Another nice day.

Back in the fifties, our little hut, the 'reserve house', was used to store provisions, stoves, spare sleeping bags and clothing in case of fire in the main hut. The electricity to the hut was disconnected and only torchlight inside was allowed. They had had a fire. One of the men had gone to the sauna to check his laundry in the washing machine (ooh, what luxury) and noticed a fire just beginning to get going in the motor house. The alarm was raised and the fire extinguished before it had a chance to take hold. It was the reason we turned off our paraffin heater every night. Every Saturday in Kinnvika had been sauna day, followed by 'delicacies' and wine with the evening meal. Thirteen men had sweated it out together on the tiered wooden benches in the little room. Of course, in those days, the doors hadn't warped and twisted in the weather and still sealed properly, keeping in the heat and steam. But we decided we'd give it a try. A two-and-a-half-metre-deep snow bank surrounded the sauna hut, keeping the light breeze at bay. A central door led into a narrow cloakroom, behind which lay the now dingy changing room. Through a second door was the sauna with the wooden benches mounted against the end wall. Mid morning we started taking in armfuls of logs and put a match to the dried coils of beach-found birch bark kindling. We allowed several hours for it to heat the hut and the sea-smoothed rocks sitting in an old saucepan on the stove. We kept an eye on the white smoke emerging from the crooked chimney and restocked the fire as the smoke died away. It was almost impossible to get the sauna very hot, but for us, just being very warm was a luxury.

After lunch, we stripped off, dumping our clothes on the rickety bench in the changing room, and shot inside the sauna in an effort to stop the heat escaping. We sprinkled water on the stones and stretched out our towels and pretended we were sitting in a highly efficient, steamy sauna. We had to use our imagination a bit, but it was relaxing none the less to be able to lie naked and not risk freezing to death within a couple of minutes.

I was quite content to lie there for hours, but no, Hauke insisted I run around outside with him for five minutes in −20°C. Balto couldn't believe his eyes as we whooped it up and jumped around in the snow wearing our big, well-insulated boots. Hauke was a bit mad, doing forward rolls in the snow while Balto was trying to have a good sniff at all the exposed flesh. As soon as the cold began to bite my skin, I declared I'd had enough of this masochistic behaviour and ran back inside to the relative heat of the sauna. It really wasn't up to much, and after another half-hour, we gave in, declaring it probably was much warmer in our own hut after all. We'll do it again, we said; but we never did.

*　　*　　*

Visibility was the best it had been so far this year. The twenty-sixth of February saw the undersides of the pillowed, dark grey clouds, dusted a shimmering mother-of-pearl pink as the sun crept towards the horizon. The sky started to take on that golden orange glow of the approaching sphere.

'I think we'll see the sun this morning.' I yawned over my cup of tea, still wrapped in my quilt.

'Not sure,' mused Hauke, picking up his steaming mocha coffee and heading for the door and Balto's walk. 'Don't think we will.'

When he returned, breakfast was leisurely as usual; Hauke had finished off his honey and chocolate drenched muesli and I was drinking yet another mug of tea when Hauke leaned across the table to peer out of the window. He jumped up as if a bear was coming. No, it was the sun! The sun was coming! There was a mad scrabble to put on thick jumpers, jackets, boots, hats and gloves, gather up all available cameras and get outside before we missed the event we had waited so long for. The clouds had momentarily broken up just above the mountains and the orange light had deepened and started to take on a metallic, molten glow that could only herald the imminent arrival of the sun.

So we stood around for half an hour, video cameras trained on the distant horizon, SLRs ready focused, fingers crossed. There was a narrow ridge of dark cloud hanging over the horizon where the glacier split sea and sky, obscuring what we most wanted to see. Slowly, achingly slowly, it spread itself thinner as it drifted millimetre by millimetre away to our right, leaving a thin sliver of a gap above the glacier. And still we waited. Then, almost imperceptibly, a strong orange-gold light struggled to emerge above the ice, fighting the clouds. Winning. We rolled the cameras. The sun, approaching with

205

excruciating, tantalising slowness, abruptly shot out a short, stubby ray of vertical amber light, then another, longer, then another, until suddenly it fired a delicate finger of pure gold towards us, lighting up our lives for the first time since October. Clouds all around us were lit up in smoky pinks, but in front of us it was only fabulous warm oranges and amber, a thin cord of molten gold below the clouds, so beautiful we drank it in, mesmerised, struck silent and still by the intensity of our emotions.

We awoke from our reverie and ran around and leaped skywards as more and more rays of sunlight washed the grey from Kinnvika. We photographed the windows, the apricot snow, our honeyed faces, real, black shadows, Kinnberget, our little sun-bathed hut. We cheered and danced together, swinging round and round in circles, stopping, breathing rapidly, gazing as much as we dared directly at the sun, blinding our eyes, before chasing Balto about and waltzing to the incredible melody of the new, sun-blessed day.

We'd made it. We had, in my mind, overwintered. Gone through the interminably dark polar night and lived to see the sun once more. As Liljequist wrote simply in 1958, 'The sun reappeared over the horizon at midday, and the polar night was over.' The three of us had survived. We were the lucky ones, but I felt so honoured to have shared the experience of the last seven months with Hauke, and looked forward with immense pleasure to our remaining six. Being the first woman to overwinter on Spitsbergen at over 80 degrees north really didn't mean anything to me. Just being here was all that mattered. I had been given a fabulous opportunity to experience the natural beauty and raw, rugged,

Arctic life in this remote and lonely corner of the far north, and it had exceeded all expectations. Right this minute, it was heaven on earth.

CHAPTER TEN

BATTLES

'I'm not sure that I want to go back to Germany alone,' reflected Hauke without preamble as I opened a tin of mushrooms. 'I like you more and more,' he continued as he sipped at his rather cold, room temperature red wine. 'We're a good team.'

I wasn't quite sure how to respond to that. What was he suggesting? Something? Nothing? I stirred the mushrooms vigorously into the salami-tomato sauce. I agreed with him, as we'd had such an incredible time here together, and it would be very difficult to adjust to living alone again: for me, no doubt, the depression would set in once more. Perhaps that was being a bit pessimistic. I felt much better in myself since being here, but I hadn't considered what I would do with myself afterwards; whether to stay in Longyearbyen or move on. I wasn't really ready to think about an 'us' just yet. It surprised us both the way we fit together, mentally and physically. It's not as if we really had to try hard to be kind to each other for the sake of harmony in our little rabbit hutch; it came quite naturally. We were both independent people and I had learnt when to offer help and when to let Hauke get on with something by himself (though I sometimes forgot and wished I hadn't). Hauke had taken the same approach with me. I'm so used to doing things for myself, I get annoyed when people try to give me help I haven't asked for. We had worked well together most of the time, and we still did daft things together, like jumping up in the middle of working and bumping tummies like a couple of Weebles, having a silly laugh about it and then carrying on as if nothing had happened.

I gave the pasta twirls a stir with the wooden spoon, steam rising and misting my own glass of Merlot, and kept quiet.

'I still don't believe you really meant "yes" after an hour in the pub,' said Hauke, persevering, dipping the spoon into the sauce and giving it a taste. 'More pepper, I think.'

Always more pepper. It goes with his character.

'Yeah. But you know I never think about things. I just do it if I like the idea of it. I hardly ever think about the consequences. If you think about something too much you'd never do anything. Just sit on your fat bum in front of the telly.' I knew I had thought a lot about going on this expedition, had done some research into Hauke and Kinnvika, but actually, I knew in my heart of hearts that my first answer had been the right one. I drained the liquid from the pasta into Balto's bowl. 'I don't think I want another telly when I go back. Much more fun without one. People actually talk to each other.' I gave the sauce a final stir and plonked the pan on the table. I sat the pasta next to it, the steam imitating its shape as it gyrated towards the ceiling, and Hauke brought the warmed-up plates from the woodburner. I put the pepper pot on the table. Hauke would still want more. Talking together whilst I was cooking dinner had become a very special side of our life in Kinnvika, and conversation was usually relaxed. Was it because we had survived another day here and had one less to go? I wasn't counting down the days to leaving—I didn't want to think about that until I absolutely had to. I was too happy being here. Was it the wine? I don't really know. We didn't purposely avoid discussing awkward subjects, they just didn't materialise. It was the wrong time of day, maybe—too nice to spoil by being contentious. I grabbed a couple of serviettes and slid one each under our forks.

'Smells good,' sniffed Hauke hungrily, setting down his wine and pulling up his chair. 'You're a good cook.'

'And you're a liar!' I laughed. 'Dig in.'

I was relieved that Hauke hadn't pursued his unvoiced question, but I knew that one day he would come back to it. He always did. He would get his answer. I just didn't know what it would be.

*   *   *

The weather was bloody awful. It had been reasonable earlier in the day, but the wind had picked up steadily during the daylight hours and was now scraping across the hut's wires like a learner at the violin. Snow flew around the hut like shredded sheet music in the gale. For the first time, Hauke had arranged with Svalbard Radio to link up on the radiotelephone with Dietmar Wolter in Germany (the one who had sent our Christmas hamper) so that he could take part as the guest speaker at a conference, discussing the way people lived their lives in Germany: how did it affect their well-being, their standard of life; how did the welfare service help (or not); was the comfortable, secure way of life they led satisfactory, healthy? Hauke was speaking as one who had been away from all the comforts of life for more than seven months (plus his time at sea and in Mushamna) so could offer an opinion on how it felt to have almost nothing, but to have so much.

The allotted time drew close. He called up Svalbard Radio on the short-wave. Waited for a reply. Nothing. He tried again. Absolutely zilch. Shit! Two minutes to go.

'Svalbard Radio, Svalbard Radio. Come in, Svalbard Radio.' Not a dicky-bird. 'Shit! Shit! Shit!' One minute to go. The storm must be affecting the radio reception.

Pulling the satellite phone from the shelf above his bed, he dialled in Dietmar's number. We knew it didn't work well indoors, but we had to try. He managed to make contact, but it was breaking up and difficult to hear.

'I'll call you back in one minute.'

He grabbed his cold weather gear, redialled the number, waited until it was ringing, then bundled outside into the deteriorating weather. He'd no other choice. The wind howled all about the hut as he jammed the phone up against his ear, huddling low down against the snow wall at the back of the hut, the least windswept place he could find. Balto was disappearing under the snow, having more sense than to poke his nose out from under his tail. The connection was made. Hauke could hear the gentle hum of conversation and clinking glasses and cutlery as he tried to keep warm. It was –25°C. The delegates were amazed to have a contribution from the North Pole, and were sensible enough to keep the questions short and clear, but they had no idea what Hauke was going through. I was feeling the cold too, attempting to film the whole thing, protecting the video camera on its tripod as best I could with my body. The wind increased with vindictive determination, and Hauke curled up into a ball, turning away from me, trying to protect himself and the phone. We didn't have much film to spare, so as it got low, I shifted position and zoomed in on Hauke's face, his beard and eyes encrusted with a thick layer of white ice, the phone building up an insulating layer of snow by his frozen ear. As the red light blinked, telling me my battery was almost dead, I ran indoors, leaving the camera in the cold kitchen to protect it from condensation, grabbed our scooter dresses and took them out to cover up Hauke, trying to give him a bit more protection and keep him warmer. After twenty minutes, he was finally finished, and struggled back inside on cold-jammed joints. I poured him a hot coffee, but he was almost too cold to hold it, slopping it as his hands shook.

So much for saying we had it better up here.

*   *   *

The UN had asked for, and got, a document from Saddam Hussein about his so-called weapons of mass destruction. All 12,000 pages of it. In Arabic. Bush and Blair were getting worried about attacks being launched within 45 minutes, Hans Blix wanted to finish his investigation before any decision about going to war was made, and Dolly, the cloned sheep, was about the only other thing to get a mention on the news because she died. Really, I was getting a bit pissed off with it all, to put it mildly. I'm just not into politics at all. I get fed up with the evasiveness of politicians. I've never really looked at the bigger picture and tried to analyse the reason they do what they do. Because of Hauke, I was having to learn

212

and understand. There didn't seem to be anything else going on in the world that was newsworthy, nothing to lift the gloom and doom of the reports. Talk about depressing. Hauke might have loved his politics, but even he was banging the drum a bit too much for my liking, even though I agreed with most of what he was saying.

'Saddam,' he said, 'will probably hide his troops all over Iraq and run a guerrilla war. That's what I would do.'

Yeah, yeah, maybe. Right now, I thought, after nearly four months of Iraq this, Iraq that, I could stick my fingers in my ears and not listen to another word.

*   *   *

We hacked at the wall of snow with our lightweight shovels, trying to make some headway into the depths of an enormous snowdrift. A white spume flew off the summit and was lost in the endless white of the sky. The hammering wind had compacted the snow like rock; pickaxes would have been more use, but we persevered and gradually managed to excavate a short, metre-wide tunnel. Angling slightly upwards, we took it in turns at the snow-face, burrowing deeper like the hutch rabbits we were, until we could both get comfortably inside, one behind the other, out of the wind. As one worked to widen the end of the tunnel, levelling it off to create a tiny, cocoon-shaped room, the other shovelled the snow out into the daylight behind us. Small shelves or niches were cut into the rough walls for tealights, which cast their soft, weak rays across the snow, turning it a glittering gold. We

213

wriggled out backwards to push our reindeer skins up the narrow tunnel and spread them out on the cold, smooth floor, crawling up after them where they insulated our backsides admirably.

There was just enough room to sit up, so we toasted each other with a nip of schnapps (to keep out the cold) and melted a bit of crispy chocolate in our mouths before snuggling up together. The upward sloping tunnel kept the warm air in and the cold air outside where it belonged, something that female polar bears have always known when building their dens ready for giving birth in the new year. We were surprisingly cosy in our own little den, and managed to work up quite a bit of heat between ourselves, though it felt like you'd got your backside bitten if you fell off the reindeer skin. Fun though.

We built it as an experiment so that we knew how to do it properly if we were caught in bad weather conditions whilst out on a walk. In a real emergency we would close off the entrance hole with snow, leaving enough of a gap to let in fresh air, and lie there until the bad weather improved, which could be days if you were really unlucky. This time, however, we simply readjusted our clothing, blew out the candles, squirmed back down the tunnel with our reindeer skins and strolled the few short steps back to the hut, where we cooked dinner and downed an extra glass of red wine.

March. Even though the sun was back it was the coldest time of the year. One would expect temperatures to start to rise with its return, but the heat energy from the sun is absorbed by the ice and snow as it attempts to melt, leaving nothing to warm the air. We often had beautiful clear skies and windless days, but temperatures were regularly below −25°C and occasionally below −35°C. It was hard to keep warm even indoors when the wind blew strong, and wearing woolly hats inside the hut was not unusual. Our triple-glazed windows had remained comparatively see-through during the dark winter, but now fingers of frost grew longer and wider between the window panes, obscuring our vision with feathery crystals reflecting the sun. Out on Hinlopen Strait, trapped by the sea ice, numerous sculptured icebergs—one a tugboat, another a wedding cake—glowed peach and apricot in the low sun, casting long cerulean shadows over the rippled ice; snow shimmered pearlescent gold and orange as the sun sank below the distant mainland mountains. Sometimes frost smoke would drift across our bay, greying the ice, the sun an amber traffic light in thick fog.

Our last full moon before the permanent summer sun threw silver light across the shining beacon of Kinnberget and our shimmering huts. At the spring equinox, we sprang around the hut like a pair of demented kangaroos, glad that night was finally succumbing to the longer day as the sun crossed the equator, and so, like September, day and night were equal. I lay flat on the snow as the blue skies above deepened in intensity, clear and rich in a way I hadn't seen since I was a child, reflecting in the snow and turning it a tranquil powder blue. The sun and light played tricks high in the atmosphere, creating a dazzling rainbow corona around the sun; another day a spectacular fog-bow, like a rainbow in pure white, arched over Kinnvika like a heavenly, protective arm. We had almost no need of our stalwart, hard-working generator; as the sun gathered strength, the solar panels trickled energy into the storage batteries under Hauke's bed in ever-increasing quantities, so the generator became one of the first things we packed away preparatory to us leaving Paradise towards the end of August.

One amazingly clear day, we explored a narrow, deep valley running behind Kinnberget. We were well protected against the deep cold that was nudging −30°C. Apart from my down jacket and my favourite blue wool undies (not to be washed too often or they'll shrink, Randi had said), for additional warmth I wore my windproof face mask that I would normally wear when snow-scootering, my eyes just able to see out and my little snub nose tucked away out of sight under the nosepiece. I even tied a thick scarf over my chin. Mum's stupid little mittens weren't so stupid after all. Although thin, they were wool, and worn inside my leather, sheepskin-lined gauntlets, they kept my hands perfectly snug and warm. I began to think of my clothing as my three Ws: warm, wool and windproof.

We cut across the corner of the bay on the thickening ice to the mouth of the valley. Balto had fun, skipping over the hardened snowdrifts like a spring lamb, falling over onto his nose now and then as his front paws unexpectedly dug deep into soft snow, grinning as he popped up and bounded off again with high waving tail. The snow lay in great, rounded double-cream dollops as we entered the truncated valley; above us enormous pillows of meringue, beautiful but potentially deadly, overhung the vertical rock walls amongst wind-sculpted Elizabethan ruffs. A pyramidal mound of palest platinum snow filled the centre of the gently sloping, twisting valley, wind-packed and shaded from the sun. Having climbed to the top, Hauke wobbled on the apex and slid five metres down while our unimpressed dog peered down at him as if to say 'What *are* you doing, stupid man?'

Concrete-hard walls of snow barred our way at one point, and we hacked steps into them with the ice-axe to clamber over—Balto getting an unceremonious shove on the bum as his claws scrabbled uselessly at the hard wall. My boots creaked like sail ship rigging as I traversed an enormous, steep-sided embankment of hard-tamped snow with the aid of my ice-axe, which squeaked as I plunged it into the crisp surface. Leaving the ghostly grey shadows of the valley depths behind us, we emerged into dazzling sunshine, screwing up our eyes as best we could from the glare of light on white. A pelmet of snow clung to the upper edges of the incline, embellished with the most delicate of lacy, rainbow-spangled crystals, shattering into a million flashing fragments as we touched them. We sat on the lip of the valley, dangling thick-booted, double-socked feet over the four-metre drop. My black face mask was rimed in frozen breath, thickest across my mouth and nose, turning the fleecy fabric brittle. My hat was edged in fur-like frost and stray strands of hair hung white and hoary. My eyelashes twinkled in the sun as if coated in thick, crystalline mascara. Pearls of ice hung from Hauke's eyebrows and moustache, and a white patch of skin on the side of his nose warned of the first signs of frostbite. He rubbed it vigorously to return the circulation and warm it up, covering it again with his overstretched facemask. Before we got too cold, we scrambled to our feet and took the easy route back down the side

217

of Kinnberget, across the snow-glued rocks speckled dayglo yellow, cream, black and tangerine with the new spring growth; reddening stems of saxifrage poked up here and there through the sparse snow as we returned to the bay and retraced our steps homewards for a lunch of bread and cheese and hot tea.

*   *   *

Balto was starting to moult. The old fur seemed to be turning orange-brown as if he was getting a suntan, and even the fur between his pads was turning a strange, dark plum colour. Back in England I had spiked all the moulted short, soft underfur from my Bernese mountain dog on the barbed-wire fence at the top of the garden where the birds could gather it to line their nests. We were still waiting to see our first birds. Bear visits seemed to have increased with the return of the light, but maybe that was partly because we could now see them. Tiny shrimps, which had been around in the water all winter, flashing neon blue light as they were brought to the surface when Hauke bored holes through the ice, now appeared plain, uninteresting brown.

April came marching in, determined to kick out −40°C March and drape its own milder cloak around our shoulders. Our first two birds, too far away to be identified, caught the tail-end of the intense cold, but within a week we were experiencing temperatures that rocketed to a little below zero, which left the icebergs decorated with icicles dripping incredibly salty water off their tips—confirming they were made from sea ice and not a part of a calving glacier. We took two of our

218

red-Rexined chairs and set them out in a sunny, sheltered spot close to the hut. Wrapped up warm, we would sit for hours and sip our wine, binoculars round our necks, and watch and wait for our first visitors returning to the Arctic after their summer sojourn in the south.

Our first identified birds were glaucous gulls returning to their nesting sites either side of the narrow entrance to Claravågen. Kittiwakes started to arrive soon after, followed by a sprinkling of Arctic skuas, fulmars, black guillemot, Arctic terns, eider ducks, and Spitsbergen's only songbird, the black and white snow bunting, which we hadn't seen last year as they'd probably already left. Finding food locally was difficult for them as the ice remained locked fast and thick around the visible coastline, except for one small stretch of open water, hardly bigger than a boating lake, a short distance from Ruud's Hytte But flying long distances to find open water further afield presented no problems for them.

The temperature pendulum swung back the other way, dropping again at the same time as we sighted our first seal of the year. It emerged onto the ice, barely visible, looking like a mouse dropping far, far out in the bay. The reindeer had completely deserted us over the winter, finding somewhere better protected from the relentless gales and with better grazing, so it was wonderful to see them start their regular tours around Kinnvika once more. It felt good to see old friends.

*   *   *

It was unusually quiet in the hut. Hauke had been feeling unwell for a few days and had painfully jarred his shoulder when he fell whilst skiing, so now he could hardly lift his arm. There wasn't much he could do other than give it complete rest, but he was a typical man, a pain in the backside when out of sorts. And he had started to lose his voice. I wasn't too unhappy about it at first as it curtailed the amount of discussion over the Iraq war, but his ears were working fine. He'd been going to bed early and sleeping a lot, but waking up before the alarm and tuning in to Deutsche Welle at six-thirty to hear the latest on the war. I was hoping that once George Dubya had sent in the troops Hauke would ease off and calm down a bit, but if anything he just got worse. He'd been getting steadily more and more wound up, shouting about Churchill and Dresden and the hundreds of thousands of people dying in the firestorm, and how Bush and Blair were doing the same to the ordinary Iraqi people. He was complaining that not enough troops were being sent in to fight and retain control—he said you needed six times the enemy's numbers. He was flitting back and forth between Deutsche Welle, NRK from Norway, Voice of America and the BBC, getting different viewpoints and information from each one. He even managed to track down Baghdad Radio, but couldn't understand any of it. With such blanket coverage throughout the day and evening we were probably better informed than most people, but I didn't need so much of it. Hauke got cross and agitated almost as soon as he tuned in, and in the evenings, after a couple of glasses of wine, he'd rant on and on like a needle stuck in the groove. Even when we were outside, conversation frequently revolved around the war; I couldn't seem to get away from it anywhere.

Then, one evening, just before I started cooking dinner, Hauke started ranting on again in his hoarse voice about Dresden and Stalingrad, Hitler and Churchill, Bush and Blair. His croaky voice grew to a shout as he remembered all the young German soldiers of 18 years old who had been killed in the last war (nearly a hundred per cent of those in Wesel, where Hauke lived). They had no choice but to fight, he raged, slaughtered like the seals by the polar bears. What about our lads, then, I thought? It had been the same for them. They'd also received the summons to go and fight. He went on about how the old men and young boys had fought to the end to defend what was still standing in Germany, trying to protect what was left from the English and American armies after they'd already lost so much. He could understand why many of the Iraqis, no friends of Saddam, were rallying to fight the Yanks after so many of them had been killed in the bombing, and, and, and . . .

I stood up, put on my jacket, boots and gloves and walked out. I knew he wasn't getting at me personally, but I was fed up with us Brits getting the blame for everything. We had been, after all, the only European country left that was still capable of returning the fight in the Second World War. Everyone else had given in. We had no choice. And I, like most people in Britain, was against the Iraq war right from the beginning. But right now, whatever the rights and wrongs of the situation, enough was enough. Give it a rest, Hauke!

It was too bloody cold to stay out more than ten minutes, but my point had been made. Hauke apologised straight away. He wasn't getting at me, he said, very quietly. I knew that. I'll keep quiet for 24 hours, he said, not mention the war.

Having almost lost his voice helped, but he was as good as his word, never uttered another thing about the war. And when his voice improved, we discussed my dislike of the excess of information, how it made me want to explode, so we agreed to moderate the amount of war news we were listening to, and I could live with that. The BBC's loss was NRK's gain—less news, more music. But it worked, and the stress was almost immediately removed; Hauke was more relaxed (especially as he started to feel better) and I could actually start taking an interest in the Middle East once more. The crisis, for us, was over.

*　　*　　*

St George's Day, 23 April. The first thing I had to do was hang up my Union Jack. It wasn't the right flag to use but I hadn't been able to find an English one in any of the places I'd tried in England before I left. It would have to do. Hauke laughed at me as I trailed my flag along the snow, trying to find a good place to nail it up. He found me a long length of wood in the main hut (perhaps it was our chimney cleaning wood), bored a hole in the snow between the hut and the motor house and set up my flagpole. He then whacked in a couple of nails (I'd have done that first) and hooked on the flag through its two eyelet holes. It fluttered gently in the light breeze, and I said what a great attraction for the bears it was. They investigated anything out of the ordinary, being such nosy creatures, but that day my flag was safe.

Hauke decided to make a sundial. It was a fabulous day for making it, very cold but with crystal clear skies and zero wind. My huge flag hung

222

limp from the pole, a corner just touching the snow. Hauke scuffed a large circle in the snow keeping the flagpole in the centre. Using it as an hour hand, where the sun cast its shadow across the circle at midday, Hauke scored a line across the circle, then repeated the process every hour for the next few hours until we had enough marks and could fill in the remaining ones by guesswork. It wouldn't last too long—Hauke didn't want to mark the hours with sticks, as they and the grooves would soon be covered over when the wind increased—but it was yet another thing that was fun to make together, and beat telly any day.

I worried about my flag over the next few days. I really wanted to take it home again, but Hauke wouldn't let me fetch it in. 'Leave it there,' was all he kept saying. I know what you're hoping for, I thought.

And a week later his wish came true. We had another beautiful, birdwatching day, so we'd been sitting in our red-Rexined chairs, relaxing and soaking up the sun. We were dozing indoors on our bunks after lunch, Balto twitching his paws in the kitchen, when Hauke had the feeling that a bear was around outside. We peered over the table and looked at the flag. It was hanging on by a single nail near the bottom of the flagpole. No sign of the bear, but he was around somewhere. We crept about inside the hut, peering through the frosted windows, finally spotting the bear where we emptied the piss-pot. He was very dynamic, striding about confidently. We didn't like him at all. It was safer to stay inside and see what happened. The bear strode back to the flagpole and stood by my flag. The next moment he'd grabbed hold of it in paws and teeth and ripped

223

it apart like tissue paper. Bored with that, he headed off for our chairs leaving my shredded Union Jack rolling about in death throes on the ground. He tasted the chairs, pulling one over, easily splitting the Rexine with his sharp teeth. Didn't taste good, so he set the chair upright again and came and sat in front of our door; at least we couldn't see him from either side window, so we reckoned he must have been there. I kept my rifle with me all the time and fetched Hauke's, very quietly, from the nail just inside the door. After a few minutes, the bear hopped up onto the snow bank and, sitting on his bum, played with my flag again, then rolled over onto his back, paws in the air, ripping it still further. Bored again, he nosed around the hut, with us creeping from window to window, trying to follow his movements. We decided that if this one broke into the hut, we'd shoot it. He was obviously dangerous. Was it the time of year for excessive ursine testosterone? Judging from the number of very active bears we'd seen lately, it seemed like it.

He was getting too comfortable around the hut, Hauke decided. Time to go into attack mode. Checking he was away from the door, Hauke sprung out. The bear heard him and lunged towards him, but Hauke fired the warning pen and slammed the door shut. I was right behind him with the rifle. Hauke peeked out again through the door. The bear hadn't come too close, so he loosed off another warning pen. Mr Bear wasn't as brave as he looked (I thought, hopefully) and ran off pretty smartly, followed by Hauke banging the dog bowls together, the rifle and I close by. Balto, as had become the norm, was left inside the living room, imprisoned by the kitchen door.

The bear decided to stop and observe us from up in the rocks below Kinnberget, but that wasn't allowed. It was a long shot, maybe half a kilometre, but Hauke took careful aim, allowing for windage and fall of shot as I observed through the binocs. He fired, and a puff of smoke plumed into the air a couple of bears' lengths to the right of our furry friend, about two metres above his head. He got the hint, and took off at a run, heading left across the ridge and disappeared, departing up what we were now calling The Bear Road to the north.

The wind had picked up a little and my flag bits were rolling merrily away after the bear. We galloped after them, not wanting to lose them, retrieving them for souvenirs. We mended the chair with silver tape, writing 'Bear' and dating it. We left it a while before going back to our birdwatching, just in case.

*   *   *

After a run of these bear attacks I suffered a bad dream, the first one concerning bears since I'd been there. I dreamt one was coming in through the roof and I cried out in my sleep, waking myself and Hauke. I hated it when my sleep was disturbed as I felt so tired the next day, so grumpy and irritable. I couldn't get my brain in gear and discuss anything with Hauke and was easily upset, often bursting into silly tears for no real reason. Hauke was always sympathetic, at least for a short while afterwards, and showed amazing tolerance with me in my rat mode. He got a bit anxious about these aggressive bears, too.

The only time we got particularly crabby with each other was when we were preparing the final report of the expedition. It was a lot of long, hard work, and with neither of us having any experience with the programs that had been loaded onto the laptop at the university, it led to a fair bit of discord between us. We started to limit the total time spent with the computer at any one sitting and I tried, once again, to work more systematically, and eventually we smoothed out the work process and set a new level of understanding between us. Hauke was feeling better and was soon a happy bunny again as he'd had news of another grandchild on the way, his eighth. He was a very proud father of two daughters, and a son who was a third generation physicist— though he'd yet to father a child. That would be a very special moment for Hauke. I had seen lots of photos of the grandchildren who looked so cute with their blond hair and cheeky faces. There were pictures of them all above Hauke's bed. None of my family above mine. But that was me.

I'm sure he thought I was a bit of a nutcase at times. We were playing the 'William Tell Overture' on a CD, the theme music to the old TV show *The Lone Ranger*, and Hauke thought it was hilarious as I rode Silver, my horse, furiously across the range, jumping over ditches and hedges in time to the music. (It was my chair actually—cream legs and a red saddle.) Another time, he provided disco lighting while I was dancing to 'Lady Marmalade' on the radio by flashing his torches around the darkened hut.

As we munched on our Kinder Easter eggs (Hauke had a Smurf and I had a flying machine with boggle eyes), he said he was glad I had come with him; it probably wouldn't have worked with anyone else. 'Thanks,' I said, spinning the propeller, and shooting his Smurf with my invisible machine guns.

CHAPTER ELEVEN

LIFE ON ICE

The back of the main hut almost completely disappeared under hard, wind-packed snow at the beginning of June. It swept up over the roof and smothered half the western side of its 30-metre length like smooth royal icing. Being able to climb up the snowdrift to the roof afforded us a wonderful vantage point to look out towards Hinlopen Strait and watch the angular icebergs, enmeshed in the loose, broken ice, drifting back and forth with the currents. Out across the bay of Kinnvika, still covered in thick but rotting ice (caused by the salt leaching out, leaving it full of holes and crumbly), puddles of water reflected the silvery clouds and occasional sunshine. The seawater temperature had crept up slowly and Mark and Marina on *Jonathan* were almost afloat again and beginning to think of home. Above the ice, air temperatures were a balmy 3°C; the snow was sublimating, going from solid to vapour without bothering to melt in between, leaving more brown patches of rock and shingle near the beach. Icicles were crashing down from the roof of our little hut, making us jump and think polar bears were trying to break in. Before they finally disappeared, we broke some off and used them one more time to decorate our gin fizzes. With frequent new falls of snow over the icy ground, it became slippery underfoot, catching us out frequently and dumping us unceremoniously on our backsides as

227

we wandered about the terrain to observe our changing world. Tiny black spiders with beetle-like bodies scurried between the warming stones and fulmars flew overhead, their wings audible in the silence.

From the height of our eyrie, we were able to watch the comings and goings of both bears and reindeer while they were still several kilometres away, just a slight movement amongst the ice and snow enough to give away their position. Reindeer varied in colouring, their dense coats ranging from creamy greys towards a rich, dark mouse colour, but generally their fur was paler in winter. Our old adage, generally, still stood: if you thought it was a bear, it was a bear. Occasionally, when viewed through our binoculars, the small speck of yellow reindeer turned into a bear, or a pale bear became a reindeer. But we weren't often wrong.

One morning after breakfast, whilst sweeping the ice for seals with my binoculars, I thought I spotted three reindeer far out, though it was hard to see clearly. I called Hauke as it was rather an unusual sight. We climbed up onto the roof of the main hut to get a better view, and thought that it was in fact a family of three bears; a mother and her two well-grown cubs. We watched them for a long time. They seemed to be zigzagging about the ice, gradually working their way to our left towards a small ice-clamped island called Hvaløya. On reaching the island, they crossed to the opposite side and carefully crept back onto the ice—a seal disappeared below the surface as they approached—apparently heading for the land on the northern side of Murchisonfjord. Were they bears, or reindeer after all? We rested our eyes for a few minutes, looked again through the binocs. The more we looked the more confused we became, but in the end we decided they were reindeer, much to my relief. Hauke didn't like encountering three-bear families where the cubs were around two years old, as they would have honed their hunting skills and would be a formidable team; he had felt a lot of anxiety in Mushamna whenever such families were around.

As they worked their way closer to Kinnvika, we could now see clearly how our three reindeer carefully picked their way across the frozen sea, each choosing their own, independent route, detouring left and right, backwards and forwards, to ensure good ice under their hooves, taking their time, not hurrying, keeping safe. Sometimes they would leap across a patch of water or thin ice or backtrack to take a different route. One, with pale brown fur, was a bit bolder or more experienced than the others and made land first. He was followed a little later by the biggest and palest of the three— sporting antlers—and eventually the third and smallest of the group with spiky growths on its head as tall as its ears. The bucks lose their antlers early in the winter but they start to grow again from April to July, shedding their velvet in August and September. The hinds start their antler growth in June, but often keep them a whole year before starting to grow new ones. They foraged among the rocks, nibbling at the new shoots, before splitting up; one turned right and headed back towards Murchisonfjord and the other two came towards Kinnvika to excite Balto, fast on his long line and out of trouble.

Babies arrive in June, so we were careful with Balto when he was off the lead during our walks. At the beginning of the month we went to see how many kittiwakes had returned to the bird cliff on Hunnberget, about five kilometres away on the northern coastline of Murchisonfjord. A few kittiwakes were sailing through the air in lazy circles as we drew near, drifting on the updraught. At the top of the cliff, attached to a big, heavy boulder, a length of rope was still firmly tied and coiled neatly around its base. We had no idea how long it had lain there, weathered grey and slightly fluffy—perhaps fifty years, maybe longer—but we had no intention of using it for its given purpose; to dangle a man down the cliff face so he could collect the birds' eggs.

We counted around a hundred birds perched on the tiny white-edged ledges of the dark expanse of rock. They were coming and going, squabbling with a neighbour as they tried to find a place to land, launching into the air on black-tipped wings, or fighting—spiralling downwards grappling each other's beaks. I thought they'd crash to the ground, but they released each other moments before and flew their separate ways. As we left them to their aerial gyrations, Balto sniffed out some fresh reindeer tracks, so Hauke kept a firm hold on his line as we tried to find them. Sure enough, we spotted one of our 'house' deer, a pale female with a hooked antler, and her soft-brown companion. To our surprise, both had babies alongside, already browsing the new growth, one almost pink and the other cocoa coloured. They must have been born very early, but perhaps that was just the way they did things here on Nordaustlandet, getting a jump-start on summer.

Between April and June we'd often see a fine pair of bucks grazing companionably on our walks up the

Bear Road. One day, a pair of them had been rubbing their antlers, trying to remove the velvet, on some blue plastic, heavy-duty fishing nets that they'd found on the beach. As a result they had become tangled together in the strong mesh, their heads firmly fastened together by the unbreakable coils. Hauke tried to approach them with a view to cutting them free, but they were too scared and skittered away like conjoined twins. They were lucky in that they could at least feed fairly comfortably together, so had a chance of surviving. Yet it was almost a common sight to find horns lying around entangled in sturdy plastic fishing nets, so we had little cause for optimism. The males loose their horns naturally at the beginning of the winter, but we couldn't say with certainty that some survived enmeshed until this time. By the time the bears and foxes had been about and cleaned up, only the antlers remained. Our analysis of the rubbish on the beach showed only ten per cent was made up of fishing industry rubbish if you counted each individual item, but the nets and lengths of rope were far bigger than anything else we found, and the annual beach clean-up on Spitsbergen was mostly for this kind of stuff.

Eero over in Mushamna had had a hard time hunting reindeer. Perhaps they had learnt to keep away from the hunters, whereas ours had no reason to fear us, being completely protected on Nordaustlandet. But he had bagged one or two, and told us over the radio that he'd sent a nice leg for us back to the Governor's office where it was now lying in the freezer waiting to be delivered on the next helicopter visit, whenever that was going to be.

                                *   *   *

Our friends had been very generous to us (Randi
must have spent a small fortune on us over the year)
with the supply of fresh fruit and salad, milk and
cream, ham, cakes and biscuits delivered by the
occasional helicopter, but usually it was just the post
they brought. (Three months was the longest we
went without someone dropping in; the other
overwinterers were more or less en route from
Longyearbyen to the research station in Ny Ålesund,
so had many more visits, but we would have
managed perfectly without these little luxuries. The
best part was getting letters from home.) The only
other fresh food we were eating were bean sprouts,
though I wasn't always successful growing them as
it often got too cold in the hut overnight and they
died off. Our dried fish were tied by the tails in pairs
and were hanging over a long rope up in the main
hut, stinking the place out. We weren't too fond of
them, and Balto ended up eating the most. The salted
fresh salmon from the Longyearbyen lads on their
fishing expedition kept well and, if well soaked
beforehand to remove the excess of salt, were
extremely tasty and a real treat.

We didn't manage to drink our way through all
the alcohol, especially the strong spirits. The rum
was good to warm us up after being out in the cold,
added to hot tea to brace us again, or for soaking a
cut finger, and the champagne was reserved for
Sunday breakfasts. It stored remarkably well just
above the kitchen floor where we were a bit worried
about it freezing solid, but we only lost one bottle to
the extreme cold. In fact, over the whole time in

Kinnvika, we only had three duff bottles of champagne where the corks had sprung slightly and it had gone flat.

There was hardly any red wine left; it seemed we'd taken such a lot, but it was actually less than a bottle a day between us. As I cooked the dinner, we would invariably drink a glass of wine while talking together, and an additional glass with the meal. A frozen box of wine might have made a good weapon against the polar bears, but we never thought to try it. It was too late now, it had all defrosted.

* * *

Whenever possible we walked in the afternoon, down to the beach and back if the weather was unfriendly, or further afield, up over Kinnberget or across Twillingneset and on to Hinlopen Strait and beyond. We took much pleasure in our local walks and had no inclination to go much further. We were happy to stay close to home watching our piebald snow buntings chirruping around Kinnvika, flitting from roof to rock and back again, hunting for old seeds and somewhere to nest, or competing with each other in an aerial ballet, dancing together in the air, flying back and forth, up and down in a synchronised *pas de deux* before separating and flitting away in the annual mating game. Purple sandpipers arrived in ones and twos, widely scattered across the tundra, and searched for a meagre supply of food. Up on the Bear Road one day, we lay on our backs in the snow, listening to the sound of granular snow landing on our jackets, and, hearing the windy whoosh of wings, we rolled over to watch a small flock of geese land and take a breather below us, pick through the newly budded saxifrage, before loping downhill, wings aflap and lifting off in search of better grazing.

*   *   *

I couldn't blame the geese for moving on—the weather was pretty miserable of late; grey and overcast, depressing despite the mildness with just occasional glimpses of the sun. One day, it would be foggy, windy, snowy, cold and cloudy; but the next, warm and sunny with a rainbow-kissed blue sky. British weather would have a hard job competing with that. By midsummer's day, the consistency of the new snow changed, too. Normally it was very dry and crystalline, almost like sand, and couldn't be compacted together, but of late it was much wetter and heavier, and, for the first time since we'd arrived in Kinnvika, we could have snowball fights. I just wished my aim was as accurate and painful as Hauke's. Behaving like a couple of kids, we built our one and only snowman of the year. Even between us it was almost impossible to lift the two, big balls of snow for his head and body onto the enormous base. Our Anglo-German snowman got coal buttons; stones for eyes and nose; a curvy piece of wood for his mouth; a soggy, cardboard oil-filter for a hat; a ski stick and a shovel pushed under his arms; and a rope belt round his fat middle to finish him off.

And just to remind us that winter really was retreating, we found our first saxifrage flower wide open, its five glossy, puce-coloured petals a brave splash of colour defying the cold.

234

With a break in the gloomy weather, the sun rose on a sparkling, cloud-free day, and a stranger appeared in Kinnvika. Armed with a mirror and a large pair of scissors, Hauke was hacking away at his straggly beard, snipping away at the grey-blond growth as close as he dared, before finally lathering up and scraping away the stubble with a plastic razor. He looked weird. Even Balto thought so. I had grown so used to Hauke with his insulating whiskers over the last nine months that I had forgotten what he'd looked like before. I'd sit and watch him across the table in the evenings as he read a book, trying to get used to the new look, but it was over a week before I stopped feeling the smooth, pale skin and Hauke became Hauke again.

Having cheered himself up with a shave, he started emptying our museum of its exhibits. We hadn't heard a thing from the Governor or his advisors—they hadn't bothered to write back to us—so, as promised, we returned the items to where we found them. We didn't want to fall foul of the stringent laws on Spitsbergen protecting such items. It would be easier to transport the heavier items while there was still smooth snow to drag them along.

I helped Hauke carry or drag the heavy ships' timbers, but otherwise he preferred to work alone. He found it a depressing task; especially returning the half sledge to the ice, where a polar bear found it to play with, and it eventually disappeared with the retreating ice, perhaps lost forever. It took him two days to finish the task, getting plenty of exercise towing the pulka around the area, dropping off the various items as he went. Sad as it was, we'd spent many enjoyable hours looking for the pieces in the first place. Trying to identify them and display them to their best advantage in the museum had given us a deeper insight into the history of Spitsbergen and the difficult and dangerous lives of its transient visitors. Something the visitors to the museum in Longyearbyen now wouldn't get.

*　　*　　*

Hauke had been reading the old diary of a Norwegian hunter who had shared his hut with a female companion, but after one short month, they were already arguing with each other and didn't get on at all. Over a glass of wine, we talked about how well we'd gelled, relieved that we'd had no major upsets and remained amicable throughout the year. It was hard to imagine transferring our relaxed companionship and extraordinary lifestyle back to civilisation, though. We tried to evaluate what effects outside influences such as friends, family and work would have on us. Here we'd been almost entirely alone, and although welcoming the occasional visitors, we were glad to be rid of them again, even if we liked them. There was no way we could be that isolated back home. It would be too selfish not to see family and friends and hide away from people, and not practical anyway. Hauke had to go back to the university and work on the scientific results amassed during the expedition, meet his new grandchild, pick up the threads of his old life. I had to find a new one. We were so protective of our Kinnvika life but it seemed impossible to us to recreate it elsewhere, so

236

we made no plans to be together afterwards. We wanted to have a chance but would quit while we were ahead. We kept repeating to ourselves that here in Kinnvika, it wasn't 'real life', and outside influences on our return would only tarnish our special relationship. Maybe he was also having second thoughts about us going back to Germany together having had no positive reply from me (or a negative one), or was he trying to let himself down gently if I decided not to go with him? I just wanted to preserve in my memory this extraordinary, incredible adventure we'd had together, to hold it close to my heart and remember it forever. I think we were trying to hang on to our original decision, that we would treat the whole thing as time restricted, no pressure at the end of it to stay together, but it still left me feeling emotionally confused. I couldn't, or wouldn't, find the words to argue against Hauke's reasoning. I didn't want to face the future alone, to go back to square one and start again, and I guess I didn't dare to think about a future together for fear of being disappointed again. It seemed a logical decision, and not one I felt I should argue against.

Would anyone understand our decision? How could they? They didn't have what we had; couldn't begin to imagine it. So after telling everyone what a great time we had had up here, they wouldn't comprehend why we should go our separate ways. Neither of us were looking forward to the adventure coming to an end, but agreed we would see each other now and then. I hoped so. We had had a lot of fun and enjoyed being together. It seemed a shame not to find another solution, really, but there you go. 'It is as it is,' he said.

Maybe we were just afraid to lose the magic.

I started to pack away things: wool, books, extreme weather clothing, old letters and anything else I didn't think I'd need over the final two months. My worries about being bored in Kinnvika had proved unfounded. We'd spent a lot of time outside when the weather was favourable and worked on our diaries, books and reports, scientific experiments and an occasional, tiny bit of housework. I'd also devoured many books, especially over the winter, though perhaps without absorbing them too much. I seem to have lost the knack of remembering things. I think I've learned to read just to pass the time, to be entertained, not to educate myself. It probably just needs retraining. Hauke had enjoyed reading the reproductions of several hunters' diaries, and was currently dipping into a three-volume series of letters, dating from the 1780s, by a German called Georg Christoph Lichtenberg (1742–1799), a writer and fellow physicist.

I had certainly taken far too much craftwork to do, but had got quite a lot done nonetheless. Apart from running repairs and the mammoth task of knitting Hauke's jumper, plus matching mittens, I managed a Norwegian cardigan for myself—black with white snowflakes, which seemed appropriate—as well as a child's jumper with a reindeer motif, plus several other pairs of patterned mittens. I tried my hand at silk painting, starting off with a kit for a scarf with mice and snakes all over it, which was fun and easy to do. I tried creating my own patterned scarves, but couldn't get the gutta outliner to penetrate the silk properly; either it was too cold and thick or I wasn't

238

doing it correctly, so instead I did a large cross-stitch picture of old sewing equipment that Hauke called my road map. He reckoned I'd finish it long before George Dubya finished his; and he was right. I rummaged through my boxes of fabric for all the pinks and greens that I had planned on turning into a 'log cabin' quilt. Even using a rotary cutter, it took an age to cut each strip of fabric to its required length to give me more accuracy when piecing it together. In all, 1,872 individual pieces were sewn into 144 unique squares, the seams smoothed with my borrowed flat iron which warmed up on the paraffin heater. Unfortunately, the floor was far too small and dirty for me to sandwich the wadding between backing and top and pin it all together, so the top had to be folded up in a box, waiting for me to finish it. For years I'd fancied making a 'bear's paw' quilt and never got around to it, but it crossed my mind that as a thank you to Hauke for looking after me and giving me such a wonderful time here in Kinnvika, I would make him one as a present, in midnight blues and ice white. But not here. When I was back in England. I didn't want him to see me make this one. It had to be a surprise.

*   *   *

It was not quite flaming June, but as the month drew to a close, the snow started to melt in earnest, and we worried about being flooded out. A pool of melt water had formed in front of the hut and was growing deeper and bigger daily and we were still surrounded by high hills of dense snow. Around the sauna it was still dry, as the water could flow away downhill, so we decided to move in there if we had to. At least we knew the oven was operable and would keep us warm.

Ice on Kinnvika's two lagoons turned blue, emerald green and turquoise with the effects of algae, like giant opals. A dozen eider ducks, a mixture of dull brown females and striking black and white males, their heads looking a bit comical as the bill joins the head in an almost straight line, paddled about in the milky surface water, but on the small stretch of open water in front of Ruud's Hytte there were over four hundred of them. Kinnvika looked dead by comparison. But more flowers were opening around Kinnvika: white, yellow-centred tuesildre (*Saxifraga cespitosa*); golden puterublom—cushioned whitlowgrass (*Draba corymbosa*); and the greenish-white of lappmarksrublom—Lapland whitlowgrass (*Draba lacteal*); all low growing and hugging the ground. An impressive thunderclap boomed around Kinnvika, echoing off the rocks as the snowy dam at the foot of the canyon gave way and tons of ice and water spewed out into the bay, shattering the sea ice for over 200 metres with its sheer force.

Balto tried following the noisy, plashing streams, a treat to our eyes and ears, as they twisted here and there and disappeared underground to re-emerge a few metres further on. We laughed at him as he peered up holes and down them, quizzical and confused, trying to work out where the rivulets were going as they tumbled into the now snow-free, icy bay, streaked green and blue and silvery shades of pewter. The seals had all but disappeared. Summer was on its way.

We switched on the short-wave radio promptly at nine o'clock and Mark immediately called us up, much to our surprise. He said the ice in Nilspollen, where they were staying, had broken up and disappeared in the last two days and they were now swinging free off one anchor.

'We waited just to say goodbye, and now we're leaving,' he told us excitedly.

Well! That was a shock! We thought their ice would remain a lot longer, keeping them trapped and in danger of missing some of their early bookings; they had planned to ferry a group of scientists about Spitsbergen in *Jonathan*. He and Marina had mixed feelings about leaving, their big adventure drawing to a close, but we wished them bon voyage and a safe journey back to Longyearbyen, feeling a little sad to lose contact with such good friends, ones that understood and had shared what we were going through alone.

Mark signed off. 'Over and out from Nilspollen!'

'Out and over from Kinnvika!' said Hauke, getting it back to front as usual.

I sat on my bed, back against the cold wooden wall, head brushing the underside of my bookshelf, hugging my moose. Their departure made me consider my own imminent leave-taking. It really wasn't something I wanted to think about, not wanting to break the spell. I felt as if some invisible hand had hold of the door and had slowly started to close it on my incomparable year. Thinking and talking about what to do after Kinnvika was one thing, but the actual departure, the thought of closing up the hut and locking the door for the last time, of saying goodbye to Hauke, my good friend and expedition partner, just made me want to cry.

I knew I didn't want to go.

CHAPTER TWELVE

SUMMER

Ah-ooo! Ah-ooo! Ah-ooo! Looking like aquatic magpies, male eider ducks bobbed up and down, flicking back their triangular heads as they called to the brown females paddling about on the open stretch of water. With ice still decking the sea, only a few pairs seemed tempted to breed and we watched as the females waddled over the tundra, males lagging behind like bored husbands out shopping, looking for a suitable hollow near our hut in which to make a nest. Ordinarily, only the females incubate the eggs, being well camouflaged, but there was one male that seemed to like helping out, sticking out like a sore thumb in his black and white plumage to any egg-hungry passers-by, usually bears, foxes and seagulls. Eiders often nest close to human habitation in the hope of gaining extra protection and build up large colonies which are carefully harvested for their down. Our local birds had managed to hatch a dozen or more youngsters last year, but now we could only see two.

More successful were the Arctic skuas. As the snow rapidly disappeared, fortunately not flooding us out, a pair had scraped out a shallow depression in the bare ground and had nested about 50 metres away from our hut where we could easily watch them. We still had a few very old hens' eggs that we were now reluctant to eat, so Hauke left one out every day for the skuas. It was comical to watch

242

them nodding their heads, taking aim at the egg, before giving it a smart whack with their strong beaks, breaking off pieces of shell to enlarge the hole and sharing the contents. Mrs Skua was not so confident, but her husband was eventually feeding out of Hauke's hand or sitting on his shoulders. He would follow us as we took our walks, swooping out of the sky on narrow black wings, trailing long, central tail feathers, to alight on a rock close by and wait for us to catch him up; or meet us on top of Kinnberget before roaring off and pulling up into a spectacular vertical ascent.

When his own eggs appeared, Mr Skua remained at home on guard duty. He and Balto had an understanding. If Balto stayed away from the nest site, he'd stop attacking him; though just to remind him, he'd sometimes fly in and flick him on the ears with his wings, just for the fun of it, Balto ducking his head in submission. Reindeer got the same treatment if they wandered too close, and an attack by both parents pecking at their heads and bums soon had them running for shelter. Even bears were subjected to the aerial onslaught. We were hoping that the first chick would hatch on 23 July, to celebrate our anniversary in Kinnvika, but it missed it by two days. The tiny ball of black fluff was soon up on his long legs, tottering about and falling over, or snuggling up under his mother's wing. His sibling joined him after a couple of days, by which time he was already trying to fly, jumping into the air and flapping his stubby winglets. Once both were steady on their feet, they left the nest and ran about everywhere, blending into the landscape so we could only spot them when the parents came back to feed them.

The skua parents were perfectly capable of catching their own food, but why bother when you could launch an aerial attack and scare the living daylights out of some poor kittiwake? In fright he would cough up his last meal so the skua could catch it in mid-air and take it home to the youngsters. We hadn't realised that there were at least three more successful breeding pairs of skuas around until we also came under attack as we inadvertently wandered into their territory. As their chicks fledged and took wing, four or five of them raced about the sky together in tight formation, wingtip to sooty black wingtip, sharp beak to pointed tail, swooping and diving and twisting in the air like swallows, before stooping into a spectacular dive and disappearing against the sun.

*   *   *

Up on the slopes below Kinnberget, snow had revealed our old friend, Sako. He'd only been given the shallowest of graves in December because of the hard frozen ground, and the stones that had been piled over him at the time had settled with the wind, and now the disappearance of the snow revealed his head and bony back, just as we'd left him. He still looked fast asleep, ready to wake up at any time and chase away a bear. I stroked his soft black fur and pulled gently at his stiffened ear, almost expecting him to roll over and have his white tummy tickled. He appeared peaceful and undisturbed, so giving him a final rub on his head, we gathered loose flakes of rock and covered him over once more with a thick layer, topping it off with large, heavy slabs of stone and rimming the grave with pink and grey pebbles.

We had our last contact over the short-wave radio with Eero, as he left Mushamna shortly afterwards, cadging a lift home on a tourist boat heading back to Longyearbyen. There were just ourselves and Stein and his family left now, and they were due to leave on 24 July. We were hoping that the *Nordsyssel*, the Governor's new ship, would be able to drop off our last post before collecting them, as we'd had none delivered for almost five months, but the ice around the north coast of the mainland and in Hinlopen Strait was still dense and impenetrable, so we could only hope. We felt quite alone now that our regular on-air friends had departed, and receiving the mail took on a new, almost obsessive, importance that it hadn't had before. We hoped to hear from friends and family and get a giant repair kit for the inflatable. We had been keeping our fingers crossed that the ice would disappear so that we could visit a couple of special places before we left. We kept climbing up onto our roof and surveying Hinlopen Strait through our binocs, obsessively watching the ice and the open water come and go, contracting and expanding. Luckily for Stein, the ice thinned enough for the ship to get through and for them to leave, but there was absolutely no way the ship could get over to us, despite trying both before and after picking him up, as the ice was still tight packed. It was a great disappointment to us.

As the *Nordsyssel* returned home with our post we could see, from the roof of our hut, that the sea ice in Hinlopen Strait had dissipated, leaving great expanses of open water between the disintegrating lumps of ice. Feeling a bit despondent, the first feelings of isolation in Kinnvika crept in. We kept in touch with the *Nordsyssel* by short-wave radio,

245

discussing the ice conditions, and heard that they would try again five days later on the 29 July when they were again in the area.

It was nearly midnight by the time the *Nordsyssel* nudged as close as it could, still a long way from the shore off Ruud's Hytte, the nearest it could come to us. It dropped an inflatable over the side, which took about half an hour to zigzag through the maze of ice blocks, retracing its course often, until eventually finding a way through. A friendly shout and wave, and there, much to my surprise, was my survival-suited friend Leif, along with our parcels. He was helping with the annual beach clean-up, the reason the *Nordsyssel* was in the area, and had managed to get a ride with the 'postmen'. It was a very brief reunion, barely ten minutes, and then they were off again, racing through the ice back to the ship. We waved a final farewell as they regained the red-hulled ship, then we loaded up an old plastic fishing box with our somewhat heavy parcels and tramped back to the hut, towing it behind us. The following day the ice closed in and packed tight into an impenetrable barrier once more. We didn't care. We had our post.

*   *   *

It was a bit of a squeeze with all the cameras, rifles and plastic bags of boots, but with me sitting in the bows, Balto in the middle and Hauke steering, we motored slowly out of the bay, dodging the rapidly disappearing ice, and turned left into Murchisonfjord, leaving its sprinkle of islands to our right. After half an hour, I attacked the foot pump and topped up the air in the soft rubber bags of the

246

boat as the extensive repair job wasn't quite airtight; but it was good enough. The kittiwakes were still busy around Hunnberget, but didn't show any obvious signs of feeding youngsters. Strings of pearly-white birds lined the smooth boulders at the water's edge, chattering away to each other in kittiwakeese, ignoring us as we burbled past under their feet. Black-eyed seals surfaced curiously ahead of us, whiskers dripping, before diving below the surface as black guillemots, with red wellingtons and white-splashed wings whirring like clockwork, crossed our wake. We beached the boat in Florabukta (Flora Bay) and stripped off our survival suits. It was springy and luxuriantly green underfoot, fertilised with years of accumulated guano, and a mass of flowers, many unknown in Kinnvika, spangled the rich emerald carpet. The high cliffs, some sections red, others green or yellow-brown, muted the sound of falling water that we could hear further on. Leaving the dandelions and buttercups to soak up the sun, we crossed the narrow neck of Floraodden (Flora Point) to locate the waterfall.

It was tucked away in a sunlit corner, an unspectacular slip of a thing, writhing over a lip of reddish rock about 25 metres above our heads. It descended opaque and sinuous into a short, plaited rill, before frothing through the ancient russet seaweed on the beach and trickling into the silver-rippled bay. The driftwood was clearly very old, light in both weight and colour, and there was a distinct absence of modern flotsam and jetsam. Sauntering back towards the boat, we discovered the foundations of an old trapper's hut, maybe from the 1930s, but probably much older as so little remained, perhaps built over the ruins of one of even greater age. Scattered all around were bits of sawn-up antlers and bones, interspersed with shards of old bottles and blue-patterned crockery. The site was reasonably well protected from the awful winds by the cliffs of Floraberget behind, and, across the bay, by the massive red-brown bulk of Celciusberget. It was probably quite a sensible place to build a hut if you were planning to spend a winter trapping foxes and hunting bears; far less exposed to the foul elements than Kinnvika, and with much more bird life to eat and to interest. The view was spectacular, if not as far reaching as ours, taking in the wide dispersal of bare rock islets in the bay and the green sweeps below the variegated bird cliffs. Being encircled by high walls of rock, just like Longyearbyen, the site would spend much longer in the shadows until the sun was quite high in the sky. Having an extensive view before us was part of Kinnvika's special charm and allowed us to see the sun as soon as it popped above the horizon.

Back in the boat, Balto sat quietly, appearing to enjoy the ride. A thrill of pleasure, fear or cold shivered his body occasionally as we skimmed across the wavelets; his additional weight slowed us appreciably and burned up our precious, limited supply of fuel. Hauke steered lazy curves around the floating white obstacles and headed back to our home on the moon.

The excursion had been a reminder that there was another world out there, green and sweet scented, colourful and warm. It would be nice to see it again, to feel the soft wind stroke my bare arms and legs, to be able to soak and swim in warm water, to feel more than the bare rock under my boots and a woolly hat on my head. There was much more to life than Kinnvika. Much more to life than Spitsbergen. But here was home. Here was peace of mind and a calmness of spirit, a tuning-in with nature and one's self. When things were going so well, it was almost impossible to contemplate leaving it. A beautiful day like today didn't help much.

*   *   *

The sawhorse was finally back as the last of the snow disappeared from its feet and I could now calculate the depth of snow we'd had outside our door. Several lengths of driftwood were still propped up against it, and the tip of a particularly long one had remained poking up above the snow throughout the depths of winter. With the help of one of the chairs, I dropped an expanding steel ruler to the ground and read off the depth. Six foot ten inches (two metres eight centimetres). Over 18 inches (45 centimetres) higher than me. Deep enough, I thought, especially when we were cutting steps in it nearly every day so that we could get from our door to the main hut or the loo.

Early in August our little pond reappeared and swelled with the melt water and inevitable assorted bugs and green, hairy stuff. Boggy areas, some distance from the hut, were already starting to dry out again as their source of moisture disappeared into the atmosphere. The sky was already hinting at the coming winter with unusual tinges of yellow, gold and turquoise discolouring the blue, and fog and rain drifted in fine gauze curtains across the huts, obscuring the sun and wilderness. Plants were flowering rapidly and brightening up the landscape with small splashes of yellow, purple, pink and white. Except for the dark winter months, Hauke had conducted his plant safari every Saturday since we'd arrived, photographing all the lichens and flowers we could find as they started to grow, bloom and set seed. He'd tried marking the position of specific plants with bamboo sticks to ensure a year-long run of photos, but the weather, bears and reindeer were active in thwarting his plans. It had become obvious to us that the plants were triggered into new growth by light and not warmth, as we found them growing even at the coldest time of the year. Reindeer weren't the only animals to eat them. Near the outside loo we watched a medium-sized, confident but respectful bear delicately nibbling at the pink-knotted knoppsildre (*Saxifraga cernua*) like an overgrown sheep. We immediately christened him Polar Baa.

August seemed to be a busy month for bears. Hardly a day seemed to go by without at least one around; at one point we had five of them about the huts. A mum and two small babies had arrived first, coming very near to us, giving us our closest outdoor encounter with an adult bear. There was just over seven feet (2.25 metres)—I know because I measured it—between her nose and Hauke's left foot, and only the video camera between them and the hut door, and me and a rifle right behind them both. A mum and an almost full grown cub then arrived. They were a threat to our very young family, who, after spending the night thinking about the situation—bears are great thinkers if you ask me—decided it was safer to depart up the Bear Road.

Glancing out of the kitchen window one lunchtime, I spotted a big, thin bear ambling down the Bear Road, unusual on both counts, and approaching us from behind the main hut, a bit nervous, gaping and flicking his black tongue in and out.

'Can I scare this one away?' I asked Hauke.

'Why?'

'Well, I haven't done one before. Not on my own. You've always been the bear scarer.'

'Haven't you?' He looked at me, rapidly searching his memory. 'OK. I'll film it.'

Hauke stood with his rifle propped up by the corner of the main hut, camera ready to go, hanging on to Balto on his short lead. I had my rifle draped over my right shoulder, the stainless steel dully glinting in the sunlight, the metal dog bowls clutched in my sweaty hands. We waited until he got closer, started to come down off the ridge behind the hut.

'Go!' hissed Hauke, thumbing the camera switch to red.

I stepped out from behind the hut, walking slowly but with a confidence I didn't really feel towards the surprised bear, swinging my arms in slow, regular arcs above my head and banging the bowls together with as much noise as I could make. Mr Bear stopped, but wasn't at all impressed, looking at me with typically unreadable bears' eyes.

'Don't go too far,' called Hauke. Not bloody likely, I thought, but I still walked towards the bear. He made a sudden start. Oo, er. Coming my way or not? I could feel my heart thump, a sudden injection of adrenalin as the two of us confronted each other. Keep walking towards him, I told myself, don't stop, don't hesitate. You can see he's more nervous than you. Show him you're not scared of him. Don't run away.

Balto wanted to help me and Hauke was shouting at him to stay put. This was my bear. Then, as I found myself halfway between Hauke and the bear, it decided that it really didn't like this crazy little woman, turned tail, and ran off as fast as his legs would carry him.

'Yeah!' I whooped. 'First bear scare!' But it had been a bit lonely out there in no-man's-land, even if Hauke was not far behind me. I wouldn't forget that experience in a hurry. It made my spine tingle. But I had finally done it all by myself; not something I would have done a year ago. No way. It seemed to mark a change in me. An assertiveness that hadn't been there before. I was quite proud of myself. I remembered how much I shook when I saw my first bear. How scared I was. Perhaps if I had problems with awkward people in the future I could just think of them as a kind of two-legged polar bear. I could deal with those.

*   *   *

This late flurry of bears had given us a wonderful opportunity to see how they reacted with each other. Generally, the bigger bears were given a lot of respect by the younger or smaller ones, who gave them a fairly wide berth if they encountered each other. We didn't get to see an encounter with two bears of equal standing, but we assumed that they wouldn't waste energy fighting and would steer clear of each other. There seemed to be a minimum distance of about 25 metres which they'd tolerate, and quite often, just the smell of another bear was enough to have those lower down in the hierarchy disappearing to the north. It was almost comical.

A large bear strolled in one day like an old Wild West sheriff hearing about a spot of bother in town. He was tall and slim and angular (a bit like Gary Cooper), and knew the difference between a good guy and a bad guy. He headed straight into the middle of town, hips swinging, and headed for the bad guy, a not very nice bear who'd been hanging around like a bad smell for a couple of days. (It was his own fault, sleeping in his own shit which left a very obvious brown smear down his left rear leg.) The good folks of Kinnvika were pleased to see him as they hadn't been able to persuade the bad guy to leave town and were reluctant to go out of doors alone.

The sheriff strode straight up to the bad guy and shot him a penetrating stare, scaring him badly, and had him running off to hide behind the storehouse. Not good enough! The sheriff followed, eyes blazing, running him out of town and up to the ridge, where he waited for a while, got his breath back and considered his options. This town wasn't big enough for the both of them. It was time the youngster high-tailed it out of Kinnvika. He left. Our hero made himself at home on the edge of town and went to sleep for the day. Job done.

But our peace didn't last for long. About nine o'clock in the evening that same day, a young, compact and stocky bear strode arrogantly into town. He looked powerful despite his age and size; a real bruiser. We took an instant dislike to him and stayed indoors to watch what would happen. He strutted around town, investigating the buildings near our hut, pushing at doors, sniffing at window shutters, before he turned his attention to us. He circuited the hut a couple of times, had us leaping across from window to window, shadowing his movements, our pulses racing. We were trying to take photos and film him, despite our anxiety, and I kept my rifle close by me, safety catch off as normal; all I had to do was chamber a round and shoot if I had to. The bear stopped by a side kitchen window and chewed on the red fuel cans stored a few metres away, before turning back to us. He about-faced and shoved his wet black nose up against the window glass, just inches from us, sniffing and prodding. Was he going to try and break in? We made a lot of noise to try and frighten him away. He didn't give a shit and went round to the rear window, peering in at us, and we stood our ground and stared back at him. Then, slowly and effortlessly, he lifted his front paws off the ground and stretched up to his full height, swaying slightly side to side to get a better view or a better aim. I stood transfixed; Hauke, with his steady nerves, continued to film.

'Shoot him if he comes in,' he told me calmly. I didn't need telling twice. I chambered a round. There'd be no time to load up if he smashed his way through the glass. It was him or us. Seconds passed like an eternity; time stretched like our nerves as we out-stared each other. We hardly breathed. The bear dropped to his feet, swung away and peered in at the last kitchen window. We followed, defending our hut with as much noise as possible, banging the walls, the rickety table and the dog bowls. A bit difficult with our hands full of rifle or camera. The bear slunk off again. I followed his movements rapidly. Hauke stayed in the kitchen and hefted his rifle.

'I'm going to open the door and fire a warning

shot. Tell me when you can see him and it's safe to go out.'

Some responsibility! I watched the bear carefully as he looked in the hut again, this time at the front window. I waited until he moved off to one side. He turned his back to the hut.

'Now!' I shouted. I heard the door open and Hauke jump out, firing off a round just beside the bear, which whined and kicked up moss and stones around his feet as I watched through the glass; he ran off at a gallop. I rushed out to Hauke as he fired a second shot to keep him moving towards the beach. He looked as tense and nervous as I felt. I ejected the round in my rifle and reset it, making it safe.

We had a slug of red wine. I reckoned I could have done with a whisky.

About 10 p.m. that evening, the bruiser decided to come back again, and tried his luck against Gary Cooper, circling him and trying it on. But the old bear was having none of it and chased him off again, his long, fine leg fur flying. Early next morning, we awoke to hear the bruiser's paws thudding against the hut walls, but we had the shutters closed and we remained quiet until he grew bored and wandered off, and we kept him at bay with a few well-aimed rifle shots kicking up the ground near his back legs. By evening, he was back again, and Gary Cooper had had enough of the noise and interruptions and decided to see him off again, walking steadily towards him and forcing him out of town once more.

But the next day was a different story. By early morning, the bruiser was feeling confident, arrogant, and several times walked by Gary Cooper, invading his personal space, getting very close, to within ten metres. Gary Cooper failed to impose his great size,

255

and Bruiser had now worked out that although he was smaller, he was much bulkier and stronger and was therefore determined to be the main man. The old bear had no inclination to fight, and after a few attempts at bravado, wearily turned around and sedately, and somewhat sadly, disappeared up the Bear Road and was gone. And so the new displace the old.

A day later, a red cruise ship came into the bay, but decided against landing tourists after Hauke had spoken to them over the radio. Bruiser was not impressed, and, as they departed, swam after the ship, desperate for something to eat, maybe, and was gone. Just like that.

*　　　*　　　*

There was a humming noise in my head that wouldn't go away. I drifted slowly to consciousness and looked at my watch on the table. Half past four. Ugh. I snuggled down under my quilt again, tucking it around my neck. I wasn't about to look out of the window. I knew what it was. The *Nordsyssel*. I didn't want it to be there. Go away!

I glanced around the bare walls, smiling at the few male faces and bare bums I'd pasted up there over the last year in between the girlie photos. I wondered how long it would be before they too were covered by strange mould and fungi. I'd grown to like my funny little rabbit hutch in this strange, lunar land. It had kept us safe and kept us warm, albeit lukewarm during the foul winter gales, and it had been a happy home. Longyearbyen had seemed almost like a prison to me at times, a golden cage, but in Kinnvika, I felt free as a bird. I had grown with the

256

wide open spaces and learned to love the place I had almost despaired of when I first set eyes on it.

The year had flown by, leaving many special memories and feelings. I had no real idea how it had affected me and hoped I would find out more when I returned to England and could see the different way I dealt with people and situations. I'd probably grown up a bit, become a bit more open, but I'd kept my silly sense of humour.

It had been a steep learning curve at the beginning; learning to live with Hauke; how to film; how to face up to bears; how to talk about myself and the way I felt; how to anticipate situations and deal with them. Over the months, with Hauke's unfailing and untiring help, I had started to discover the person I really wanted to be; or at least I had tried to. It would be an ongoing process, and not easy. Walls would have to be knocked down, rebuilt, and knocked down again when things were not quite right. Foundations have to be solid.

It was hard to talk about what I liked and wanted. I didn't really know myself. I never had a plan for the future, a life plan. I just wanted to be happy; nothing else seemed important. But I was just waiting for 'happy' to come along by itself. I didn't go looking for it or work out what being happy meant to me. Talking with Hauke, I realised that I knew what I liked and what I didn't want—I could have made a 'for and against' list quite easily if I'd thought about it. Perhaps being in Kinnvika distilled those thoughts and the whole process of trying to discuss them with Hauke clarified them a little. He'd worked hard to get me to talk about myself; he's interested in people and helping them sort themselves out. I loved the life I'd had here, and I wanted to recreate it in some small way in my future life. I suppose for me home would always be a place in the country with roses round the door, something a bit bigger than my rabbit hutch here, fields and trees close by, and good walks to be had. I still liked the idea of living by the sea, watching seagulls wheeling overhead and the crash of waves on a windblown beach. Anything was possible if you wanted it enough. And it looked as if I'd be doing it on my own, but someone like Hauke to share it with would be much nicer. Dream on, I thought, wriggling further down my bed, pulling my pillow after me (it always seemed easier than pulling up the quilt). I couldn't escape the dull, low, background hum however much I wrapped the pillow around my ears. After a year of near silence or natural noises, it was beginning to irritate me on my last morning. I tried going back to sleep, but didn't have much luck. Maybe I needed my moose for a cuddle but he was squashed up in a rucksack somewhere, ready for the off.

I'm not sure if I could have spent a whole year here on my own, I thought; I don't think I would have chosen to do it, anyway. Maybe I could do something similar in the future, only sans polar bears. I had always told myself that if Hauke had been taken ill and had to go back to Longyearbyen temporarily, I would have wanted to stay in Kinnvika alone, but I assumed I would have had two good dogs for protection and company then. Poor old Sako. I know I'd have found it hard and scary, but I was quite determined. Easy to say when you're snug in bed and you're not in the middle of winter with a bear knocking at your door.

I looked across to Hauke's half of the room. The

empty shelves; no radio; no CD player; no books; no bear-chewed woolly hat hanging off a nail. My shelves were empty, too. A bit like how I was feeling. I'd been packing again. I rolled over onto my side and peeked out from my quilt, looking under the table at Hauke. He was still fast asleep, blowing out little explosive puffs of breath. He never snored. Not like me. I smiled to myself as I looked at him. It's funny how things turn out. If I hadn't come to Spitsbergen and things had gone well with Edwin, I probably would never have met Hauke and had this once-in-a-lifetime experience. Life is all about being in the right place at the right time. Everything in our past lives leads us to this present moment. There was no point in worrying about life's what-might-have-beens, the ifs and the buts. We'd had a fantastic time together; it had gone much better than either of us had imagined, both on a personal level and on a scientific level. We'd tried to keep optimistic and happy for each other, to get us through the year, so I'd done all my crying in the hour Hauke was out walking the dog(s) in the morning. I don't think he ever guessed. Not that I cried for anything in particular. Probably just hormones. I must have been a real pain in the arse at times, I know I was, but he'd been patient and kind. We'd had fun together and given each other time to be alone, even when sitting across from each other at the table. He'd been encouraging and given me the figurative boot up the backside when I'd needed it, getting me more organised and making me get stuck into jobs I didn't want to do, getting it done and behind me. Sticking to our daily routines and our own jobs throughout the year had been perfectly natural, without a need for enforced 'equality'; I've always believed the best

259

'man' for the job is the one most capable of doing it. It didn't stop us having a partnership and harmony and a sharing of responsibility.

I sat up and reached for the tea flask. It was empty. Poo! I ducked back under the quilt, disappointed, wishing it was windy for once to drown out the drone of engines. Silence was precious here. I'd miss it. I'd miss everything about this place. The wildlife; the weather; the polar lights dancing and flowing between the stars in the coal black sky; the scary stuff; the romance of living with nature; the hard times, the good; Sunday champagne; even the ice and the cold. Maybe not the bears, but without them, it would have been decidedly less exciting. It really was an unforgettable year.

I sighed heavily, tugging the duvet tighter. And I'll miss you too, Professor Trinks, I thought, flicking my tear-blurred eyes across to him and back again. What were we going to do? We'd not discussed a continuing relationship. We'd avoided it; skirted around the edges of it, speculated a little, tentatively broached the subject, but it was probably the one thing we hadn't properly talked about while we'd been here. Everything for me felt so unsettled. Uncertain. So much to sort and get straight in England. I needed time to settle again, finish with Spitsbergen, readjust to a normal life. I was sure Hauke still wanted more, but I wasn't sure I could cope with it outside of Kinnvika. We'd been a fairly intense 'couple' here, and we'd have to share ourselves with other people, so it wouldn't be the same, but whether the change of circumstances would enhance or detract I couldn't tell. I liked things just as they were. I really couldn't decide what to do for the best. I was trying to convince myself of something, but hadn't worked out what. Maybe I was waiting for Hauke to suggest something more permanent, but I had the feeling that the ball was very definitely in my court. It was my decision, but I think I still had this hang-up about relationships ending, and felt it was better to let it come to a natural end, here, keeping it 'time restricted', than have it all go pear-shaped again later on. The trouble was, we were similar in so many ways; the same view of life; the things we like to do. Both a bit sporty and adventurous, both happy in each other's company. I didn't really want to give all that up. Those crinkly, twinkly blue eyes still attracted. I would say 'Yes!' all over again.

I'd not felt lonely once; never wanted to leave. Still didn't. Those lonely, empty spaces within had been absent for the last thirteen months, quickly filled with the magic of Kinnvika. I'd absorbed some of that indescribable inner peace that Hauke talked about in *Svalbardposten*, the tuning-in with yourself and nature.

What would I remember most, I wondered? I felt indescribably filled with warmth and happiness, and as usual, whenever I thought of it, it made me cry. I made a pyramid of my duvet with my knees. The first snow of winter had fallen yesterday, 24 August, just a light dusting, setting the seal on our year, telling us it was time to go.

Out and over from Kinnvika.

EPILOGUE

WHAT NEXT?

There wasn't much more I could do. I only needed to make sure the windows were all closed properly and I hadn't left anything behind that I shouldn't have. Apart from the two bags of food sitting on the floor, everything else was already on board, ready for departure. I was feeling nervous but looking forward to going nonetheless. I was just waiting for Hauke now.

*   *   *

It had been strange at first, being back in England. Everything was so noisy, dirty and bright. Everywhere was too warm. There were too many people, either in a hurry to get somewhere, or sitting glued to the television, with nothing to say. Like overpowering perfume, the warm and humid air was heavy with the stink of fuel, offending my nose and making me nauseous. Conversely, the scent of flowers in gardens and meadows was sweet and powerful and I couldn't get enough of it. It took me a couple of weeks to stop checking for bears every time I stepped through the door and looking all around me when I went for walks. At least a shoulder bag was lighter than a rifle.

I'd gone back to live with my parents for a short while and then moved in with my friend Caroline in the New Forest as I went back to work at the

National Motor Museum at Beaulieu. I'd taken a temporary part-time job working in the museum stores, recording exhibits and using my sewing talents to make bespoke, environmentally friendly protective covers for the exhibits in the stores. It was there I discovered that I had returned from Kinnvika a different person. I found I treated people like lesser polar bears, much to their surprise. They expected the same person that they'd known three years before, not the one that stuck up for herself and answered back, looked people in the eye and stood taller—every extra millimetre helping in my case. It boosted my already buoyant confidence. I wondered what else I would discover about myself. Time would reveal all.

It was nice to see all my family and friends and old workmates, to tell stories about Kinnvika and my adventures with the bears and surviving the long polar night. But no one really understood what it all meant to me and how I could possibly have loved the experience so much. In many ways, by being away from Kinnvika, I was just starting to learn what it had done for me. I wished I was still there. Wished I was home.

*　　*　　*

'What are you doing on Friday?' enquired Hauke down the phone. His phone bills must have sky-rocketed with all the calls to England. Once we'd settled down to our new routines, both going back to work again, we'd been in frequent communication with each other. We could reminisce about Kinnvika and know exactly how each other was feeling about not being there. About not being together.

263

'Nothing planned,' I replied, wondering why he was asking. I was flying out to Germany to see him in three weeks' time.

'Three weeks is too long before I see you again. I've booked a flight to Heathrow, but I have to leave again on Sunday afternoon. Can you pick me up?'

I went warm all over and my face turned red.

'Of course I can. It'll be great to see you again. I can't wait either!'

What a mad 48 hours. We stayed with Caroline overnight—I was pleased that he got the thumbs up from her—then took a return ferry trip from Lymington to the Isle of Wight for lunch, just to be silly, then whizzed up the motorway to arrive in time for dinner and see my parents. They were tickled pink by his very polite, very German manners and also gave him the thumbs up. Next morning we had time for a walk around the green, wooded countryside before I drove him back to Heathrow to catch his plane. I was sad to wave him off as our time together had been so short. But I'd see him again soon.

After a few visits to Germany, it became harder and harder for me to leave again. We would hug each other hard at the airport and I would burst into tears. We talked about the situation. It had been good to spend time apart from each other, trying to introduce some form of normality into our daily life without the additional stress of having to work at a 'new' relationship. But we missed each other. The separation had made me realise how much Hauke really meant to me. The intervening months since leaving Spitsbergen had allowed me to put Longyearbyen behind me, to close the book on that part of my life, and look ahead with a positive and clearer frame of mind without the fetters of old hopes and dreams. Perhaps we had a chance after all. Were we prepared to take it?

It was another big step for me to take, but a bigger, more scary one for Hauke, who was just about to give up half his home and all of his private life to this mad Englishwoman, after living alone in Germany for several years. A brave decision.

And here I am. Waiting for Hauke.

I sit at the huge oak table in the middle of the garden. The long summer grass is waving gently at my feet, dotted about with tall, purple lupins, foxglove spikes, pot marjoram and a kaleidoscope of delicate wild flowers. In September we would give it its annual haircut. Swallows swoop across the lily-padded pond, chaffinches splash about in the shallows amongst the reeds, scattering the newts. A black redstart is perched on one of the carved horse heads on the gable, crackling like a short circuit. It's a beautiful house. My dream house. Oak framed with red brick infill and topped off with a thick reed thatch. A trailing, ruby-leaved vine and delicate red roses creep over the door and under the eaves, shedding petals on the whitewood seat below. It's a small house. A simple house. A cosy house. There's no central heating, just a big, brick-encased woodburning stove; no television; no oven either, just a four-ringed electric hob sat above a defunct Buderus oven from the 1930s. A stuffed barn owl is perched amongst books on a tall, dark cupboard surrounded by an eclectic mix of old curios. Some of my sewing machines keep company with a straw bee skep, moose antlers and a wooden penguin on the exposed beams, and our tattered Kinnvika flags, dusty in retirement, hang from an old wooden yoke.

265

Draped over the banister is Hauke's bear's paw quilt—a hundred blue paws on an ice-white ground (with two more embroidered on the back), representing the total number recorded in Kinnvika. A labour of love.

As I wait for Hauke, I can still feel the buzz from the breakfast champagne, a Kinnvika tradition we soon resurrected for Sundays. I think of our last boat trip in Kinnvika, to Russøya, where an old Russian cross still stands near the foundations of an old hut, erected to ward off evil spirits by the trappers who endured dreadful winters on that unprotected, stony islet. We saw our only rust-gold-coloured great skuas with their vicious, hooked beaks. Balto had been with us. I sighed. He was dead too, having suffered from the same kind of lymph cancer as his brother and dying 18 months later. What a sweet dog he'd been.

My ears prick at the sound of a familiar engine. Here comes Hauke. I hop off the oak bench and go to greet him as he emerges from the car. He's been to visit one of his daughters and her happy brood of five children, to say farewell before we leave.

A new adventure starts today. Hauke's sailing boat *Mesuf* is all spruced up with a new coat of paint, ready to take us on our journey to Iceland. I'm feeling nervous and will be glad when I get the first storm under my belt. It's a long trip, starting here in Germany and calling in along the Danish and Norwegian coasts before crossing to the Shetlands, the Faeroe Islands and then a two-day sail to Iceland. Hauke's picked out some interesting little harbours to visit where we'll explore the landscape and talk to the people, practising the Icelandic he's been learning at evening classes. We're thinking

266

about buying a small farm there, having a horse or two, and dogs, of course, *Mesuf* riding the waves in some well-protected harbour. Not another Kinnvika, but another adventure, a new experience. I can't wait to start my new diary, to record my adventures, to write about whales and dolphins, seascapes and light, people and places. No bears this time.

APL		CCS	
Cen		Ear	6 2 09
Mob		Cou	
ALL		Jub	
WH		CHE	
Ald		Bel	
Fin		Fol	
Can		STO	
Til		HCL	